Version 2.0

EXPLORING MICROSOFT ACCESS®

Robert T. Grauer

Maryann Barber

University of Miami

Prentice Hall, Englewood Cliffs, New Jersey 07632

Library of Congress Cataloging in Publication Data

Grauer, Robert T. [date]
    Exploring Microsoft Access, version 2.0 / Robert T. Grauer,
    Maryann Barber.
    p. cm.
    Includes index.
    ISBN 0-13-079492-9
    1. Microsoft Access. 2. Business—Databases.
    I. Barber, Maryann M. II. Title.
HF5548.4.M523G72 1994
005.369—dc20

94-12937
CIP

Microsoft Access is a registered trademark and
Windows is a trademark of Microsoft Corporation.

Acquisitions editor: P. J. Boardman
Editorial /production supervisor: Greg Hubit Bookworks
Interior and cover design: Suzanne Behnke
Production coordinator: Patrice Fraccio
Managing editor: Maureen Wilson
Developmental editor: Harriet Serenkin
Editorial assistants: Renée Pelletier / Dolores Kenny

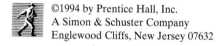
©1994 by Prentice Hall, Inc.
A Simon & Schuster Company
Englewood Cliffs, New Jersey 07632

Printed in the United States of America
10 9 8 7 6 5

ISBN 0-13-079492-9

Prentice Hall International (UK) Limited, *London*
Prentice Hall of Australia Pty. Limited, *Sydney*
Prentice Hall of Canada Inc., *Toronto*
Prentice Hall Hispanoamericano, S.A., *Mexico*
Prentice Hall of India Private Limited, *New Delhi*
Prentice Hall of Japan, Inc., *Tokyo*
Simon & Schuster Asia Pte. Ltd., *Singapore*
Editora Prentice Hall do Brasil, Ltda., *Rio de Janeiro*

Contents

3

Information from the Database: Reports and Queries 85

4

One-to-many Relationships: Subforms and Multiple Table Queries 127

Preface

Exploring Microsoft Access 2.0 is one of several books in the Prentice Hall *Exploring Windows* series. Other modules include *Microsoft Word for Windows 6.0, Microsoft Excel 5.0, PowerPoint 4.0, WordPerfect for Windows 6.0, Lotus for Windows 4.0,* and an introductory module, *Exploring Windows 3.1.* The books are independent of one another but possess a common design, pedagogy, and writing style intended to serve the application courses in both two- and four-year schools.

Each book in the series is suitable on a stand-alone basis for any course that teaches a specific application; alternatively, several modules can be bound together for a single course that teaches multiple applications. The initial component, *Exploring Windows 3.1,* assumes no previous knowledge and includes an introductory section for the individual who has never used a computer.

The *Exploring Windows* series will appeal to students in a variety of disciplines including business, liberal arts, and the sciences. Each module has a consistent presentation that stresses the benefits of the Windows environment, especially the common user interface that performs the same task in identical fashion across applications. Each module emphasizes the benefits of multitasking, demonstrates the ability to share data between applications, and stresses the extensive on-line help facility to facilitate learning. Students are taught concepts, not just keystrokes or mouse clicks, with hands-on exercises in every chapter providing the necessary practice to master the material.

The *Exploring Windows* series is different from other books, both in its scope as well as the way in which material is presented. Students learn by doing. Concepts are stressed and memorization is minimized. Shortcuts and other important Windows information is consistently highlighted in the many boxed tips that appear throughout the series. Each chapter contains an average of three directed exercises at the computer, but equally important are the less structured end-of-chapter problems that not only review the information but extend it as well. The end-of-chapter material is a distinguishing feature of the entire series, an integral part of the learning process, and a powerful motivational tool for students to learn and explore.

FEATURES AND BENEFITS

➤ *Exploring Microsoft Access* presents concepts as well as keystrokes and mouse clicks, so that students learn the theory behind the applications. They are not just taught what to do but are provided with the rationale for why they are doing it, enabling them to extend the information to additional learning on their own.

➤ *Exploring Microsoft Access* provides a much more comprehensive treatment of relational databases than competing books. At the same time, it is an introductory book that develops a database based on one table in Chapters 1, 2, and 3 before moving on to more complex systems in Chapters 4 and 5.

➤ *Exploring Microsoft Access* emphasizes the importance of database design. Appendix A contains a modular introduction to one-to-many and many-to-many relationships that can be covered at any time. Chapters 4 and 5 present additional examples of relational databases.

➤ *Exploring Microsoft Access* exposes students to many different applications. The data disk that is available contains seven different databases that are used in hands-on exercises or assigned as end-of-chapter problems. Students are able to explore a wide variety of applications but are spared the tedium of data entry.

➤ Problem solving and troubleshooting are stressed throughout. The authors are constantly anticipating mistakes that students may make and tell the reader how to recover from problems that invariably occur.

ACKNOWLEDGMENTS

We want to thank the many individuals who helped bring this project to its successful conclusion. We are especially grateful to our editors at Prentice Hall, P. J. Boardman and Carolyn Henderson, without whom the series would not have been possible, and to Harriet Serenkin, the developmental editor, whose vision helped shape the project. Gretchen Marx of Saint Joseph College produced an outstanding set of Instructor Manuals. Greg Hubit was in charge of production. Deborah Emry, our marketing manager at Prentice Hall, developed the innovative campaign that helped make the series a success.

We also want to acknowledge our reviewers, who through their comments and constructive criticism made this a far better book:

Lynne Band, Middlesex Community College
Stuart P. Brian, Holy Family College
Kimberly Chambers, Scottsdale Community College
Alok Charturvedi, Purdue University
Jerry Chin, Southwest Missouri State University
Dean Combellick, Scottsdale Community College
Cody Copeland, Johnson County Community College
Paul E. Daurelle, Western Piedmont Community College
David Douglas, University of Arkansas
Raymond Frost, Central Connecticut State University
James Gips, Boston College
Vernon Griffin, Austin Community College
Wanda D. Heller, Seminole Community College
Bonnie Homan, San Francisco State University
Ernie Ivey, Polk Community College
Mike Kelly, Community College of Rhode Island
Jane King, Everett Community College
John Lesson, University of Central Florida
Alan Moltz, Naugatuck Valley Technical Community College
Delores Pusins, Hillsborough Community College
Gale E. Rand, College Misericordia
David Rinehard, Lansing Community College
Marilyn Salas, Scottsdale Community College
John Shepherd, Duquesne University
Sally Visci, Lorain County Community College
David Weiner, University of San Francisco
Connie Wells, Georgia State University
Jack Zeller, Kirkwood Community College

A final word of thanks to the unnamed students at the University of Miami who make it all worthwhile. And, most of all, thanks to you, our readers, for choosing this book. Please feel free to contact us with any comments and suggestions. We can be reached most easily on the Internet.

Robert T. Grauer
RGRAUER@UMIAMI.MIAMI.EDU

Maryann Barber
MBARBER@UMIAMI.MIAMI.EDU

5

Many-to-many Relationships: A More Complex System   175

Appendix A: Database Design: Getting the Most from Microsoft Access   229

Appendix B: Toolbars 241

Index 247

1

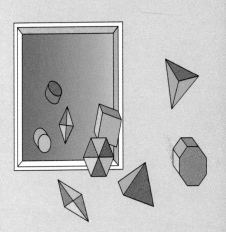

Introduction to Microsoft Access: What Is a Database?

CHAPTER OBJECTIVES

After reading this chapter you will be able to:

1. Describe the basic mouse operations; use a mouse and/or the equivalent keyboard shortcuts to select commands from a pull-down menu.
2. Discuss the function of a dialog box; describe the different types of dialog boxes and the various ways in which information is supplied.
3. Access the on-line help facility and explain its capabilities.
4. Define the terms field, record, table, and database.
5. Load Microsoft Access; describe the Database window and the objects in an Access database.
6. Add, edit, and delete records to a table within a database; use the Find command to move to a specific record.
7. Describe the record selector; explain when changes are saved to a database.
8. Explain the importance of data validation in table maintenance.
9. Describe a relational database; distinguish between a one-to-many and a many-to-many relationship.

OVERVIEW

This chapter reviews basic Windows concepts, applicable to Windows applications in general, and to Microsoft Access in particular. The emphasis is on the common user interface and consistent command structure that facilitate learning within the Windows environment. Indeed, you may already know much of this material, but that is precisely the point. Once you know one Windows application, it is that much easier to learn the next.

The chapter also provides a broad-based introduction to database processing and Microsoft Access. We begin by showing how the principles of manual record keeping can be extended to a computerized system. We discuss the basic operations in table maintenance and stress the importance of data validation. We define basic terms such as field, record, table, and database. We describe the objects within an Access database—which, in addition to tables, include forms, queries, and reports. Most significantly, we show how the real power of Access is derived from a database with multiple tables and from the relationships between those tables.

The entire chapter is built around the example of a database for a college bookstore. The two hands-on exercises in the chapter enable you to apply all of the material at the computer, and are indispensable to the learn-by-doing philosophy we follow throughout the text.

THE WINDOWS DESKTOP

The *desktop* is the centerpiece of Microsoft Windows and is analogous to the desk on which you work. There are physical objects on your real desk and there are *windows* (framed rectangular areas) and *icons* (pictorial symbols) displayed on the Windows desktop. The components of a window are explained within the context of Figure 1.1, which contains the opening Windows screen on our computer.

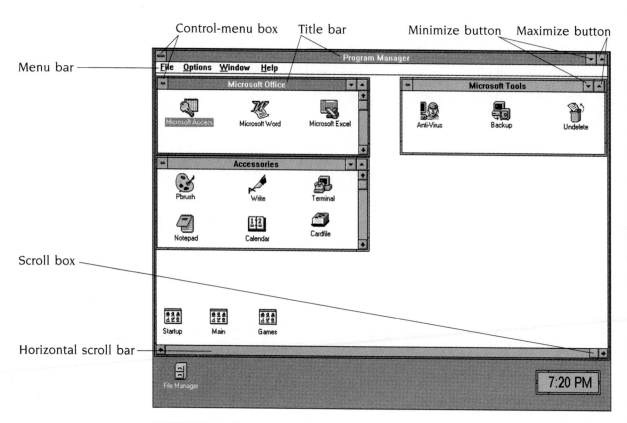

FIGURE 1.1 Program Manager

Your desktop may be different from ours, just as your real desk is arranged differently from those of your friends. You can expect, however, to see a window titled Program Manager. You may or may not see other windows within Program Manager such as the Microsoft Tools and Microsoft Office windows shown in Figure 1.1.

Program Manager is crucial to the operation of Windows. It starts automatically when Windows is loaded and it remains active the entire time you are working in Windows. Closing Program Manager closes Windows. Program Manager is in essence an organizational tool that places applications in groups (e.g., Microsoft Office), then displays those groups as windows or group icons.

Regardless of the windows that are open on your desktop, every window contains the same basic elements: a title bar, control-menu box, and buttons to minimize and to maximize or restore the window. The *title bar* displays the name of the window—for example, Microsoft Office in Figure 1.1. The *control-menu box* accesses a pull-down menu that lets you select operations relevant to the window. The *maximize button* enlarges the window so that it takes up the entire desktop. The *minimize button* reduces a window to an icon (but keeps the program active in memory). A *restore button* (a double arrow not shown in Figure 1.1) appears after a window has been maximized and returns the window to its previous size (the size before it was maximized).

Other elements, which may or may not be present, include a horizontal and/or vertical scroll bar and a menu bar. A horizontal (vertical) *scroll bar* will appear at the bottom (right) border of a window when the contents of the window are not completely visible. The *scroll box* appears within the scroll bar to facilitate moving within the window. A *menu bar* is found in the window for Program Manager, but not in the other windows. This is because Program Manager is a different kind of window, an application window rather than a document window.

An *application window* contains a program (application). A *document window* holds data for a program and is contained within an application window. (The document windows within Program Manager are known as group windows.) The distinction between application and document windows is clearer when we realize that Program Manager is a program and uses commands contained in pull-down menus to manipulate its document (group) windows.

MICROSOFT TOOLS

The Microsoft Tools group is created automatically when you install (or upgrade to) MS-DOS 6.0 or higher. The name of each icon (Antivirus, Backup, and Undelete) is indicative of its function, and each program is an important tool in safeguarding your data. The Antivirus program allows you to scan disks for known viruses (and remove them when found). The Backup utility copies files from the hard disk to one or more floppy disk(s) in case of hard disk failure. The Undelete program allows you to recover files that you accidentally erased from a disk.

WORKING IN WINDOWS

The next several pages take you through the basic operations common to Windows applications in general, and to Access in particular. You may already be familiar with much of this material, in which case you are already benefiting from the *common user interface.* We begin with the mouse and describe how it is used to access pull-down menus and to supply information in dialog boxes. We also emphasize the on-line help facility, which is present in every Windows application.

The Mouse

The mouse (or trackball) is essential to Microsoft Access as it is to all other Windows applications, and you must be comfortable with its four basic actions:

- To *point* to an item, move the mouse pointer to the item.
- To *click* an item, point to it, then press and release the left mouse button. You can also click the right mouse button to display a shortcut menu.
- To *double click* an item, point to it, then click the left mouse button twice in succession.
- To *drag* an item, move the pointer to the item, then press and hold the left button while you move the item to a new position.

The mouse is a pointing device—move the mouse on your desk and the **mouse pointer,** typically a small arrowhead, moves on the monitor. The mouse pointer assumes different shapes according to the nature of the current action. You will see a double arrow when you change the size of a window, an I-beam to insert text, a hand to jump from one help topic to the next, or a circle with a line through it to indicate that an attempted action is invalid.

The mouse pointer will also change to an hourglass to indicate that Access is processing your last command, and that no further commands may be issued until the action is completed. The more powerful your computer, the less frequently the hourglass will appear. Conversely, the less powerful your system, the more you will see the hourglass.

A right-handed person will hold the mouse in his or her right hand and click the left button. A left-handed person may want to hold the mouse in the left hand and click the right button. If this sounds complicated, it's not, and you can master the mouse with the on-line tutorial provided in Windows (see step 2 in the hands-on exercise on page 14).

MOUSE TIP FOR LEFTIES

Customize the mouse to reverse the actions of the left and right buttons. Double click the Main group icon in Program Manager to open the group, then double click the Control Panel icon. Double click the Mouse icon, click the Swap Left/Right Buttons check box, then click OK.

Access is designed for a mouse, but it provides keyboard equivalents for almost every command. Toolbars offer still other ways to accomplish the most frequent operations. You may (at first) wonder why there are so many different ways to do the same thing, but you will come to recognize the many options as part of Access's charm. The most appropriate technique depends on personal preference, as well as the specific situation.

If, for example, your hands are already on the keyboard, it is faster to use the keyboard equivalent. Other times, your hand will be on the mouse and that will be the fastest way. It is not necessary to memorize anything, nor should you even try; just be flexible and willing to experiment. The more you do, the easier it will be!

MOUSE TIP: PICK UP THE MOUSE

It seems that you always run out of room on your real desk just when you need to move the mouse a little further. The solution is to pick up the mouse and move it closer to you—the pointer will stay in its present position on the screen, but when you put the mouse down, you will have more room on your desk in which to work.

Pull-down Menus

Pull-down menus, such as those in Figure 1.2, are essential to all Windows applications. A pull-down menu is accessed by clicking the menu name (within the menu bar) or by pressing the Alt key plus the underlined letter in the menu name; for example, Alt+H to pull down the Help menu.

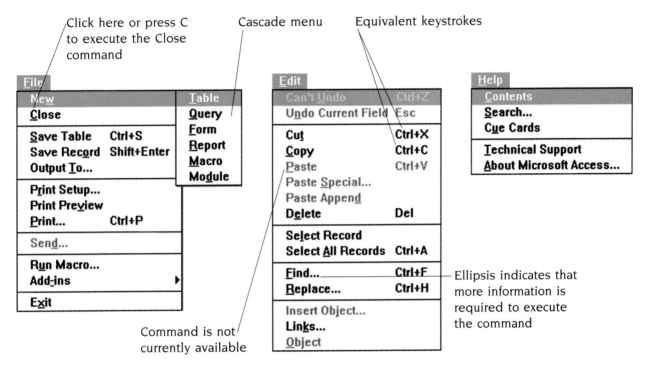

FIGURE 1.2 Pull-down Menus

Menu options (commands) are executed by clicking the command once the menu has been pulled down or by pressing the underlined letter (e.g., press C to execute the Close command in the File menu). You can also bypass the menu entirely if you know the equivalent keystrokes shown to the right of the command in the menu (e.g., Ctrl+X, Ctrl+C, and Ctrl+V in the Edit menu to cut, copy, and paste text, respectively).

A *dimmed command* (e.g., the Paste command within the Edit menu) indicates that the command is not currently available; that is, some additional action has to be taken in order to execute the command.

An arrowhead after a command indicates that a cascade menu will follow with additional choices. Clicking on the arrowhead (which is not visible for the New command in Figure 1.2) produces the *cascade menu* listing the additional choices (Table, Query, and so on).

Other commands are followed by an *ellipsis* (. . .), which indicates that more information is required to execute the command. For example, selection of the Find command in the Edit menu requires the user to specify the text to be found. The additional information is entered into a dialog box, which appears immediately after the command has been selected.

Dialog Boxes

A *dialog box* appears when additional information is needed to execute a command—that is, whenever a menu option is followed by an ellipsis. There are many different ways to supply that information, which leads to different types of dialog boxes as shown in Figure 1.3.

Text box indicates that a character string is required

Option buttons indicate mutually exclusive choices

Check boxes indicate that multiple options can be selected

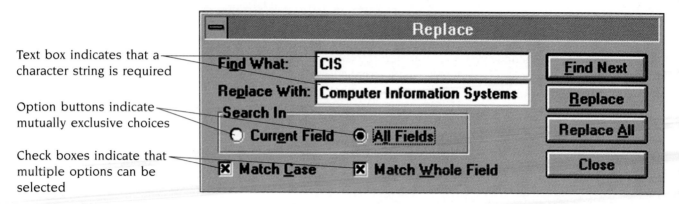

(a) Option Buttons, Check Boxes, and Text Boxes

Command buttons

Open list box displays available choices

Drop-down list box (Click arrow to display available choices)

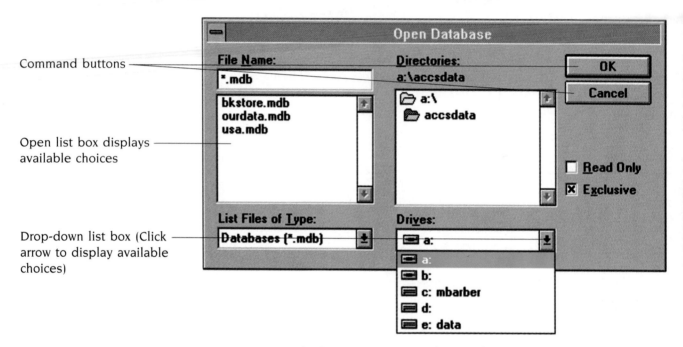

(b) Open List Boxes and Drop-down List Boxes

FIGURE 1.3   Dialog Boxes

A text box indicates that specific data is required, such as the Find and Replace character strings in Figure 1.3a. The flashing vertical bar within the text box is the *insertion point,* which indicates where new text will be entered.

Option buttons indicate mutually exclusive choices, one of which must be chosen. All Fields is selected in the dialog box in Figure 1.3a, which automatically deselects Current Field. In other words, clicking one button automatically clears the other.

Check boxes indicate that multiple options can be selected. Match Case and Match Whole Field are both checked in Figure 1.3a, so both options are in effect. Unlike option buttons (one of which is always selected), it is not necessary to select any check boxes. The individual items are selected (or cleared) by clicking on the appropriate check box.

List boxes allow you to choose from a predetermined set of choices. An *open list box,* such as the list of file names in Figure 1.3b, displays the available choices, any of which is selected by clicking the desired item. A *drop-down list box,* such as the list of available drives or file types, conserves space by showing only the current selection. Click the arrow of a drop-down list box to produce a list of available options.

All dialog boxes contain one or more **command buttons** to initiate an action. The function of a command button is generally apparent from its name. The Replace All command button in Figure 1.3a, for example, replaces all occurrences of CIS with Computer Information Systems.

On-line Help

Access provides extensive on-line help, which is accessed by pulling down the **Help menu.** The Access Help menu was shown earlier in Figure 1.2 and contains the following choices:

Contents	Provides access to all elements within Help
Search . . .	Searches for help on a specific subject
Cue Cards	Activates on-line coach that steps you through a specific task
Technical Support	Describes the different types of technical support available
About Microsoft Access . . .	Indicates the specific release of Access you are using

The Contents command displays the window of Figure 1.4a and provides access to all elements within the Help facility. A Help window contains all of the

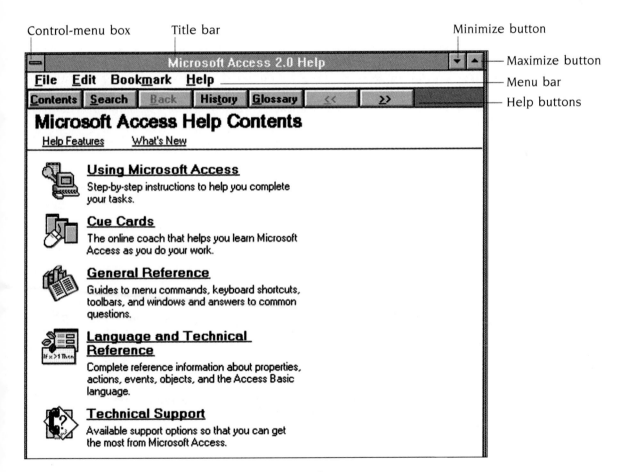

(a) Contents Command

FIGURE 1.4 On-line Help

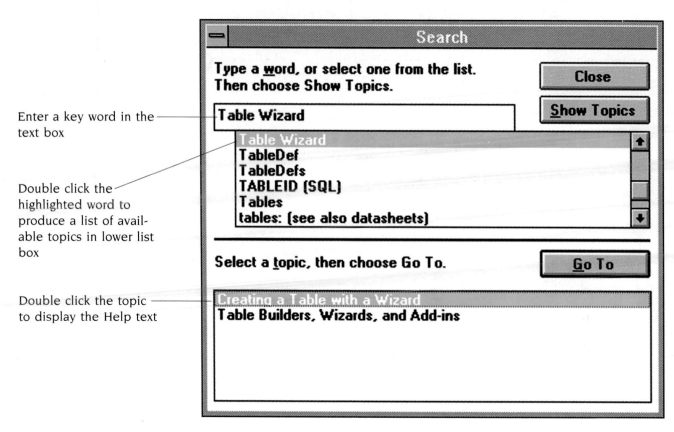

Enter a key word in the text box

Double click the highlighted word to produce a list of available topics in lower list box

Double click the topic to display the Help text

(b) Search Command

FIGURE 1.4   On-line Help (continued)

elements found in any other application window: a title bar; minimize and maximize or restore buttons; a control-menu box; and optionally, a vertical and/or horizontal scroll bar. There is also a menu bar from which you open menus and access commands.

The help buttons near the top of the Help window enable you to move around more easily; that is, you can click a button to perform the indicated function. The Contents button returns to the screen in Figure 1.4a from elsewhere within Help. The Search button produces the screen of Figure 1.4b and allows you to look for information on a specific topic. Type a key word in the text box and the corresponding term will be selected in the adjacent list box. Double click the highlighted item to produce a list of available topics in the lower list box. Double click the topic you want (or select the topic and click the Go To command button) to see the actual help text, such as the screen shown in Figure 1.4c.

The Back button returns directly to the previous help topic. The History button is more general as it displays a list of all topics selected within the current session and makes it easy to return to any of the previous topics. The Glossary button enables you to obtain a working definition of important terms within Access as shown in Figure 1.4d.

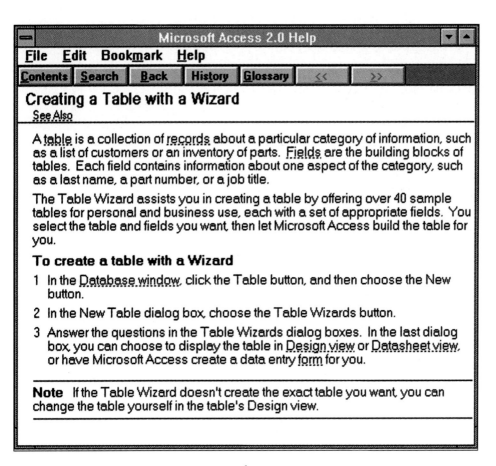

(c) Help Text

Definition of term

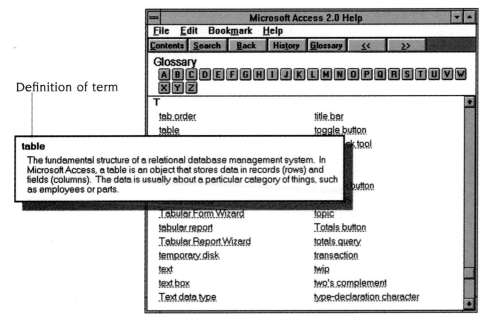

(d) Glossary

FIGURE 1.4 On-line Help (continued)

INTRODUCTION TO ACCESS

A ***database*** is a collection of related data. A ***database management system***
(DBMS) stores and manipulates the data in a database. ***Microsoft Access*** is the
DBMS you will study throughout this book.

The Database Window

An Access database stores not only data but also ***objects*** associated with that data.
There are six different types of objects in an Access database: tables, forms,
queries, reports, macros, and modules.

- A ***table*** stores data about a particular subject and is the basic element in any
  database. The data in a table is organized in rows (records) and columns (fields)
  as will be explained in the next section.
- A ***form*** provides a more convenient and attractive way to enter, display, and/or
  print the data in a table. Forms are discussed in Chapter 2.
- A ***query*** answers a question about the database. The most common type of
  query specifies a set of criteria, then searches the database to retrieve the
  records that satisfy the criteria. Queries are described in Chapters 3 and 4.
- A ***report*** presents the data in a table or query in attractive fashion on the
  printed page. Reports are described in Chapter 3.
- ***Macros*** and ***modules*** automate the process of working with a database. A macro
  is a list of commands for Access to execute. A module provides a greater degree
  of automation through programming in Access Basic. Both macros and modules are beyond the scope of this book.

The objects in an Access database are listed in the ***database window*** as
shown in Figure 1.5. The command buttons enable you to create new objects or
to work with existing objects. The ***object buttons*** list the objects of a given type.
For example, click the Query button to show queries within the database.

The desktop in Figure 1.5 contains an application window for Microsoft
Access. You should also recognize many of the elements described earlier in the
chapter such as the minimize and maximize or restore buttons, a menu bar, and
control-menu boxes. The toolbar provides access to the most commonly executed
commands. (The icons on the toolbar are unique to Access and differ from those
in other Microsoft applications.)

CASE STUDY: THE COLLEGE BOOKSTORE

Imagine, if you will, that you are the manager of your college bookstore and that
you manually maintain data for every book in the store. You have recorded the
specifics of every book (the title, author, publisher, price, and so on) in a manila

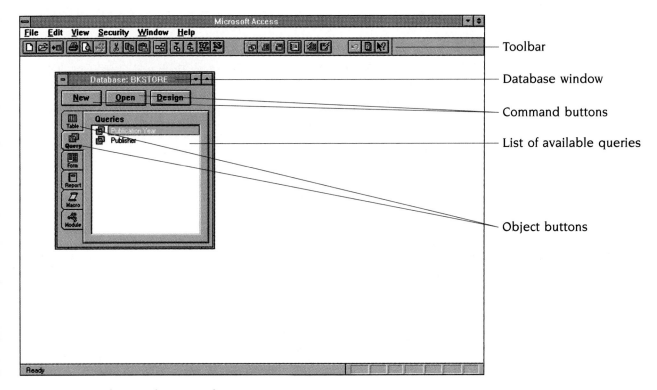

Toolbar

Database window

Command buttons

List of available queries

Object buttons

FIGURE 1.5 The Database Window

folder, and have stored the folders in a file cabinet. The set of manila folders corresponds to a *table* within an Access database. Each individual folder corresponds to a *record* in that table. Each fact or data item in a folder corresponds to a *field* in a record.

Normal business operations will require you to make repeated trips to the filing cabinet to maintain the timeliness and accuracy of the data. You will have to add a folder whenever a new book is received. You will also have to modify the data in a folder to reflect a price increase or other change in the data. And you will need to remove the folder of any book that is no longer carried by the bookstore. Each of these operations, additions, changes, and deletions must also be done in a computerized database.

In order for the system we have described to be truly useful, you will need to maintain an additional set of folders for publishers, containing the address and phone number for each publisher. How else would you be able to place an order? You will most likely have to maintain another set of folders to keep track of the orders: to know when an order was placed, the status of the order, which books were ordered, how many copies, and so on.

Each set of folders corresponds to a different table within a single database. For the time being, however, we will focus on a single table (on one set of folders) so that you can learn the basics of Access. After you are comfortable working with a single table, we will show you how to work with multiple tables.

TABLES

A table (or set of tables) is the heart of any database as it contains the actual data. In Access, a table is displayed in one of two views—the design view or the datasheet view. The *design view* is used to define the table initially and to specify the fields it will contain. It is also used to modify the table definition if changes are subsequently necessary. The design view is discussed in Chapter 2. The *datasheet view* is the view you use to add, edit, or delete records. It is the view we focus on in this chapter.

Figure 1.6a shows the datasheet view of the Books table in our bookstore. The first row in the table contains the *field names.* Each additional row contains a record (the data for a specific book). Each column represents a field (one fact about a book). Every record contains the same fields in the same order: ISBN number, Title, Author, Year, List Price, and Publisher.

The status bar at the bottom of the figure shows there are four records in the table and that you are positioned on the first record. This is the record you are working on and is known as the *current record.* (You can work on only one record at a time.)

The datasheet view displays a *record selector symbol* (either a triangle or a pencil) next to the current record to indicate its status. A *triangle* indicates that you have not changed the data since the table was last saved. A *pencil* indicates that you are entering or changing data and that these changes have not yet been saved. An *asterisk* appears next to the blank record at the end of every table.

Figure 1.6a shows the table as it would appear immediately after you opened it. The first field in the first record is selected (highlighted), and anything you type at this point will *replace* the selected data. (This is the same convention as in any other Windows application.) The triangle next to the current record (record one) indicates changes have not yet been made. An asterisk appears as the record selector symbol next to the blank record at the end of the table. The blank record is used to add a record to the table but is not counted in determining the number of records in the table.

Figure 1.6b shows the table in the process of entering data for a new record at the end of the table. The current record is now record five. The *insertion point* (a flashing vertical bar) appears at the point where text is being entered. The record selector for the current record is a pencil indicating that its data has not yet been saved. The asterisk has moved to the blank record at the end of the table, which now contains one more record than the table in Figure 1.6a.

WHEN IS DATA SAVED?

There is one critical difference between Access and other Windows applications such as Word for Windows or Microsoft Excel. *Access automatically saves any changes in the current record as soon as you move to the next record or when you close the table.* You do *not* have to execute the Save command.

THE INTERNATIONAL STANDARD BOOK NUMBER

The International Standard Book Number (ISBN) is an internationally recognized number that uniquely identifies a book. The first part of the number indicates the publisher; for example, every book by Prentice Hall begins with 0-13. The assignment of the number 13 was not an accident. Prentice Hall was founded in 1913, its first office was on 13th street in New York City, and its first phone number ended in 1300. The original name of the company included a hyphen. Prentice-Hall (including the hyphen) is thirteen characters.

Field names

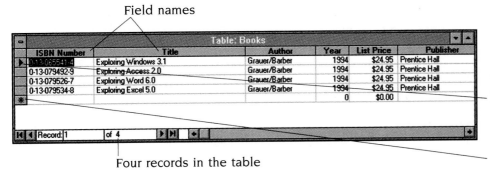

Triangle indicates the record has not been changed

Indicates the blank record present at the end of the table

Four records in the table

(a) All Data Has Been Saved

Insertion point indicates where text is entered

Pencil indicates the data has not been saved

Indicates the blank record at the end of the table

Five records in the table (one record has been added)

(b) Current Record Has Not Been Saved

FIGURE 1.6 Tables

LEARNING BY DOING

We come now to the first of two hands-on exercises that implement our learn-by-doing philosophy. The exercise shows you how to load Windows and practice with the mouse, then directs you to load Microsoft Access and retrieve the Bookstore database from the *data disk* that is available from your instructor.

Remember that Access provides different ways to accomplish the same task. Commands may be accessed from a pull-down menu, from a shortcut menu, through keyboard equivalents, and/or from a toolbar. The various techniques may at first appear overwhelming, but you will be surprised at how quickly you learn them. There is no need to memorize anything nor is there a requirement to use every single technique. Just be flexible and willing to experiment.

CREATE A WORKING DISK

The data disk is almost full and should not be used to add or modify data files referenced in the hands-on exercises. There is no problem if you install the data disk onto your hard drive. If you do not install the data disk to the hard drive, then you must copy the files needed for each exercise from the data disk to a second floppy disk known as a working disk.

Introduction to Microsoft Access

Objective To load Windows and Microsoft Access; to open an existing database; to add a record to a table within the database. The exercise introduces you to the data disk provided by your instructor. It also reviews basic Windows operations: pull-down menus, dialog boxes, and the use of a mouse.

Step 1: Load Windows

➤ Type **WIN,** then press the **enter** key to load Windows if it is not already loaded. The appearance of your desktop will be different from ours, but it should resemble Figure 1.1 at the beginning of the chapter.

➤ You will most likely see a window containing Program Manager, but if not, you should see an icon titled Program Manager near the bottom of the screen; double click on this icon to open the Program Manager window.

DOUBLE CLICKING FOR BEGINNERS

If you are having trouble double clicking, it is because you are not clicking quickly enough, or more likely, because you are moving the mouse (however slightly) between clicks. Relax, hold the mouse firmly in place, and try again.

Step 2: Master the mouse

➤ A mouse is essential to the operation of Microsoft Access as it is to all other Windows applications. The easiest way to practice is with the mouse tutorial found in the Help menu of Windows itself.

➤ Pull down the **Help menu.** Click **Windows Tutorial.** Type **M** to begin, then follow the on-screen instructions.

➤ Exit the tutorial when you are finished.

Step 3a: Install the data disk

➤ Do this step *only* if you have your own computer and want to copy the files from the data disk to the hard drive. Place the data disk in drive A (or whatever drive is appropriate).

➤ Pull down the **File menu.** Click **Run.** Type **A:INSTALL C** in the text box. Click **OK.** (The drive letters in the command, A and C, are both variable. If, for example, the data disk were in drive B and you wanted to copy its files to drive D, you would type the command **B:INSTALL D**)

➤ Follow the on-screen instructions to install the data disk.

Step 3b: Create a working disk

➤ Do this step *only* if you are not going to use the hard drive to store the files created in this exercise. Use the Windows File Manager to copy the files **BKSTORE.MDB** and **BKSTORE.LDB** from the data disk to a formatted floppy disk known as the working disk.

Step 4: Load Microsoft Access
➤ Double click the icon for the group containing Microsoft Access if that group is not already open.
➤ Double click the program icon for **Microsoft Access.**
➤ You may or may not see the screen in Figure 1.7a, depending on the options within your system. If the screen is present, **double click** the control-menu box to close the Cue Cards window and begin working on the Bookstore database.
➤ Click the **maximize button** (if necessary) so that the window containing Microsoft Access fills the entire screen.

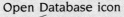

Open Database icon

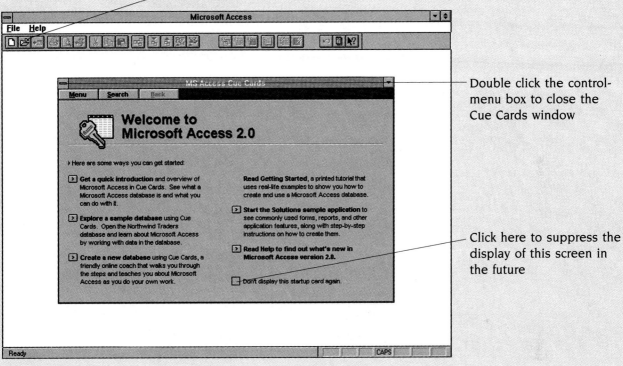

Double click the control-menu box to close the Cue Cards window

Click here to suppress the display of this screen in the future

(a) Opening Screen (step 1)

FIGURE 1.7   Hands-on Exercise 1

ABOUT MICROSOFT ACCESS

About Microsoft Access on the Help menu displays information about the specific release of Access together with a System Information command button. Click the button to learn about the hardware installed on your system, including the amount of memory and available space on the hard drive.

Step 5: Open the Bookstore database
➤ Pull down the **File menu** and click the **Open Database** command (or click the **Open Database icon** on the toolbar). You will see a dialog box similar to the one in Figure 1.7b.

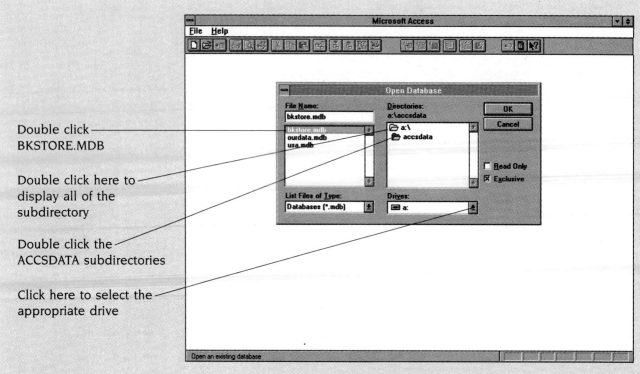

Double click
BKSTORE.MDB

Double click here to
display all of the
subdirectory

Double click the
ACCSDATA subdirectories

Click here to select the
appropriate drive

(b) Opening a Database (step 5)

FIGURE 1.7   Hands-on Exercise 1 (continued)

➤ Click the arrow on the Drives list box to select the appropriate drive—for
  example, drive C or drive A, depending on whether you installed the data
  disk.
➤ Double click the root directory (a:\ or c:\) in the Directories list box to display the subdirectories on the selected drive. Use the working disk if you
  are using drive A.
➤ Double click the **ACCSDATA** directory to make it the active directory.
➤ Double click **BKSTORE.MDB** to open the database for this exercise. The
  Open Database command has loaded the database from disk into memory,
  enabling you to work with the database.

ONE FILE HOLDS ALL

All of the objects in a database (tables, forms, queries, reports, macros,
and modules) are stored in a single file with the *MDB extension.* Execution of the Open Database command in the File menu provides access to
all of the objects via the Database window.

Step 6: Open the Books table
➤ The Table button is already selected. Double click the icon next to **Books** to
  open the table, as shown in Figure 1.7c.
➤ Move and size the window containing the Books table as follows:
  — To move the window, point to the title bar, drag the window to its new
     position, and release the mouse.

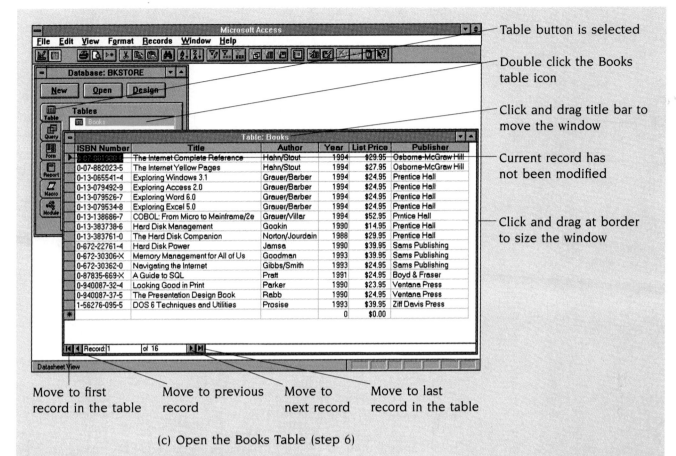

Table button is selected

Double click the Books table icon

Click and drag title bar to move the window

Current record has not been modified

Click and drag at border to size the window

Move to first record in the table

Move to previous record

Move to next record

Move to last record in the table

(c) Open the Books Table (step 6)

FIGURE 1.7 Hands-on Exercise 1 (continued)

— To size the window, point to any border or corner of the window (the pointer changes to a two-headed arrow), then drag until the window is the size you want. Dragging a border changes only one dimension. Dragging a corner changes the length and width simultaneously.

THE WRONG VIEW

If you do not see the records in the table, it is most likely because you are in the wrong view—the Design view rather than the Datasheet view. Pull down the View menu and click Datasheet, or click the Datasheet icon on the toolbar.

Step 7: Moving within a table

➤ Click anywhere in the window containing the Books table. Click the **maximize button** to reduce the clutter on the screen.

➤ Click in any field in the first record, and the status bar indicates record 1 of 16. The triangle symbol in the record selector indicates that the record has not been modified since the last time the table was saved.

➤ You can move from record to record (or field to field) by using either the mouse or the arrow keys.

— Click in any field in the second record. The status bar indicates record 2 of 16.

— Press the **down arrow key** to move to the third record. The status bar indicates record 3 of 16. Press the **left and right arrow keys** to move from field to field within the third record.

➤ You can also use the *navigation buttons* to move from one record to the next.
— Click | ◀ to move to the first record in the table.
— Click ▶ to move forward in the table to the next record.
— Click ◀ to move back in the table to the previous record.
— Click ▶ | to move to the last record in the table.

THE COMMON USER INTERFACE

Ctrl+Home and Ctrl+End are keyboard shortcuts that apply universally to every Windows application and move to the beginning and end of a document, respectively. Microsoft Access is no exception. Press Ctrl+Home to move to the first field in the first record of a table. Press Ctrl+End to move to the last field in the last record. Press Home and End to move to the first and last fields in the current record, respectively.

Step 8: Add a record
➤ Click the **New button** on the toolbar. The record selector moves to the last record (record 17). The insertion point is positioned in the first field (ISBN Number).
➤ Enter data for the new record as shown in Figure 1.7d. The record selec-

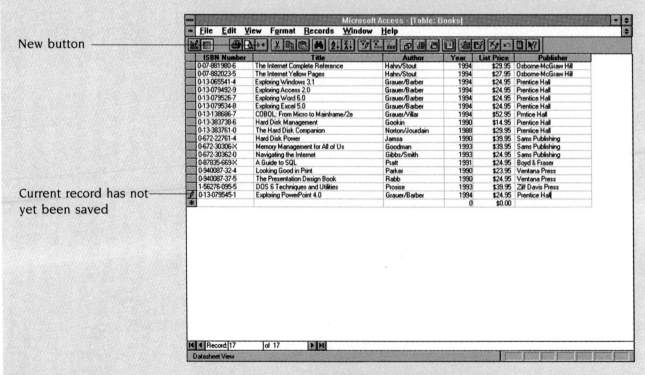

New button

Current record has not yet been saved

(d) Add a Record (step 8)

FIGURE 1.7   Hands-on Exercise I (continued)

tor changes to a pencil as soon as you enter the first character in the new record.

➤ Press the **enter key** when you have entered the last field for the record. The new record is saved, and the record selector changes to a triangle and moves automatically to the next record.

MOVING FROM FIELD TO FIELD

Press the Tab key, the right arrow key, or the enter key to move to the next field in the current record (or the first field in the next record if you are already in the last field of the current record). Press Shift+Tab or the left arrow key to return to the previous field in the current record (or the last field in the previous record if you are already in the first field of the current record).

Step 9: Print the table

➤ Pull down the **File menu** and click **Print** (or click the **Printer icon** on the toolbar). You will see the Print dialog box on your monitor as shown in Figure 1.7e.

➤ Check that the All option button has been selected under Print Range. Click the **OK** command button to accept the default options and print the table.

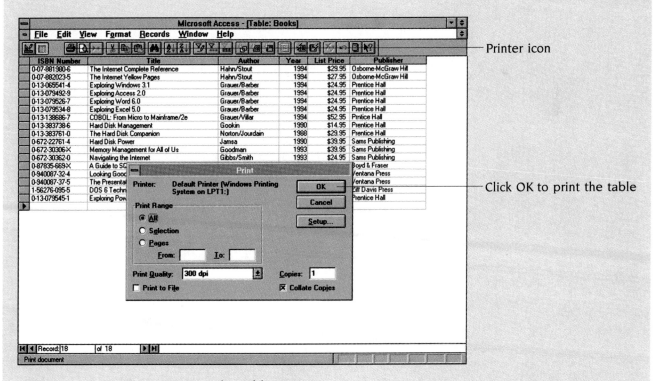

(e) Print the Table (step 9)

FIGURE 1.7 Hands-on Exercise 1 (continued)

Step 10: Exit Access and Windows
➤ Pull down the **File menu.** Click **Exit** to close Access.
➤ Pull down the **File menu** in Program Manager. Click **Exit Windows.** You will see an informational message indicating that you are leaving Windows. Click the **OK** command button to exit.

MAINTAINING THE DATABASE

The exercise just completed showed you how to open an existing table and add records to that table. You will also need to edit and/or delete existing records in order to maintain the database as changes occur. These operations require you to search a table for a specific record in order to make the change. This is best accomplished through the ***Find command*** in the Edit menu. If, for example, you wanted to change the price of a particular book, you could use the Find command to move directly to that book rather than manually search the table.

As previously indicated, Access automatically saves changes in the current record as soon as you move to the next record. It also remembers the last change you made and allows you to undo that change. The Edit menu contains different Undo commands, depending on the nature of that change. The ***Undo Typing command*** lets you cancel your most recent change. The ***Undo Current Field command*** and ***Undo Current Record command*** cancel all changes to the current field or record, respectively. Even after the changes have been saved (i.e., when you move to the next record), the ***Undo Saved Record command*** undoes the changes to the previously edited record. Once you begin editing another record, however, changes to the previous record can no longer be undone.

Data Validation

Nor is it sufficient to simply add (edit or delete) a record without adequate checks on the validity of the data. Look carefully at the data in Figure 1.7 and ask yourself if a computer-generated report for Prentice Hall will include *COBOL: From Micro to Mainframe?* The answer is *no* because the publisher field for this book was entered incorrectly. Prentice Hall is misspelled (the first "e" was omitted). You know who the publisher is, but the computer does not because it is searching for the correct spelling.

Data validation is a crucial part of any system. Good systems will anticipate errors you might make and reject those errors prior to accepting data. Access automatically implements certain types of data validation. It will not, for example, let you enter letters where a numeric value is expected (e.g., the Year and Price fields in our example). Other types of validation are implemented by the user. You may decide, for example, to reject any record that omits the title or author. Data validation is described more completely in Chapter 2.

GARBAGE IN, GARBAGE OUT

A computer does exactly what you tell it to do, which is not necessarily what you want it to do. It is absolutely critical, therefore, that you validate the data that goes into a system, or else the associated information will not be correct. No system, no matter how sophisticated, can produce valid output from invalid input. In other words, **garbage in, garbage out (GIGO).**

We said earlier that an Access database consists of different types of objects such as tables, forms, queries, and reports. Figure 1.8 contains an example of each object as it appears in the Bookstore database.

A table stores data and is the basis for all of the other objects in a database. Figure 1.8a contains the Books table. There are 17 records and six fields for each record.

Figure 1.8b shows the result of a query to select books by a particular publisher (Prentice Hall in this example). A query resembles a table except that it contains selected records, selected fields for those records, and further may list the records in a different order.

Figure 1.8c illustrates a form that can be used to add a new book or edit data for an existing book. You enter data into a form, and Access stores the data in the corresponding table in the database. A form provides a much friendlier interface than does a table and is used for that reason.

Figure 1.8d illustrates a report that prints the books by Prentice Hall. A report may display the results of a query, as in this example, or it may produce entirely different information. All reports provide presentation quality output.

Later chapters discuss forms, queries, and reports in depth. The following exercise is intended as an introduction to what can be accomplished in Access.

Table: Books

ISBN Number	Title	Author	Year	List Price	Publisher
0-07-881980-5	The Internet Complete Reference	Hahn/Stout	1994	$29.95	Osborne-McGraw Hill
0-07-882023-5	The Internet Yellow Pages	Hahn/Stout	1994	$27.95	Osborne-McGraw Hill
0-13-065541-4	Exploring Windows 3.1	Grauer/Barber	1994	$24.95	Prentice Hall
0-13-079492-9	Exploring Access 2.0	Grauer/Barber	1994	$24.95	Prentice Hall
0-13-079526-7	Exploring Word 6.0	Grauer/Barber	1994	$24.95	Prentice Hall
0-13-079534-8	Exploring Excel 5.0	Grauer/Barber	1994	$24.95	Prentice Hall
0-13-079545-1	Exploring PowerPoint 4.0	Grauer/Barber	1994	$24.95	Prentice Hall
0-13-079548-3	Exploring Windows 4.0	Grauer/Barber	1994	$24.95	Prentice Hall
0-13-138686-7	COBOL: From Micro to Mainframe/2e	Grauer/Villar	1994	$52.95	Prentice Hall
0-13-383738-6	Hard Disk Management	Gookin	1990	$14.95	Prentice Hall
0-672-22761-4	Hard Disk Power	Jamsa	1990	$39.95	Sams Publishing
0-672-30306-X	Memory Management for All of Us	Goodman	1993	$39.95	Sams Publishing
0-672-30362-0	Navigating the Internet	Gibbs/Smith	1993	$24.95	Sams Publishing
0-87835-669-X	A Guide to SQL	Pratt	1991	$24.95	Boyd & Fraser
0-940087-32-4	Looking Good in Print	Parker	1990	$23.95	Ventana Press
0-940087-37-5	The Presentation Design Book	Rabb	1990	$24.95	Ventana Press
1-56276-095-5	DOS 6 Techniques and Utilities	Prosise	1993	$39.95	Ziff Davis Press
			0	$0.00	

Record: 1   of 17

(a) Books Table

Select Query: Publisher

Publisher	Author	Title	ISBN Number	Year	List Price
Prentice Hall	Gookin	Hard Disk Management	0-13-383738-6	1990	$14.95
Prentice Hall	Grauer/Barber	Exploring Access 2.0	0-13-079492-9	1994	$24.95
Prentice Hall	Grauer/Barber	Exploring Excel 5.0	0-13-079534-8	1994	$24.95
Prentice Hall	Grauer/Barber	Exploring PowerPoint 4.0	0-13-079545-1	1994	$24.95
Prentice Hall	Grauer/Barber	Exploring Windows 3.1	0-13-065541-4	1994	$24.95
Prentice Hall	Grauer/Barber	Exploring Windows 4.0	0-13-079548-3	1994	$24.95
Prentice Hall	Grauer/Barber	Exploring Word 6.0	0-13-079526-7	1994	$24.95
Prentice Hall	Grauer/Villar	COBOL: From Micro to Mainframe/2e	0-13-138686-7	1994	$52.95
				0	$0.00

Record: 1   of 8

(b) Publisher Query

FIGURE 1.8 Database Objects

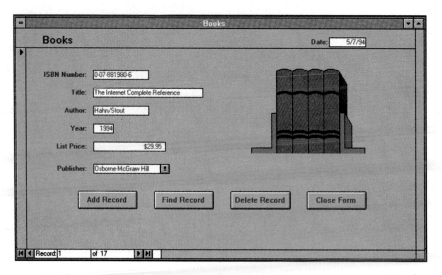

(c) Books Form

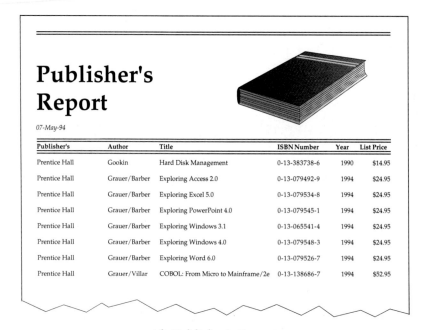

(d) Publisher's Report

FIGURE 1.8 Database Objects (continued)

Maintaining the Database

Objective To use the Find command to locate a specific record within a table; to change and delete existing records; to demonstrate data validation; to select and print a report. Use Figure 1.9 as a guide in doing the exercise.

Step 1: Open the Bookstore database
➤ Load Access as you did in the previous exercise.

- ➤ Pull down the **File menu** and click **Open Database** (or click the *Open Database icon* on the toolbar) to display the Open Database dialog box.
- ➤ Click the arrow on the Drives list box and select the appropriate drive—for example, drive C or drive A, depending on whether you installed the data disk.
- ➤ Double click the root directory (a:\ or c:\) in the Directories list box to display the subdirectories on the selected drive.
- ➤ Double click the **ACCSDATA** directory to make it the active directory.
- ➤ Double click **BKSTORE.MDB** to open the database and display the database window.
- ➤ The Table Button is already selected. Double click the icon for the **Books table** to open the table from the previous exercise.
- ➤ Click the **maximize button** to see and access all fields in all records.
- ➤ *Exploring Powerpoint 4.0,* the book you added in the first exercise, appears in the middle of the table in sequence according to the ISBN field. (This is because the ISBN field has been designated as the primary key, a concept explained in Chapter 2.)

KEYBOARD SHORTCUTS: THE DIALOG BOX

Press Tab or Shift+Tab to move forward (backward) between fields in a dialog box, or press the Alt key plus the underlined letter to move directly to an option. Use the space bar to toggle check boxes on or off and the up and down arrow keys to move between options in a list box. Press enter to activate the highlighted command button and Esc to exit the dialog box without accepting the changes.

Step 2: The Find command
- ➤ Click anywhere in the Publisher field for the first record.
- ➤ Pull down the **Edit menu.** Click **Find** to display the dialog box in Figure 1.9a.
- ➤ Type **Prntice Hall** (omit the first "e"). Check that the other parameters for the Find command match the dialog box in Figure 1.9a.
- ➤ Click the **Find First command button.** Access moves to record 8, the record containing the designated character string, and selects the Publisher field for that record. You may need to move the dialog box (by dragging its title bar) to see the selected field.
- ➤ Click the **Close command button** to exit the Find dialog box and continue working in the table.

Step 3: Change an existing record
- ➤ You should be positioned in the Publisher field of record 8. (The status bar indicates record 8 of 17.) The record selector is a triangle indicating that no changes have yet been made to this record.
- ➤ Click immediately after the *r* in Prntice to deselect *Prntice Hall* and simultaneously set the insertion point. Type an **e** to correct the publisher's name for this record. The record selector changes to a pencil, indicating that a

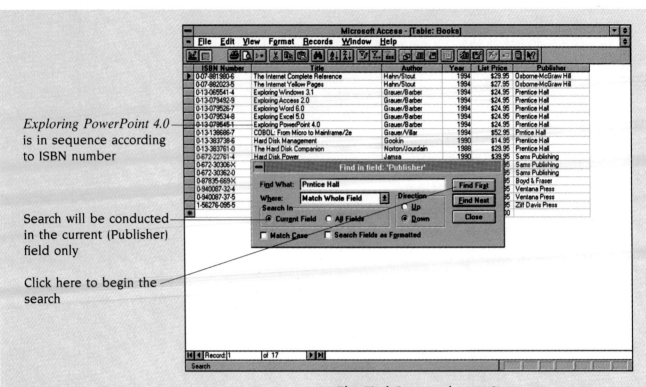

Exploring PowerPoint 4.0
is in sequence according
to ISBN number

Search will be conducted
in the current (Publisher)
field only

Click here to begin the
search

(a) The Find Command (step 2)

FIGURE 1.9   Hands-on Exercise 2

change has been made to this record, but that the change has not yet been
saved.

➤ Press the **down arrow** to move to the next record and simultaneously save
the change you just made. The record selector is again a triangle, indicating
that all changes have been saved.

TO SELECT OR NOT SELECT

The fastest way to replace the value in an existing field is to select the
field, then type the new value. Access automatically selects the field for
you when you use the keyboard (Tab, enter, or arrow keys) to move from
one field to the next. Click the mouse to deselect the field if you are
replacing only one or two characters rather than the entire field.

Step 4: The Undo command
➤ Pull down the **Edit menu.** Click **Undo Saved Record.** The Publisher field for
COBOL: From Micro to Mainframe reverts back to the incorrect spelling.
➤ Pull down the **Edit menu** a second time. The Undo command is dim, indi-
cating that you can no longer undo any changes. Press the **Esc** key twice to
continue working.
➤ Correct the Publisher field a second time and move to the next record to
save your change.

Step 5: The Delete command

➤ Click any field in the row containing the book titled *The Hard Disk Companion*. You can use the Find command as in the previous step, or you can click anywhere in record 10.

➤ Pull down the **Edit menu.** Click **Select Record** to highlight the entire record.

➤ Press the **Del key** to delete the record. You will see a dialog box as shown in Figure 1.9b, indicating that you have just deleted a record and asking you to confirm the deletion. Click **OK.**

➤ Pull down the **Edit menu.** The Undo command is dim, indicating that you cannot undelete a record. Press **Esc** to continue working.

THE ROW SELECTOR

Click the row selector (the box immediately to the left of the first field in a record) to select the record without having to use a pull-down menu. Click and drag the mouse over multiple rows to select several records at the same time.

Step 6: Data validation

➤ Click the **New button** on the toolbar as shown in Figure 1.9c. The record selector moves to the last record (record 17).

➤ Add data as shown in Figure 1.9c, being sure to enter an invalid price by typing **XXX** in the List Price field. Press the **Tab key** to move to the Publisher field.

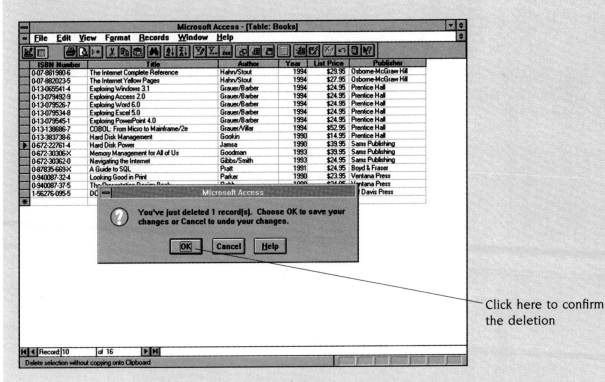

Click here to confirm the deletion

(b) The Delete Command (step 5)

FIGURE 1.9 Hands-on Exercise 2 (continued)

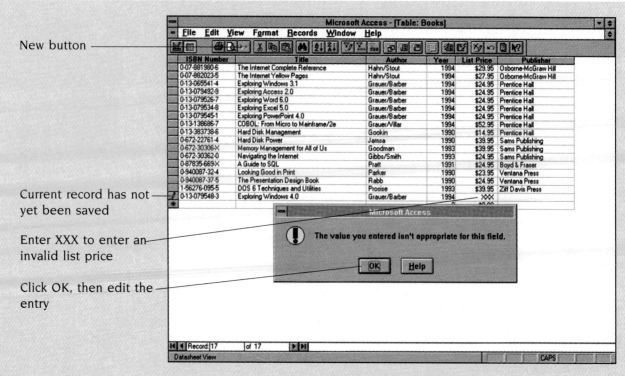

New button

Current record has not yet been saved

Enter XXX to enter an invalid list price

Click OK, then edit the entry

(c) Data Validation (step 6)

FIGURE 1.9   Hands-on Exercise 2 (continued)

➤ Access displays the dialog box in Figure 1.9c, indicating that the value you entered (**XXX**) is inappropriate for the List Price field; in other words, you cannot enter letters when Access is expecting a numeric entry.

➤ Click the **OK** command button to close the dialog box and return to the table. Drag the mouse to select XXX, then enter the correct price ($24.95).

➤ Press the **Tab key** to move to the Publisher field. Type **Prentice Hall.** Press the **Tab key, right arrow key,** or **enter key** to complete the record and move to the blank record at the end of the table.

➤ Double click the **control-menu box** to close the Books table and return to the database window.

Step 7: Open the Books form

➤ Click the **Form button** in the Database window. Double click the **Books form** to open the form as shown in Figure 1.9d.

➤ Click the **Add Record command button** to move to a new record. The status bar shows record 18 of 18.

➤ Enter data for the new book as shown in the figure. Click the **Close Form command button** when you are finished.

Step 8: Run a query

➤ Click the **Query button** in the Database window. Double click the **Publisher query** to run the query.

➤ You will see the dialog box in Figure 1.9e. Type **Prentice Hall** and press **enter** and you will see the books for the publisher you entered.

➤ Double click the **control-menu box** to close the query and return to the Database window.

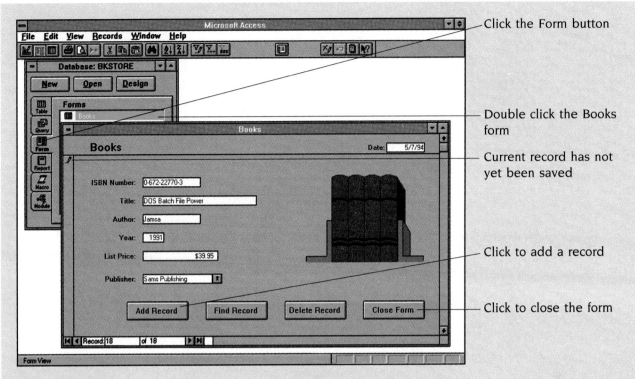

Click the Form button

Double click the Books form

Current record has not yet been saved

Click to add a record

Click to close the form

(d) The Books Form (step 7)

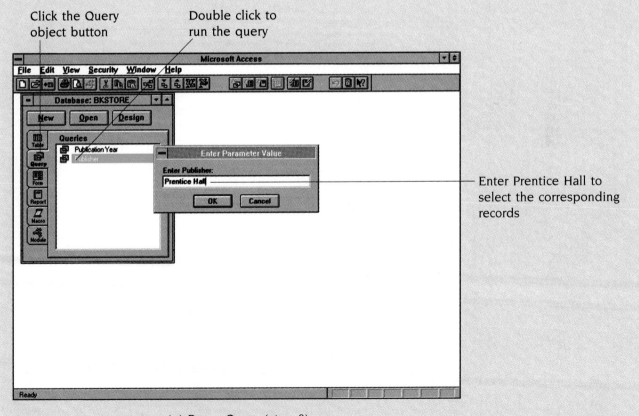

Click the Query object button

Double click to run the query

Enter Prentice Hall to select the corresponding records

(e) Run a Query (step 8)

FIGURE 1.9 Hands-on Exercise 2 (continued)

THE REPLACE COMMAND

Individuals familiar with a word processor know the advantages of the Replace command. The same capability is available in Access. Pull down the Edit menu and click Replace, then supply the necessary information in the dialog box.

Step 9: Print a report

➤ Click the **Report button** in the Database window to display the available reports.

➤ Double click the icon for the **Publishers report.** Type **Prentice Hall** (or the name of any other publisher) in the Parameter dialog box. Press **enter** to create the report.

➤ Click the **Maximize button** in the Report window so that the report takes the entire screen as shown in Figure 1.9f.

➤ Click the **Zoom button** on the Report toolbar so that you can see the entire page.

➤ Click the **Print button** on the Report toolbar to produce the Print dialog box. Click OK to print the report.

➤ Click the **Close Window button** to close the Report window.

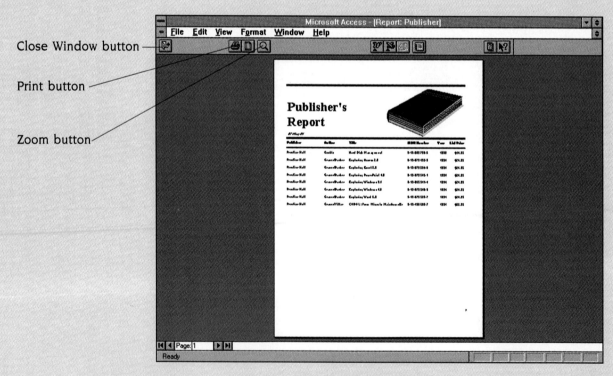

(f) Print a Report (step 9)

FIGURE 1.9   Hands-on Exercise 2 (continued)

Step 10: Exit Access
➤ Pull down the **File menu.** Click **Exit** to leave Access and return to Windows.

LOOKING AHEAD: A RELATIONAL DATABASE

The database we have been using is a simple database in that it contains only one
table. The real power of Access, however, is derived from multiple tables and the
relationships between those tables. This type of database is known as a ***relational
database.***

In this section we extend the Bookstore example by including additional
tables. We will ask you to look at the data in those tables in order to answer questions about the database. You will need to consider several tables at the same time,
but that is precisely what Access does. Once you see how the tables are related
to one another, you will be well on your way to designing your own applications.

Pretend again that you are the manager of the bookstore and think about
how you would actually use the database. You want information about the individual books, but you also need information about the publishers of those books.
At the very least you need the publishers' addresses and phone numbers so that
you can order the books. And once you order the books, you need to be able to
track the orders, to know when each order was placed, which books were ordered,
and how many. These requirements give rise to a database with several additional
tables as shown in Figure 1.10.

The Books table in Figure 1.10a is the table we have been using throughout
the chapter with one modification. This is the substitution of a PublisherID field
instead of the publisher's name. The Books table contains only fields that pertain
to a specific book such as the book's ISBN Number, Title, Author, Year (of publication), List Price, and PublisherID. The Publishers table has fields that pertain
to the publisher: PublisherID, PublisherName, Address, City, State, Zipcode, and
Phone. The PublisherID appears in both tables, which enables us to obtain the
publisher's address and phone number for a particular book. Consider:

Query: What are the address and telephone number for the publisher of the
book, *Exploring Windows 3.1?*
Answer: *Exploring Windows 3.1* is published by Prentice Hall, which is located at
113 Sylvan Avenue, Englewood Cliffs, NJ, 07632. The telephone number
is (800) 526-0485.

To determine the answer, Access would search the Books table for *Exploring Windows 3.1* to obtain the PublisherID (P4 in this example). It would then
search the Publishers table for the publisher with this PublisherID and read the
address and phone number. The relationship between the publishers and books is
an example of a ***one-to-many relationship.*** One publisher can have many books,
but a book can have only one publisher.

ISBN	Title	Author	Year	List Price	PublisherID
0-07-881980-6	The Internet Complete Reference	Hahn/Stout	1994	$29.95	P5
0-07-882023-5	The Internet Yellow Pages	Hahn/Stout	1994	$27.95	P5
0-13-065541-4	Exploring Windows 3.1	Grauer/Barber	1994	$24.95	P4
0-13-079492-9	Exploring Access 2.0	Grauer/Barber	1994	$24.95	P4
0-13-079526-7	Exploring Word 6.0	Grauer/Barber	1994	$24.95	P4
0-13-079534-8	Exploring Excel 5.0	Grauer/Barber	1994	$24.95	P4
0-13-138686-7	COBOL: From Micro to Mainframe/2e	Grauer/Villar	1994	$52.95	P4
0-13-383738-6	Hard Disk Management	Gookin	1990	$14.95	P4
0-13-383761-0	The Hard Disk Companion	Norton/Jourdain	1988	$29.95	P4
0-672-22761-4	Hard Disk Power	Jamsa	1990	$39.95	P3
0-672-30306-X	Memory Management for All of Us	Goodman	1993	$39.95	P3
0-672-30362-0	Navigating the Internet	Gibbs/Smith	1993	$24.95	P3
0-87835-669-X	A Guide to SQL	Pratt	1991	$24.95	P1
0-940087-32-4	Looking Good in Print	Parker	1990	$23.95	P2
0-940087-37-5	The Presentation Design Book	Rabb	1990	$24.95	P2
1-56276-095-5	DOS 6 Techniques and Utilities	Prosise	1993	$39.95	P6

(a) Books Table

PublisherID	Publisher Name	Address	City	State	Zipcode	Phone
P1	Boyd & Fraser	20 Park Paza	Boston	MA	02116	(800)543-8444
P2	Ventana Press	P.O. Box 2468	Chapel Hill	NC	27515	(800)743-5369
P3	Sams Publishing	11711 North College Avenue	Carmel	IN	46032	(800)526-0465
P4	Prentice Hall	113 Sylvan Avenue	Englewood Cliffs	NJ	07632	(800)526-0485
P5	Osborne McGraw-Hill	2600 Tenth Street	Berkeley	CA	94710	(800)338-3987
P6	Ziff Davis Press	5903 Christie Avenue	Emeryville	CA	94608	(800)688-0448

(b) Publishers Table

OrderID	Date	PublisherID
O1	6/12/94	P4
O2	5/31/94	P5
O3	7/01/94	P4
O4	4/30/94	P3
O5	6/18/94	P5
O6	5/22/94	P2
O7	4/18/94	P4
O8	5/01/94	P1

(c) Orders Table

OrderID	ISBN	Quantity
O1	0-13-065541-4	200
O1	0-13-079492-9	200
O1	0-13-079526-7	200
O1	0-13-079534-8	200
O2	0-07-881980-6	35
O3	0-13-065541-4	200
O3	0-13-079526-7	50
O3	0-13-079534-8	50
O4	0-672-22761-4	25
O4	0-672-30306-X	45
O5	0-07-881980-6	50
O5	0-07-882023-5	75
O6	0-940087-32-4	25
O7	0-13-138686-7	100
O7	0-13-065541-4	50
O8	0-87835-669-X	20

(d) Order Details Table

FIGURE 1.10 The Bookstore Database

Query: Which books are published by Ventana Press?

Answer: Two books, *Looking Good in Print* and *The Presentation Design Book,* are published by Ventana Press.

To answer this query, Access would begin in the Publishers table and search for Ventana Press to determine the PublisherID. It would then select all records in the Books table with a PublisherID of P2. It's easy once you recognize the relationship between the tables.

The Bookstore database in Figure 1.10 has a second one-to-many relationship—between publishers and orders. One publisher can receive many orders, but a given order goes to only one publisher. Use this relationship to answer the following queries:

Query: Which publisher received Order number O2?

Answer: Osborne McGraw-Hill received Order number O2.

To determine the publisher for a specific order, Access would search the Orders table (Figure 1.10c) for the specific order (order number O2 in this example) and obtain the corresponding PublisherID (P5). It would then search the Publishers table for the matching PublisherID and return the publisher's name.

You probably have no trouble recognizing the need for the Books, Publishers, and Orders tables in Figure 1.10. You may be confused, however, by the presence of the Order Details table, which is made necessary by the ***many-to-many relationship*** between orders and books. One order can specify several books, and at the same time, one book can appear in many orders. Consider:

Query: Which books were included in Order number O1?

Answer: *Exploring Windows 3.1, Exploring Excel 5.0, Exploring Word 6.0,* and *Exploring Access 2.0.*

To answer the query, Access would search the Order Details table for all records with an Order-ID of O1. Access would then take the ISBN number for each of these records into the Books table to obtain the title. Can you answer the next query, which is also based on the many-to-many relationship between books and orders?

Query: How many copies of *Exploring Windows 3.1* were ordered in all?

Answer: A total of 450 copies.

This time, Access searches the Books table to obtain the ISBN number for *Exploring Windows 3.1.* It then searches the Order Details table for all records with this ISBN number (0-13-065541-4) to add the individual quantities.

We trust that you were able to answer our queries by intuitively relating the tables to one another. You will also learn how to do this in Microsoft Access when we address this topic in Chapters 4 and 5 and Appendix A. You must first, however, develop a solid understanding of how to work with one table at a time, which is the focus of Chapters 2 and 3.

SUMMARY

The common user interface ensures that all Windows applications are similar in appearance and work basically the same way, with common conventions and a consistent menu structure. It provides you with an intuitive understanding of any application, even before you begin to use it, and means that once you learn one application, it is that much easier to learn the next.

The mouse is essential to Microsoft Access as it is to all other Windows applications, but keyboard equivalents are provided for virtually all operations. Toolbars provide other ways to execute common commands. On-line help provides detailed information about all aspects of Microsoft Access.

The database window displays the objects in a database, which include tables, forms, queries, reports, macros, and modules. The database window enables you to create a new object or to open an existing object.

A table is displayed in one of two views—the design view or the datasheet view. The design view is used to define the table initially and to specify the fields it will contain. The datasheet view is the view you use to add, edit, or delete records.

Each column represents a field. The first row in the table contains the field names. Each additional row contains a record. Every record contains the same fields in the same order.

A record selector symbol is displayed next to the current record and signifies the status of that record. A triangle indicates that you have not changed the data in the current record. A pencil indicates that you are in the process of entering (or changing) the data but that the changes have not yet been saved. An asterisk appears next to the blank record present at the end of every table where you add new records to the table.

A computer does exactly what you tell it to do, which is not necessarily what you want it to do. It is absolutely critical, therefore, that you validate the data that goes into a system, or else the associated information will not be correct.

Access automatically saves any changes in the current record as soon as you move to the next record or when you close the table. The Undo Saved Record command cancels (undoes) the changes to the previously saved record so long as no editing has been done to yet another record.

The real power of Access is derived from multiple tables and the relationships between those tables. This type of database is known as a relational database and is covered later in the text after you have mastered a single table.

 ## Key Words and Concepts

Application window	Datasheet view	Help menu
Asterisk (record selector)	Design view	Icon
Cascade menu	Desktop	Insertion point
Check box	Dialog box	Macro
Click	Dimmed command	Many-to-many relationship
Command button	Document window	Maximize button
Common user interface	Double click	MDB extension
Control-menu box	Drag	Menu bar
Cue Card	Drop-down list box	Microsoft Access
Current record	Ellipsis	Minimize button
Data validation	Field	Module
Database	Field name	Mouse pointer
Database Management System (DBMS)	Find command	Navigation button
Database window	Form	Object
	GIGO (garbage in, garbage out)	Object button

One-to-many
   relationship
Open list box
Option button
Pencil (record selector)
Point
Program Manager
Pull-down menu
Query
Record
Record selector symbol
Relational database

Report
Restore button
Scroll bar
Scroll box
Table
Text box
Title bar
Triangle (record
   selector)
Undo Current Field
   command

Undo Current Record
   command
Undo Saved Record
   command
Undo Typing command
Window

Multiple Choice

1. Which of the following will execute a command from a pull-down menu?
   (a) Clicking on the command once the menu has been pulled down
   (b) Typing the underlined letter in the command
   (c) Both (a) and (b)
   (d) Neither (a) nor (b)

2. Which program is always active during a Windows session?
   (a) Program Manager
   (b) Microsoft Access
   (c) Both (a) and (b)
   (d) Neither (a) nor (b)

3. What is the significance of three dots next to a menu option?
   (a) The option is not accessible
   (b) A dialog box will appear if the option is selected
   (c) A help window will appear if the option is selected
   (d) There are no equivalent keystrokes for the particular option

4. What is the significance of a menu option that appears faded (dimmed)?
   (a) The option is not currently accessible
   (b) A dialog box will appear if the option is selected
   (c) A help window will appear if the option is selected
   (d) There are no equivalent keystrokes for the particular option

5. Which of the following elements may be found within a help window?
   (a) Title bar, menu bar, and control-menu box
   (b) Minimize and maximize or restore buttons
   (c) Vertical and/or horizontal scroll bars
   (d) All of the above

6. Which of the following is true regarding a dialog box?
   (a) Option buttons indicate mutually exclusive choices
   (b) Check boxes imply that multiple options may be selected
   (c) Both (a) and (b)
   (d) Neither (a) nor (b)

7. Which of the following is true about moving and sizing a window?
    (a) The title bar is used to size a window
    (b) A border or corner is used to move a window
    (c) Both (a) and (b)
    (d) Neither (a) nor (b)

8. Which of the following objects are contained within an Access database?
    (a) Tables and forms
    (b) Queries and reports
    (c) Both (a) and (b)
    (d) Neither (a) nor (b)

9. The Open Database command:
    (a) Loads a database from disk into memory
    (b) Loads a database from disk into memory, then erases the database on disk
    (c) Stores the database in memory on disk
    (d) Stores the database in memory on disk, then erases the database from memory

10. Which of the following is true regarding the record selector symbol?
    (a) A pencil indicates that the current record has already been saved
    (b) A triangle indicates that the current record has not changed
    (c) An asterisk indicates the first record in the table
    (d) All of the above

11. Which view is used to add, edit, and delete records in a table?
    (a) The Design view
    (b) The Datasheet view
    (c) Either (a) and (b)
    (d) Neither (a) nor (b)

12. Which of the following is true with respect to a table within an Access Database?
    (a) Ctrl+Home moves to the last field in the last record of a table
    (b) Ctrl+End moves to the first field in the first record of a table
    (c) Both (a) and (b)
    (d) Neither (a) nor (b)

13. Which of the following is true of an Access database?
    (a) Every record in a table contains the same fields as every other record
    (b) Every table contains the same number of records as every other table
    (c) Both (a) and (b)
    (d) Neither (a) nor (b)

14. Which of the following best describes the relationship between publishers and books as implemented in the Bookstore database within the chapter?
    (a) One to one
    (b) One to many
    (c) Many to many
    (d) Impossible to determine

15. Which of the following best describes the relationship between books and orders as implemented in the Bookstore database within the chapter?

    (a) One to one

    (b) One to many

    (c) Many to many

    (d) Impossible to determine

ANSWERS

1. c	**9.** a
2. a	**10.** b
3. b	**11.** b
4. a	**12.** d
5. d	**13.** a
6. c	**14.** b
7. d	**15.** c
8. c	

EXPLORING ACCESS

1. Use Figure 1.11 to match each action with its result. A given action may be used more than once or not at all.

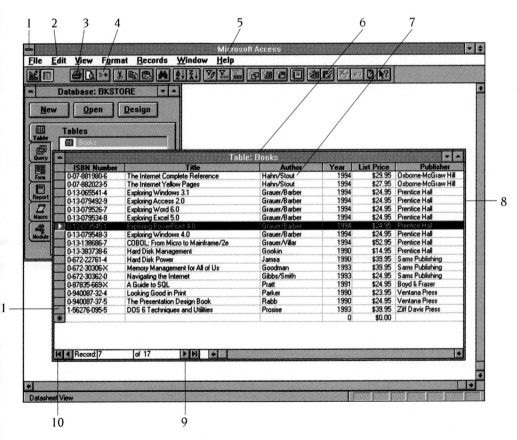
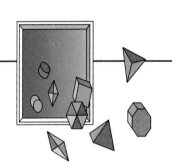

FIGURE 1.11 Screen for Problem 1

Action	Result
a. Double click at 1	___ Go to the first record in the table
b. Click at 3	___ Size the window
c. Click at 4	___ Exit Access
d. Click at 5	___ Add a new record to the table
e. Click and drag at 6	___ Move the window
f. Click at 7, click at 2	___ Go to the next record in the table
g. Click and drag at 8	___ Print the table
h. Click at 9	___ Delete *DOS 6 Techniques and*
i. Click at 10	*Utilities* from the table
j. Click at 11, then press the Del key	___ Find the book written by Jamsa
	___ Search for help on adding records

2 Exploring help: Answer the following with respect to Figure 1.12:
  a. What is the significance of the scroll box that appears within the scroll bar?
  b. What happens if you click on the down (up) arrow within the scroll bar?
  c. What happens if you click the maximize button? Might this action eliminate the need to scroll within the help window?
  d. How do you print the help topic shown in the window?
  e. Which entries in the help screen are underlined? What happens if you click an underlined entry?

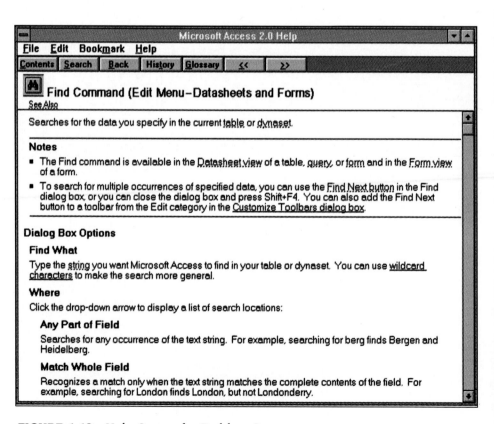

FIGURE 1.12 Help Screen for Problem 2

3. The error messages in Figure 1.13 appeared or could have appeared in conjunction with the hands-on exercises in the chapter. Indicate a potential cause of each error and a suggested course of action to correct the problem.

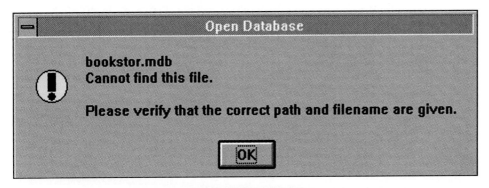

(a) Informational Message 1

(b) Informational Message 2

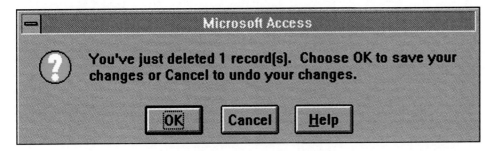

(c) Informational Message 3

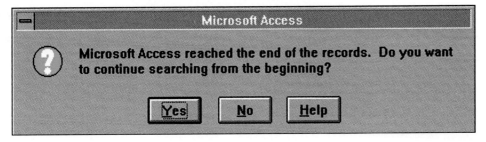

(d) Informational Message 4

FIGURE 1.13 Error Messages for Problem 3

4. The Replace command: The table in Figure 1.14 is a modified version of the Books table used in the chapter.

    a. Can the Current Field and All Fields option buttons in the Replace dialog box be checked simultaneously?

    b. Can the Match Case and Match Whole Field boxes in the Replace dialog box be checked simultaneously?

    c. Assume that the user clicks the All Fields option button, but makes no other changes to the dialog box. Which record will be returned when the user clicks the Find Next command button? Will you need to continue the search from the beginning of the table?

    d. Assume that the user clicks the Replace All command button. Will the replacement be made for the character string, *Prentice Hall Publishers*? for the character string, *prentice hall*?

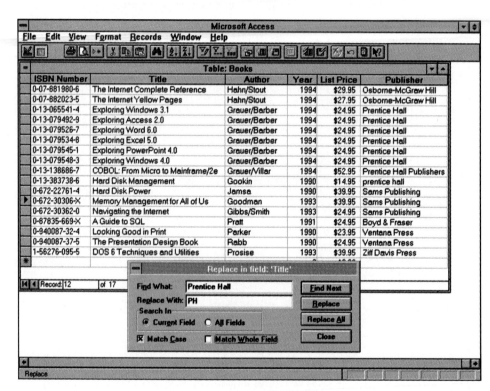

FIGURE 1.14 Screen for Problem 4

5. Data validation: Open the Bookstore database that was used in the chapter to add the book *Excel 4 for Windows,* by Hergert, published by Sybex in 1992, and priced at $14.95. The ISBN number is 0-7821-1016-9. First, however, we want you to enter the data *incorrectly* in order to evaluate the data validation capability that is built into the system. What happens if you:

    a. Omit the title or author field?

    b. Enter a duplicate value for ISBN?

    c. Enter a nonnumeric value for the year or price?

    d. Enter an inappropriate year (e.g., a year in the future)?

    Do you think that additional data validation should be built into the system?

6. Answer the following with respect to the Bookstore database in Figure 1.10:

    a. Which publisher received order number O8?

    b. How many orders have been placed by the bookstore?

c. How many orders were sent to Prentice Hall?

d. What is the price of *A Guide to SQL*? Who is the author? Who is the publisher? How many copies of this book have been ordered?

Which table (or tables) have to be modified to accommodate the following changes in the Bookstore database?

e. The phone number for Sams Publishing is changed to (800) 526-1000.

f. The price of *Exploring Windows* is increased to $25.95.

g. Order number O3 was modified to include 500 copies of *Exploring Windows 3.1* rather than the original 200.

h. Order number O9 was placed on June 6, 1994. The order is for 1,000 copies of *Exploring Windows, Exploring Word for Windows, Exploring Excel,* and *Exploring Access.*

i. The book, *Looking Good in Print,* is no longer carried by the bookstore.

j. Order number O7 is cancelled. Which record(s) have to be deleted from which table(s)?

k. What problems, if any, would be caused by deleting the record for Osborne McGraw-Hill from the Publishers table?

7. The EMPLOYEE.MDB database: The table in Figure 1.15 exists within the EMPLOYEE.MDB database on the data disk. Open the table and do the following:

a. Add a new record for yourself. You have been hired as a trainee earning $20,000 in Boston.

b. Delete the record for Kelly Marder.

c. Change Pamela Milgrom's salary to $59,500.

d. Use the Replace command to change all occurrences of "Manager" to "Supervisor".

e. Print the table after making the changes in parts a through d.

f. Print the All Employees Report after making the changes in parts a through d.

g. Print the Location Report after making the changes in parts a through d.

h. Create a cover page, then submit the output from parts e, f, and g to your instructor.

SocialSecurityNumber	LastName	FirstName	Location	Title	Salary	Sex
255-09-4456	Johnson	James	Chicago	Account Rep	$47500	M
255-69-7854	Marlin	Billy	Miami	Manager	$125000	M
265-30-9876	Manin	Ann	Boston	Account Rep	$49500	F
267-44-9850	Frank	Vernon	Miami	Manager	$75000	M
269-57-4322	Charles	Kenneth	Boston	Account Rep	$40000	M
279-85-2345	Adamson	David	Chicago	Manager	$52000	M
279-85-7644	Marder	Kelly	Chicago	Account Rep	$38500	F
388-56-3443	Brown	Marietta	Atlanta	Trainee	$18500	F
565-87-9002	Adams	Jennifer	Atlanta	Trainee	$19500	F
595-34-0289	Milgrom	Pamela	Boston	Manager	$57500	F
596-84-3222	Rubin	Patricia	Boston	Account Rep	$45000	F
598-65-8994	Coulter	Tracey	Atlanta	Manager	$100000	F
800-39-8764	Smith	Frank	Atlanta	Account Rep	$65000	M
800-56-8944	James	Mary	Chicago	Account Rep	$42500	F

Table: EMPLOYEE

Record: 1 of 14

FIGURE 1.15 Screen for Problem 7

8. Exploring Cue Cards: The best way to learn about Cue Cards is to use them.

a. What are Cue Cards supposed to do?

b. Which command, in which menu, will produce the opening Cue Card?

c. What is the corresponding toolbar icon?

d. Use either the Menu command (in part b) or the corresponding toolbar icon (in part c) to produce the opening Cue Card in Figure 1.16a.

e. Click the arrow next to "See a quick overview" to access the Cue Card in Figure 1.16b.

f. Click the arrow next to "Tables" to learn about this feature in Access. Follow the on-screen instructions to review the material that was presented in the chapter.

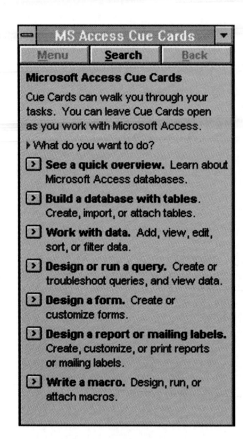

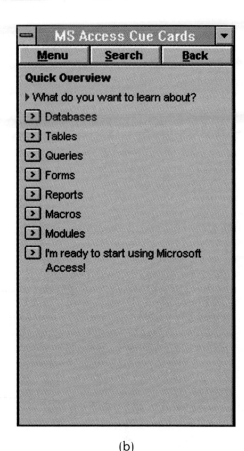

(a)   (b)

FIGURE 1.16 Cue Cards for Problem 8

 Case Studies

Planning for Disaster

This case has nothing to do with a database per se, but it is perhaps the most important case of all, as it deals with the question of backup. Do you have a backup strategy? Do you even know what a backup strategy is? You should learn, because sooner or later you will wish you had one. You will erase a file, be unable to read from a floppy disk, or worse yet, suffer a hardware failure in which you are unable to access the hard drive. The problem always seems to occur the night before an assignment is due. The ultimate disaster is the disappearance of your computer, by theft or natural disaster (e.g., Hurricane Andrew, the floods in the Midwest, or the Los Angeles earthquake). Describe in 250 words or less the backup strategy you plan to implement in conjunction with your work in this class.

Your Own Reference Manual

The clipboard is a temporary storage area available to all Windows applications. Selected text is cut or copied from one document into the clipboard from where it can be pasted into another document altogether. Use on-line help to obtain detailed information on several topics in Microsoft Access, copy the information to the clipboard, then paste it into a Word for Windows document, which will become your personal reference manual. To really do an outstanding job, you will have to format the reference manual after the information has been copied from the clipboard. Be sure to include a title page.

The Common User Interface

One of the most significant benefits of the Windows environment is the common user interface, which provides a sense of familiarity when you go from one application to another—for example, when you go from Excel to Access. How many similarities can you find between these two applications? Which menus are common to both? Which keyboard shortcuts? Which formatting conventions? Which toolbar icons? Which shortcut menus?

The Database Consultant

The university's bookstore manager has gone to your instructor and asked for help in improving the existing database. The manager needs to know which books are used in which courses. One course may require several books, and the same book is often used in many courses. A book may be required in one course and merely recommended in a different course. The manager also needs to be able to contact the faculty coordinator in charge of each course. Which additional table(s) should be added to the database in Figure 1.10 to provide this information? Which fields should be present in those tables?

2

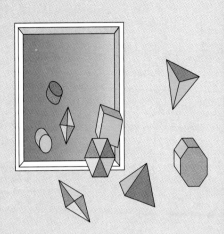

Tables and Forms: Design, Properties, Views, and Wizards

CHAPTER OBJECTIVES

After reading this chapter you will be able to:

1. Describe in general terms how to design a table; discuss three guidelines you can use in the design process.
2. Describe the field types and properties available within Access and the purpose of each; set the primary key for a table.
3. Use the Table Wizard to create a table; add and delete fields in an existing table.
4. Discuss the importance of data validation and how it is implemented in Access.
5. Use the Form Wizard to create one of several predefined forms.
6. Distinguish between a bound control, an unbound control, and a calculated control; explain how each type of control is entered on a form.
7. Modify an existing form to include a combo box, command buttons, and color.
8. Switch between the Form view, Design view, and Datasheet view; use a form to add, edit, and delete records in a table.

OVERVIEW

This chapter introduces a new case study, that of a student database, which we use to present the basic principles of tables and forms. The database has only a single table and is the focus of all examples in Chapters 2 and 3. Databases with multiple tables are covered in Chapters 4 and 5.

The first half of the chapter shows you how to create a table using the Table Wizard, then shows you how to modify the table by changing the properties of fields within the table. It stresses the importance of data validation during data entry. The second half of the chapter introduces forms as a more convenient way to enter and display data. You use the Form Wizard to create a basic form, then modify that form to include command buttons, a combo list box, color, and formatting.

The success of any database depends heavily upon the design of the underlying table(s). Thus, you should pay close attention to the conceptual discussion following the case study.

CASE STUDY: A STUDENT DATABASE

As a student you are well aware that your school maintains all types of data about you. They have your social security number. They have your name and address and phone number. They know whether or not you are receiving financial aid. They know your major and the number of credits you have completed.

Think for a moment, then write down all of the fields that might be stored in a student table. Try to include all of the data that is necessary for the school to produce the information it needs. Think how you should characterize each field according to the type of data it contains, such as text, numbers, or dates.

Our solution is shown in Figure 2.1, which may or may not correspond with what you have written. (The order of the fields within the table is not significant.) Whether or not your list of field names is the same as ours is not really important, because there are many acceptable solutions. What is important is that the table contain all necessary fields so that the system can perform as intended.

Figure 2.1 may seem obvious upon presentation, but it does reflect the results of a careful design process based on three essential guidelines:

1. Include the necessary data
2. Store data in its smallest parts
3. Avoid calculated fields

Each guideline is discussed in turn. As you proceed through the text, you will be exposed to many different applications that help you develop the experience necessary to design your own systems.

Field Name	Type
SocialSecurityNumber	Text
FirstName	Text
MiddleName	Text
LastName	Text
Address	Text
City	Text
State	Text
PostalCode	Text
PhoneNumber	Text
Major	Text
BirthDate	Date/Time
FinancialAid	Yes/No
Sex	Text
Credits	Number
QualityPoints	Number

No spaces are used in the field names

FIGURE 2.1 The Student Table

Include the Necessary Data

How do you determine the necessary data? The best way is to create a rough draft of the reports you will need, then check the table to be sure it contains the fields necessary to produce those reports. In other words, ask yourself what information will be expected from the system, then determine the data required to produce that information. Put another way, determine the input needed to produce the required output.

Consider, for example, the type of information that can and cannot be produced from the table in Figure 2.1:

➤ You can contact a student by mail or by telephone. You cannot contact the student's parents if the student lives on campus and thus has an address different from his or her parents' address.

➤ You can calculate a student's grade point average (GPA) by dividing the quality points by the number of credits. You cannot produce a transcript listing the courses a student has taken.

➤ You can calculate a student's age from his or her date of birth. You cannot determine how long the student has been at the university because the date of admission is not in the table.

Whether or not these omissions are important depends on the objectives of the system. Suffice it to say that you must design a table carefully, so that you are not disappointed when it is implemented. *You must be absolutely certain that the data entered into a system is sufficient to provide all necessary information;* otherwise the system is almost guaranteed to fail.

Store Data in Its Smallest Parts

Figure 2.1 divides a student's name into three fields (first, middle, and last) to reference each field individually. You might think it easier to use a single field consisting of the entire name, but that approach is inadequate. Consider the consequences of a single field with respect to the following names:

Allison Foster
Brit Reback
Carrie Graber
Danielle Ferrarro

Whether you realize it or not, the names are listed in alphabetical order (according to the design criteria of a single field). This is because the records are sorted according to the leftmost position in the designated field. Thus the "A" in Allison comes before the "B" in Brit, and so on. The proper way to sort is on last name, which can be done only if last name is stored as a separate field. At other times you may want to reference just the first name, perhaps to send informal letters with a salutation of the form, "Dear Allison" or "Dear Brit".

CITY, STATE, AND ZIP CODE—ONE FIELD OR THREE?

The city, state, and zip code should always be stored as separate fields. Any type of mass mailing requires you to sort on zip code to take advantage of bulk mail. Other applications may require you to select records in a particular state (or combination of states). The guideline is simple: store data in its smallest parts.

Avoid Calculated Fields

A *calculated field* is a field whose value is derived from an existing field or combination of fields. Calculated fields should not be stored in a table because they are subject to change, waste space, and are otherwise redundant.

Grade Point Average (GPA) is an example of a calculated field because it is computed by dividing the number of quality points by the number of credits. It is unnecessary, however, to store the GPA in the Student table since we store the fields on which it is based, and thus can instruct Access to calculate the GPA when it is needed.

BIRTH DATE VERSUS AGE

A person's age and date of birth provide equivalent information as one is calculated from the other. It might seem easier, therefore, to store the age rather than the birth date, and thus avoid the calculation. That would be a mistake because age changes continually, whereas the date of birth remains constant. Similar reasoning applies to an employee's length of service versus the date of hire.

CREATING A TABLE

There are two ways to create a table. The easiest way is to use the *Table Wizard,* an interactive coach that lets you choose from several predefined tables. The Table Wizard asks you questions about the fields you want to include in your table, then creates the table for you. Alternatively, you can create a table yourself by defining every field in the table. Regardless of how a table was created, you can modify it to include a new field or to delete an existing field.

Every field in a table has a field name and a data type. The *field name* should be descriptive of the data that will be entered into the field. It can be up to 64 characters, including letters, numbers, and spaces. We do not use spaces in our field names, which is consistent with the default names provided by Access in its predefined tables. LastName, BirthDate, and Credits are examples of field names in Figure 2.1.

Data Types

The *data type* indicates the nature of the data in the field and determines how Access processes that data. Text, Date/Time, and Number are examples of data types used in Figure 2.1.

The data type determines the values allowed in a field. It controls the amount of space allocated to a field and the types of operations that can be performed. There are eight different data types: Number, Text, Memo, Date/Time, Currency, Counter, Yes/No, and OLE Object.

A *number field* contains a value that can be used in a calculation such as the number of quality points or credits a student has earned. The contents of a number field are restricted to numbers, a decimal point, and a plus or minus sign.

A *text field* stores alphanumeric data such as a student's name or address. It can contain alphabetic characters, numbers, and/or special characters (e.g., an apostrophe in O'Malley). Fields that contain only numbers, but which are not used in a calculation (e.g., social security number, telephone number, or zip code), should be designated as text fields for efficiency purposes. A text field can hold up to 255 characters.

A *memo field* can be up to 64,000 characters long. Memo fields are used to hold descriptive data (several sentences or paragraphs).

A *Date/Time field* holds formatted dates or times (e.g., mm/dd/yy) and allows the values to be used in date or time arithmetic.

A *currency field* can also be used in a calculation and is used for fields that contain monetary values.

A *counter field* is a special data type that causes Access to assign the next consecutive number each time you add a record. By definition, the value of a counter field is unique for each record in the file, and thus counter fields are frequently used as the primary key.

A *Yes/No field* (also known as a Boolean or Logical field) assumes one of two values such as Yes or No, or True or False. A Yes/No field is preferable to one-position text fields because it is more efficient.

An *OLE field* contains an object created by another application. OLE objects include pictures, sounds, or graphics.

Primary Key

The *primary key* is a field (or combination of fields) that uniquely identifies a record. Every table must have a primary key, and there can be only one primary key per table.

A person's name is not used as the primary key because names are not unique. A social security number, on the other hand, is unique and is a frequent choice for the primary key. Social security number is the primary key in the Student table. The primary key emerges naturally in many applications such as a part number in an inventory system, or the ISBN number in the book table of Chapter 1.

Views

A table has two views—the Datasheet view and the Design view. The *Datasheet view* is the view you used in Chapter 1 to add, edit, and delete records. The *Design view* is the view you will use in this chapter to create a table.

Figure 2.2a shows the Datasheet view corresponding to the table in Figure 2.1. (Not all of the fields are visible.) The Datasheet view displays the record selector symbol for the current record (a pencil or a triangle). It also displays an asterisk as the record selector symbol next to the blank record at the end of the table.

Figure 2.2b shows the Design view of the same table. The Design view displays the field names in the table, the data type of each field, and the properties of the selected field. The Design view also displays a key indicator next to the field (or combination of fields) designated as the primary key.

Current record (has been saved)

SocialSecurityN	First Name	Middle Name	Last Name	Address	City	State	Postal Code	Phone Number
111-11-1111	Benjamin	David	Harrison	1718 Rodeo Drive	Coral Springs	FL	33071-8346	(305) 753-1098
222-22-2222	Juliette	Laura	Masters	8900 Main Highway	Chicago	IL	60620-4565	(312) 455-6521
333-33-3333	Patricia	Renee	Jones	500 Park Avenue	New York	NY	10020-0300	(212) 667-4848
444-44-4444	Matthew	James	Baldwin	3433 College Terrace	Baltimore	MD	21224-3443	(410) 444-8712
555-55-5555	Jessica	Lewis	Warner	426 Hardee Avenue	San Francisco	CA	94114-0876	(415) 677-4545
666-66-6666	Karen	Anne	Cutler	13601 S.W. 92 Avenue	Miami	FL	33176-6235	(305) 233-2020
777-77-7777	Kenneth	Neil	Irwin	900 Alamo Drive	Houston	TX	77090-0475	(713) 757-8400

Table: All Students

Blank record at end of table

Record: 1 of 7

(a) Datasheet View

FIGURE 2.2 The Views of a Table

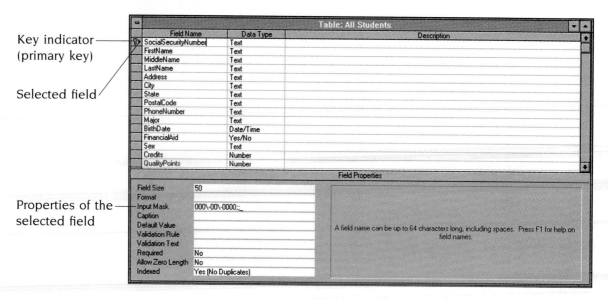

Key indicator (primary key)

Selected field

Properties of the selected field

(b) Design View

FIGURE 2.2 The Views of a Table (continued)

Property	Description
Field Size	Adjusts the size of a text field or limits the allowable value in a number field. Microsoft Access uses only the amount of space it needs even if the field size allows a greater number.
Format	Changes the appearance of number and date fields but does not affect the stored value.
Decimal Places	Controls the number of places after the decimal point for a Number or Currency field.
Input Mask	Displays formatting characters, such as hyphens in a social security number, so that the formatting characters do not have to be entered; imposes data validation by ensuring that the data fits in the mask size.
Caption	Specifies a label other than the field name for forms and reports.
Default Value	Automatically assigns a designated (default) value for the field in each record that is added to the table.
Validation Rule	Rejects any record where the data does not conform to the specified validation rule.
Validation Text	Specifies the error message that is displayed when the validation rule is violated.
Required	Rejects any record that does not have a value entered for this field.
Allow Zero Length	Allows text or memo strings of zero length.
Indexed	Increases the efficiency of a search on the designated field; the primary key is always indexed.

FIGURE 2.3 Field Properties

Field Properties

A *property* is a characteristic of an object that determines how the object appears or works. All Access objects (tables, forms, queries, and reports) have properties that control their behavior.

Each field also has a set of field properties that determine how the data in the field is stored and displayed. The properties are set to *default values* according to the data type but can be modified as necessary. The properties for each field are displayed in the Design view as shown in Figure 2.2b. The properties are described briefly in Figure 2.3 and illustrated in the hands-on exercise that follows.

HANDS-ON EXERCISE 1:

Creating a Table

Objective Use the Table Wizard to create a table; add and delete fields in an existing table; change the primary key of an existing table; establish an input mask and validation rule for fields within a table; switch between the design and datasheet views of a table. Use Figure 2.4 as a guide in the exercise.

Step 1: Create a new database

➤ Pull down the **File menu** and click **New Database** (or click the **New Database icon** on the toolbar). The New Database dialog box will appear as shown in Figure 2.4a.

➤ Click the Drives drop-down list box to specify the appropriate drive, drive C or drive A, depending on whether or not you installed the data disk in Chapter 1.

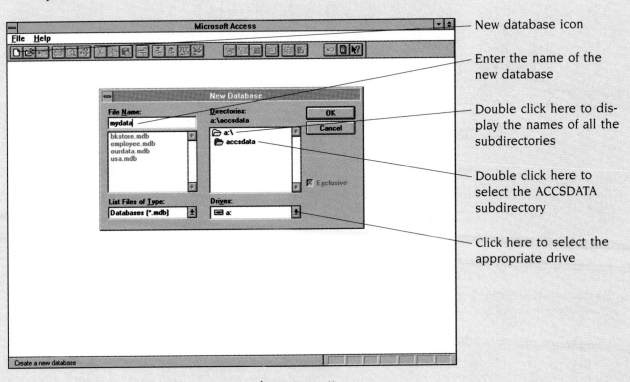

(a) Create a New Database (step 1)

FIGURE 2.4 Hands-on Exercise 1

➤ Double click the root directory (a:\ or c:\) to display the subdirectories on the selected drive. Use the **working disk** created in Chapter 1 (page 14) if you are not using the hard drive.

➤ Scroll through the Directories list box until you come to the **ACCSDATA** directory. Double click this directory to make it the active directory.

➤ Click in the **File Name text box** and drag to select **db1.mdb.** Type **MYDATA** as the name of the database you will create. (The MDB extension is added automatically.) Press **enter** or click **OK.**

CHANGE THE DEFAULT DIRECTORY

The default directory is the directory Access uses to retrieve (and save) a database unless it is otherwise instructed. To change the default directory, pull down the View menu, click Options, and select the General category. Click the down arrow in the Items list box and scroll to Default Database Directory. Enter the new directory (e.g., C:\ACCSDATA) and click OK. The next time you access the File menu the default directory will reflect the change.

Step 2: Create the table
➤ The Database window for the database MYDATA should appear on your monitor as shown in Figure 2.4b. (The table button is selected by default.)

Click here to create a new table

Table object is selected

Click here to enter selected field in the new table

Click here to scroll through available tables

Click here to select business-related tables

Click here to select a field

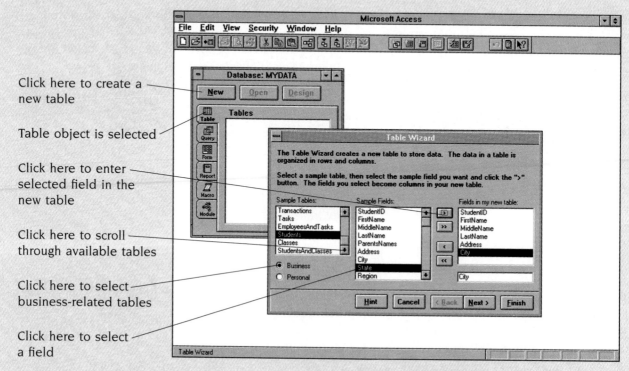

(b) The Table Wizard (step 3)

FIGURE 2.4 Hands-on Exercise 1 (continued)

➤ Click the **New command button** to create a table within the MYDATA database. Click the **Table Wizards button** in the New Table Dialog box to use the Table Wizard. You should see a dialog box similar to Figure 2.4b.

Step 3: The Table Wizard
➤ If necessary, click the **Business option** button. Click the **down arrow** on the Sample Table list box to scroll through the available business tables. (The tables are not in alphabetical order.) Double click the **Students table.**
➤ Click the **StudentID field** in the Sample Fields list box, then click the **> button** to enter this field in the new table list as shown in Figure 2.4b.
➤ Enter the remaining fields: **FirstName, MiddleName, LastName, Address, City, State, PostalCode, PhoneNumber,** and **Major.** Click the **Next command button** when you have entered all the fields.

WIZARDS AND BUTTONS

Many Wizards present you with two open list boxes and expect you to copy some or all fields from the list box on the left to the list box on the right. The > and >> buttons work from left to right. The < and << buttons work in the opposite direction. The > button copies the *selected* field from the list box on the left to the box on the right. The >> button copies *all* of the fields. The < button removes the *selected* field from the list box on the right. The << removes *all* of the fields.

Step 4: The Table Wizard (continued)
➤ The next screen in the Table Wizard asks you to name the table and determine the primary key.
  — The Table Wizard suggests Students as the name of the table. Change the name to **All Students.**
  — Make sure that the option button **Let Microsoft Access set a primary key for me** is selected.
  — Click the **Next command button** to accept both of these options.
➤ The final screen in the Table Wizard asks what you want to do next.
  — Click the option button to **Modify the table design.**
  — Click the **Finish command button.** The All Students table appears.
➤ Pull down the **File menu** and click **Save** (or click the **Save icon** on the Table Design toolbar) to save the table.

Step 5: Add the additional fields
➤ Click the **maximize button** to give yourself more room to work.
➤ Click the cell immediately below the last field in the table. Type **BirthDate** as shown in Figure 2.4c.
➤ Press the **Tab key** to move to the Data Type column. Click the **down arrow** on the drop-down list box. Click **Date/Time** as the field type for the BirthDate field.
➤ Add the remaining fields with the indicated field types to the Students table:
  — Add **FinancialAid** as a Yes/No field. (There is no space in the field name.)
  — Add **Sex** as a Text field.
  — Add **Credits** as a Number field.

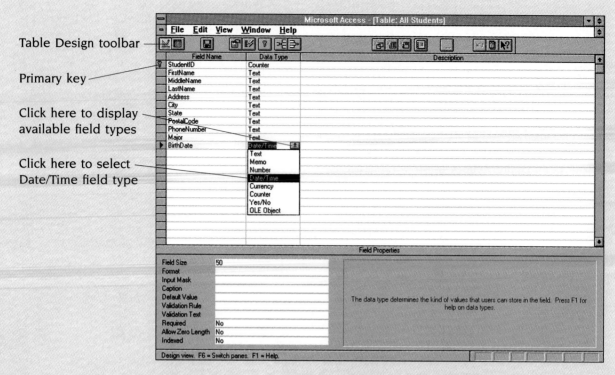

Table Design toolbar

Primary key

Click here to display
available field types

Click here to select
Date/Time field type

(c) Add the Additional Fields (step 5)

FIGURE 2.4 Hands-on Exercise I (continued)

— Add **QualityPoints** as a Number field. (There is no space in the field name.)
➤ Save the table.

CHOOSING A FIELD TYPE

The fastest way to specify the *field type* is to type the first letter; type T for text, D for date, N for Number, and Y for Yes/No. Text is the default data type.

Step 6: Change the primary key

➤ Point to the first row of the table and click the **right mouse button** to produce the shortcut menu in Figure 2.4d. Click **Insert Row** to insert a row.

➤ Click the **Field Name column** in the new row. Type **SocialSecurityNumber** (without spaces) as the name of the new field. Press **enter.** The data type will be set to Text by default.

➤ Click the **Set Primary Key icon** on the toolbar to change the primary key to social security number. The primary key symbol has moved from the StudentID field to the SocialSecurityNumber field.

➤ Point to the **StudentID field** in the second row. Click the **right mouse button** to display the shortcut menu. Click **Delete Row** to remove this field from the table definition.

➤ Save the table.

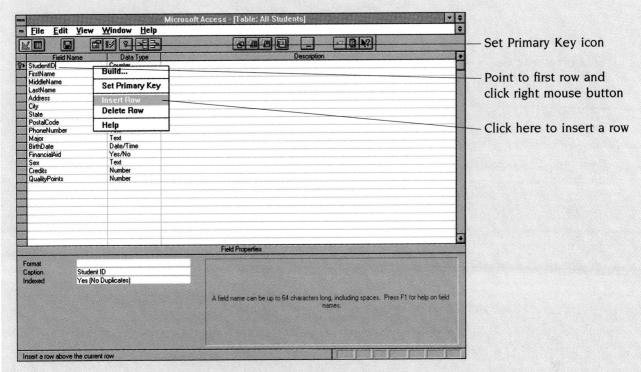

(d) Change the Primary Key (step 6)

FIGURE 2.4   Hands-on Exercise 1 (continued)

INSERTING OR DELETING FIELDS

Point to an existing field, then click the right mouse button to produce a
shortcut menu. Click Insert Row or Delete Row to add or remove a field
as appropriate. To insert (or delete) multiple fields, point to the field selector to the left of the field name, click and drag the mouse over multiple
rows to extend the selection, then click the right mouse button to produce
a shortcut menu.

Step 7: Add an input mask
➤ Click the field selector column for **SocialSecurityNumber.** Click the **Input
Mask** box in the Properties Area. (The box is currently empty.)
➤ Click the **Build button** to display the *Input Mask Wizard* as shown in Fig-
ure 2.4e. (You may see an informational message telling you to save the
table. Click **Yes.**)
➤ Click **Social Security Number** in the Input Mask dialog box. Click the **Try
It** text box to see how the mask works. If necessary, press the **left arrow key**
until you are at the beginning of the text box, then enter a social security
number (digits only). Click the **Finish command button** to accept the default
choices associated with establishing an *input mask.*
➤ Click the field selector column for **BirthDate,** then follow the steps detailed
above to add an input mask. (Choose the **Short Date** format.) Click **Yes** if
asked whether to save the table.
➤ Save the table.

Click here to select field

Click to select Social Security Number

Click here to see how the mask works

Build button

Click here to select Input Mask property

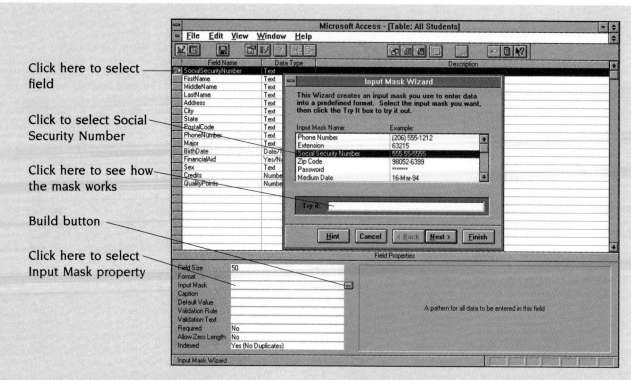

(e) Create an Input Mask (step 7)

FIGURE 2.4 Hands-on Exercise I (continued)

KEYBOARD SHORTCUTS

The keyboard is faster than the mouse if your hands are already on the keyboard. Press the Alt key plus the underlined letter to pull down the menu—for example, Alt+F to pull down the File menu—then type the underlined letter in the desired command—for example, S for Save. In other words, Alt+F, then the letter S, executes the File Save command.

Step 8: Add a Validation Rule
> Click the field selector column for the **Sex** field. Click the **Field Size box** and change the *field size* to **1** as shown in Figure 2.4f.
> Click the **Format box** in the Properties Area. Type a **>** sign to convert the data to uppercase.
> Click the **Validation Rule box.** Type **="M" or "F"** to accept only these values on data entry.
> Click the **Validation Text box.** Type **Specify M for Male or F for Female.**
> Save the table.

Step 9: Specify the required fields
> Click the field selector column for the **FirstName** field. Click the **Required box** in the Properties Area. Click the **down arrow** and select **Yes.**
> Repeat these steps to require the LastName and PhoneNumber.
> Save the table.

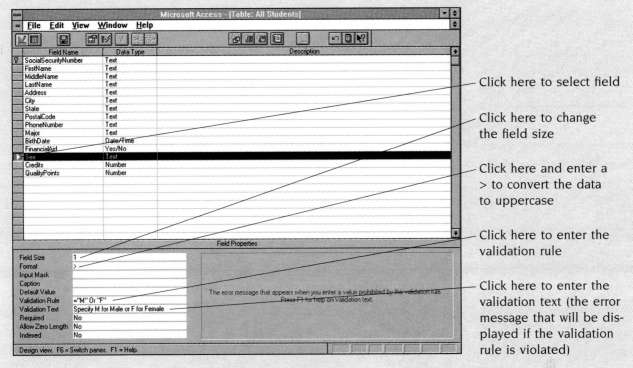

Click here to select field

Click here to change the field size

Click here and enter a > to convert the data to uppercase

Click here to enter the validation rule

Click here to enter the validation text (the error message that will be displayed if the validation rule is violated)

(f) Add a Validation Rule (step 8)

FIGURE 2.4   Hands-on Exercise I (continued)

Step 10: Change the field size

➤ Click the field selector column for the **State** field. Click the **Field Size box** in the Properties Area. Select **50** and enter **2** to limit the field to two characters corresponding to the accepted abbreviation for a state.

➤ Click the **Format box** in the Properties Area. Type a **>** sign to convert the data to uppercase.

➤ Change the field size for the **Credits** and **QualityPoints** fields to **Integer.**

➤ Save the table.

Step 11: The Datasheet view

➤ Pull down the **View menu** and click **Datasheet** (or click the **Datasheet icon** on the toolbar) to change to the Datasheet view as shown in Figure 2.4g.

➤ The insertion point (a flashing vertical line indicating the position where data will be entered) is automatically set to the first field of the first record.

➤ Type **111111111** to enter the social security number for the first record. (The mask will appear as soon as you enter the first digit.)

CHANGE THE FIELD WIDTH

Drag the border between field names to change the displayed width of a field. Double click the right boundary of a field name to change the width to accommodate the widest entry in that field.

Printer icon

Datasheet icon

Current record has not been saved

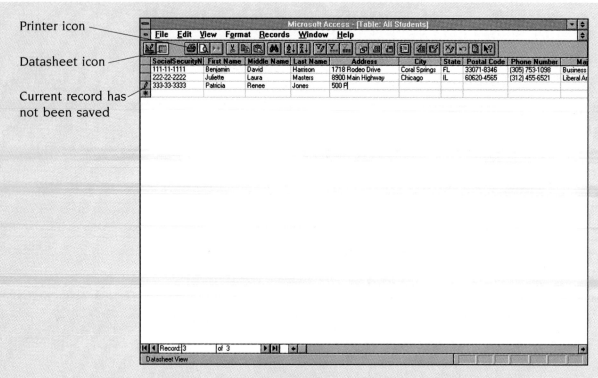

(g) Datasheet View (steps 11 and 12)

FIGURE 2.4 Hands-on Exercise 1 (continued)

➤ Press the **Tab key,** the **right arrow key,** or the **enter key** to move to the First-Name field. Enter the data for Benjamin Harrison as shown in Figure 2.4g. (Use any values you like for additional fields.)

➤ Scrolling takes place automatically as you move within the record.

Step 12: Enter additional data

➤ Enter data for the two additional students shown in the figure, but enter deliberately invalid data to experiment with the validation capabilities built into Access. Some of the errors you may encounter:

— The message, *The value you entered isn't appropriate for this field,* implies that the data type is wrong—for example, alphabetic characters in a numeric field such as Credits or something other than Yes or No for FinancialAid.

UNDO COMMAND

Access remembers the most recent change you made and enables you to undo that change. The Edit menu contains different Undo commands, depending on the nature of that change. The Undo Typing command lets you cancel your most recent change. The Undo Current Field command and Undo Current Record command cancel all changes to the current field or record, respectively. Even after the changes have been saved, the Undo Saved Record command undoes the changes to the previously edited record.

- The message, *Specify M for male or F for female,* means you entered a letter other than an "M" or an "F" in the Sex field (or you didn't enter a value at all).
- The message, *Duplicate value in index, primary key, or relationship,* indicates that the value of the primary key is not unique.
- The message, *Field 'All Students.LastName' can't contain a null value,* implies that you left a required field blank.
- If you encounter a data validation error, Press **Esc** (or click **OK**), then reenter the data.

Step 13: Print the student table

➤ Pull down the **File menu** and click **Print** (or click the **Print icon** on the toolbar).

➤ Click the **All option button** to print the entire table. Click the **OK** command button to begin printing. Do not be concerned if the table prints on multiple pages.

➤ Pull down the **File menu.** Click **Close** to close the Students table.

➤ Pull down the **File menu.** Click **Exit** if you want to leave Access.

THE PRINT SETUP COMMAND

The Print Setup command lets you change the margins and/or orientation and is helpful in printing tables with many fields. Pull down the File menu, click Print Setup, then click the Landscape option button. Change the left and right margins to .5 inch each to lengthen the print line. Click OK to exit the Print Setup dialog box.

FORMS

A *form* is an object in an Access database that provides an easy way to enter and display the data stored in a table. You type data into a form such as the one in Figure 2.5, and Access stores the data in the underlying table in the database. One advantage of using a form (as opposed to entering records in the Datasheet view) is that you can see all of the fields in a single record without scrolling. A second advantage is that a form can be designed to resemble a paper form, and thus provide a sense of familiarity for the individuals who actually enter the data.

A form may have different views, as does a table. The *Form view* in Figure 2.5a displays the completed form and is used to enter or modify data in the underlying table. The *Form Design view* in Figure 2.5b is used to create or modify the form.

A form is made up of objects called *controls.* Controls are bound, unbound, or calculated. A *bound control* (such as the *text boxes* in Figure 2.5a) has a data source (a field in the underlying table) and is used to enter or modify the data in that table. An *unbound control* has no data source. Unbound controls are used to display titles, labels, lines, or rectangles.

A *calculated control* has as its data source an expression rather than a field. An *expression* is a combination of operators (e.g., +, −, *, and /), field names, constants, and functions. A student's Grade Point Average is an example of a calculated control since it is computed by dividing the number of quality points by the number of credits.

Current record has not
yet been saved

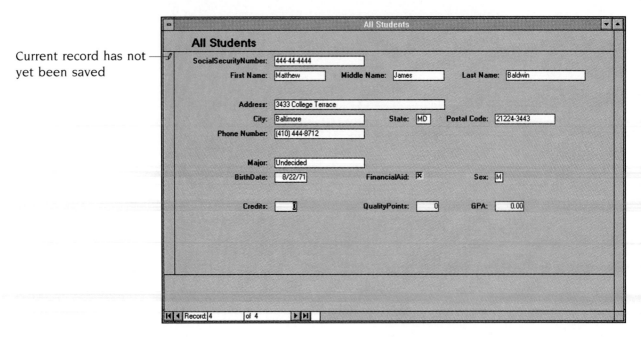

(a) Form View

Unbound control
(displays a title)

Bound control (a field
in the table is its data
source)

Calculated control (an
expression is its data
source)

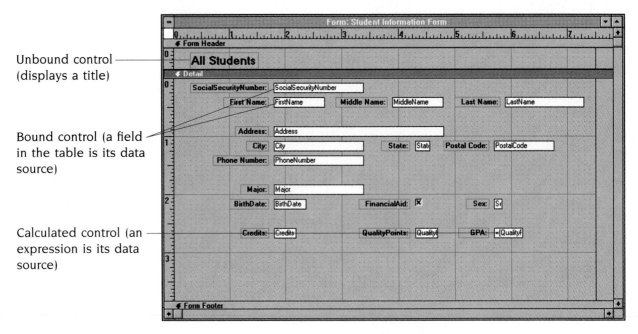

(b) Form Design View

FIGURE 2.5 Forms

Form Wizard

The easiest way to create a form is with the ***Form Wizard.*** The Form Wizard asks
questions about the form you want, then builds the form for you. You can accept
the form as it was created, or you can customize it to better suit your needs.

The controls in Figure 2.5 (except for the calculated control for GPA) were
created automatically by the Form Wizard, as you will see in the hands-on exer-

cise that follows shortly. It is up to you, however, to select, then move and/or size the controls to customize the form. Controls are treated just as any other Windows object. Thus:

To select a control—	Click anywhere on a control.
To size a control—	Click the control to select it, then drag the sizing handles. Drag the handles on the top or bottom to size the box vertically. Drag the handles on the left or right side to size the box horizontally. Drag the handles in the corner to size both horizontally and vertically.
To move a control—	Point to any border, but *not* to a sizing handle (the mouse pointer changes to a hand), then click the mouse and drag the control to its new position.

The following exercise creates a form based on the Student table from the first hands-on exercise. The Form Wizard is used to create the form initially, after which you will modify the form so that it matches the one in Figure 2.5.

INHERITANCE

A bound control inherits the same properties as the associated field in the underlying table. Due to this *inheritance* feature, changing a property setting of a field *after* the form has been created does *not* change the property of the control. Note, too, that changing the property setting of a control does *not* change the property setting of the field in the table.

HANDS-ON EXERCISE 2:

Creating a Form

Objective Use the Form Wizard to create a form; move and size controls within a form; use the completed form to enter data into the associated table. Use Figure 2.6 as a guide in the exercise.

THE TOOLBARS ARE DIFFERENT

The toolbars displayed by Access change automatically according to the view you are in. The Form Design toolbar contains icons to create or modify a form. The Form View toolbar contains icons used during data entry. Both toolbars contain icons to switch to the other view, to switch to the Datasheet view, and to display Cue Cards.

Step 1: Open the MYDATA database

➤ Load Microsoft Access. Pull down the **File menu** and click **Open Database** to display the Open Database dialog box (or click the **Open Database icon** on the toolbar).

➤ If you haven't changed the default directory:
  — Click the arrow on the Drives list box to select the appropriate drive—for example, drive C or drive A, depending on whether or not you installed the data disk.
  — Double click the root directory (a:\ or c:\) in the Directories list box to display the subdirectories on the selected drive.
  — Double click the **ACCSDATA** directory to make it the active directory.
➤ Double click **MYDATA.MDB** to open the database created in the first exercise.

Step 2: Create a new form

➤ Click the **Form button.** Click **New** to produce the New Form dialog box in Figure 2.6a.
➤ Click the **arrow** in the Select a Table/Query text box. Click **All Students** to select the All Students table created in the previous exercise.
➤ Click the **Form Wizards button** to use the Form Wizard. The first Form Wizards screen appears.

Step 3: The Form Wizard

➤ Click **Single-Column** as the type of form. Click **OK.**
➤ Click the **>> button** as shown in Figure 2.6b to enter all fields in the table on the form. Click the **Next command button.**
➤ Click the **Standard option button** to specify the style of your form. Click the **Next command button.**
➤ The next screen in the Form Wizard asks you for the title of the form and what you want to do next.

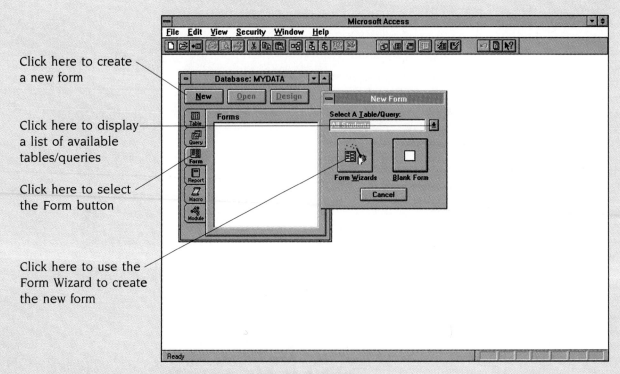

(a) Add a Form (step 2)

FIGURE 2.6   Hands-on Exercise 2

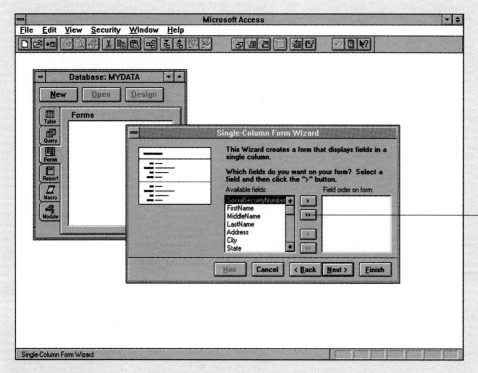

Click here to select all of the fields and enter them on the form in their current order

(b) The Form Wizard (step 3)

FIGURE 2.6 Hands-on Exercise 2 (continued)

— The Form Wizard suggests **All Students** as the title of the form. Keep this entry.

— Click the option button to **Modify the form's design.**

➤ Click the **Finish command button** to display the form in Design view. The Form Design toolbar appears automatically at the top of the window under the menu bar as shown in Figure 2.6c.

➤ The Toolbox toolbar may or may not be displayed. Click the **Toolbox icon** on the Form Design toolbar to toggle the display of the toolbox on and off. End with the toolbox hidden so you have more room to work in the next several steps.

Step 4: The Save command

➤ Click the **Maximize button** so that the form takes the entire screen.

➤ Pull down the **File menu** and click **Save** (or click the **Save icon** on the Form Design toolbar).

➤ Type **Student Information Form** in the Form Name text box as shown in Figure 2.6c. Click **OK.**

THE UNDO COMMAND

The Undo command is invaluable at any time, and is especially useful when moving and sizing controls. Pull down the Edit menu and click Undo (or click the Undo icon on the toolbar) immediately after making a mistake.

Form Design toolbar

Save icon

Toolbox icon

Undo icon

Enter name of form

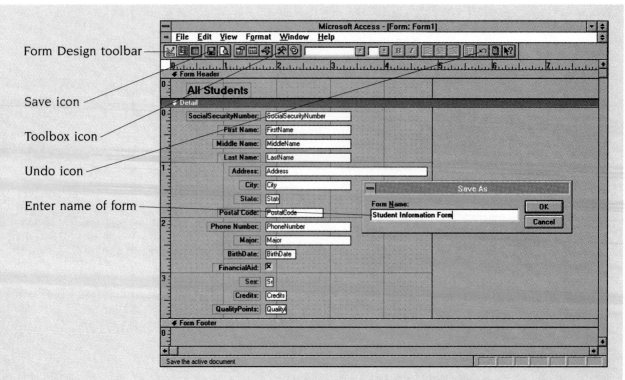

(c) The Save Command (step 4)

Click here to select the control for FirstName, then drag the sizing handle to shorten the text box

Click and drag right edge of form to 7.5"

Move handle

Sizing handle

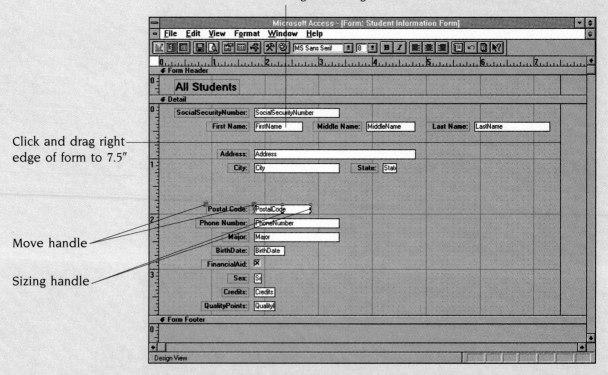

(d) Rearrange the Fields (step 5)

FIGURE 2.6   Hands-on Exercise 2 (continued)

Step 5: Move and size the controls
➤ Drag the right edge of the form so that the form is **7.5** inches wide.
➤ Click the control for **FirstName** to select the control and display the sizing handles. Be sure to click the text box and *not* the attached label. Drag the sizing handle to shorten the text box.
➤ Click the control for **MiddleName** and shorten its text box. Click and drag the border of the control (the pointer changes to a hand) to position the MiddleName field next to the FirstName field. Use the grid to space and align the controls.
➤ Size the control for **LastName,** then move it next to the MiddleName control as shown in Figure 2.6d. Be sure that the text box for LastName does not extend beyond the 7.5-inch border.
➤ Click and drag the other controls to complete the form:
— Place the controls for City, State, and PostalCode on the same line.
— Move the control for PhoneNumber up so that it is close to the address.
— Place the controls for BirthDate, FinancialAid, and Sex on the same line.
— Place Credits and QualityPoints on the same line.
➤ Do not be concerned if the size and/or placement of your text boxes differ from ours. (See tip box in the middle of page 64 to align the controls.)
➤ Save the form.

Step 6: Add a calculated control (GPA)
➤ Click the **Toolbox icon** on the toolbar to display the toolbox as shown in Figure 2.6e.
➤ Click the **Textbox tool** in the toolbox. The mouse pointer changes to a tiny cross with a text box attached.

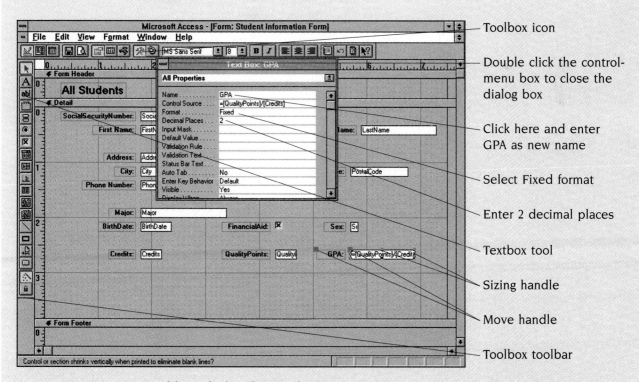

(e) Add a Calculated Control (step 6)

FIGURE 2.6 Hands-on Exercise 2 (continued)

- ➤ Click and drag in the form where you want the text box (the GPA control) to go, and release the mouse. You will see an Unbound control and an attached label containing a field number (e.g., Field42).
- ➤ Click in the text box of the control (Unbound will disappear). Type **=[QualityPoints]/[Credits]** to calculate a student's GPA. You must enter the field names *exactly* as they were defined in the table. (Do not include a space between Quality and Points.)
- ➤ Size the text box appropriately for GPA.
- ➤ Click and drag to select the text in the attached label (Field42), then type **GPA:** as the label for this control.

ALIGN THE CONTROLS

To align controls in a straight line (horizontally or vertically), press and hold the Shift key and click the labels of the controls to be aligned. Pull down the Format menu and select the edge to align (Left, Right, Top, and Bottom). Click the Undo command if you are not satisfied with the result.

SELECT THE CONTROL OR THE ATTACHED LABEL

A bound control is created with an attached label. Click the control, and the control has sizing handles and a move handle, but the label has only a move handle. Click the label (instead of the control), and the opposite occurs; the control has only a move handle, but the label will have both sizing handles and a move handle.

Step 7: Properties
- ➤ Point to the text box containing the expression =[QualityPoints]/[Credits] and click the **right mouse button** to display a shortcut menu. Click **Properties** to display the Properties dialog box in Figure 2.6e.
- ➤ Click the **Name** box. Replace the original name (Field42) with **GPA.**
- ➤ Click the **Format box.** Click the **down arrow** and select **Fixed.**
- ➤ Click the box for **Decimal places.** Enter **2** as the number of decimal places.
- ➤ Double click the **control-menu box** to close the Properties dialog box.
- ➤ Click the **Save icon** on the toolbar.

THE BORDER VERSUS THE MOVE HANDLE

You can move a control and its label together, or you can move them separately. Click and drag the border of either the control or the label to move them together. Click and drag the move handle (a tiny square in the upper-left corner) of either object to move them separately.

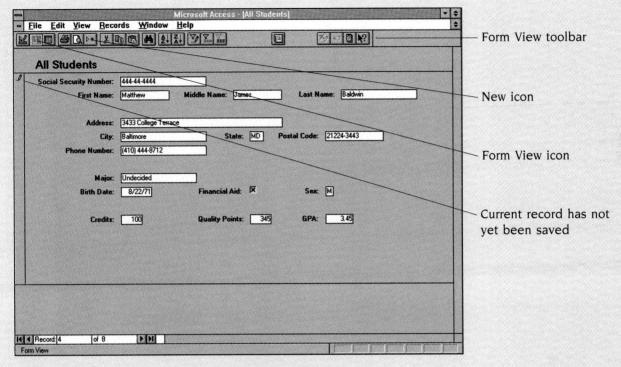

Form View toolbar

New icon

Form View icon

Current record has not yet been saved

(f) The Form View (step 8)

FIGURE 2.6 Hands-on Exercise 2 (continued)

Step 8: The Form View

➤ Click the **Form view icon** to switch to the Form view and the Form view toolbar. You will see the first record in the table (Benjamin Harrison).

➤ Click the **New icon** on the Form View toolbar to move to the end of the table and enter a new record.

➤ Enter data as shown in Figure 2.6f. The record selector symbol changes to a pencil as you begin to enter data.

— Press the **Tab key** to move from one field to the next within the form.

— Press the **space bar** or click the *check box* to toggle FinancialAid (a Yes/No field) on or off.

— All properties (masks and data validation) have been inherited from the All Students table created in the first exercise.

➤ Pull down the **File menu.** Click **Close** when you have completed the record. Click **Yes** if asked to save the changes.

➤ Pull down the **File menu.** Click **Exit** if you want to leave Access.

COMMAND BUTTONS AND COMBO BOXES

The Form Wizard provides an excellent starting point but stops short of creating the form you really want. Once you have mastered the basic operations to move and size controls, you will be looking for other ways to customize the form.

Figure 2.7a shows the Student Information Form at the end of the next hands-on exercise, which represents a marked improvement over its predecessor in Figure 2.5a. The date of execution appears near the top of the form. A combo box has been added to aid in entering a student's major. (A combo box is a combination of a list box and a table box.) Four command buttons appear at the bottom of the screen and correspond to common menu operations. The user's entries appear in blue to stand out from the rest of the form.

Figure 2.7b shows the Form Design view underlying the form in Figure 2.7a. Two additional toolbars are displayed, the *Toolbox* and the *Palette,* both of which are used to customize the form. The icons in the Toolbox enable you to add controls such as list boxes and command buttons. The Palette enables you to change the foreground or background color of text within a textbox and/or the line enclosing the textbox.

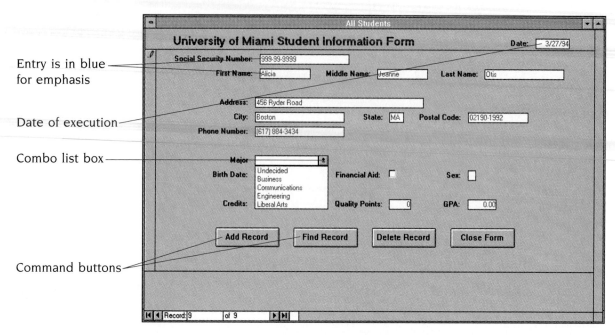

(a) The Form View

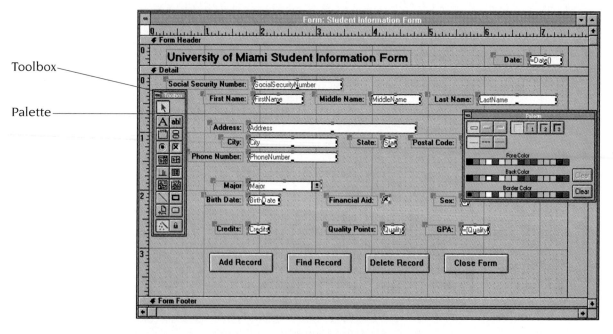

(b) The Form Design View

FIGURE 2.7   Command Buttons and Combo Buttons

HANDS-ON EXERCISE 3:

Customizing a Form

Objective Add and align command buttons in an existing form; add a combo box to facilitate data entry; use color to highlight selected controls. Use Figure 2.8 as a guide in the exercise.

Step 1: Open an existing form
➤ Open the **MYDATA** database we have been using throughout the chapter.
➤ Click the **Form button** in the Database window. The Student Information Form is already highlighted since there is only one form in the database. Click the **Design command button** to open the form from the previous exercise.
➤ If necessary:
— Click the **Maximize button** so that the form takes the entire window.
— Click the **Toolbox icon** to display the Toolbox toolbar.

FLOATING TOOLBARS

A toolbar can be docked (fixed) along the edge of the application window, or it can be displayed as a floating toolbar within the application window. To move a docked toolbar, drag the toolbar background. To move a floating toolbar, drag its title bar. To size a floating toolbar, drag any border in the direction you want to go. Double click the background of any toolbar to toggle between a floating toolbar and a docked (fixed) toolbar.

Step 2: Unbound controls
➤ Click the control in the Form Header, then click and drag to select the words **All Students.** Type **University of Miami Student Information Form** to change the text as shown in Figure 2.8a.
➤ Select the attached labels (*not* the text boxes) one at a time, to add spaces in the labels for **SocialSecurityNumber, BirthDate, FinancialAid,** and **QualityPoints** as shown in Figure 2.8a.
➤ Click the **Text box tool** in the toolbox.
➤ Click and drag in the form where you want the text box for the date. You will see an Unbound control and an attached label containing a field number (e.g., Field44).
➤ Click in the text box of the control (Unbound will disappear). Type **=Date().**
➤ Click the attached label, then click and drag to select the label. Type **Date:.**
➤ Save the form.

Step 3: Add a command button
➤ Click the **Command Button tool.** The mouse pointer changes to a tiny cross attached to a command button when you point anywhere in the form.
➤ Click and drag in the form where you want the button, then release the mouse. This draws a button and simultaneously opens the Command Button Wizard as shown in Figure 2.8b. (The number in your button may be different from ours.)

Change the text
of the title

Text box tool

Add spaces between
words in the label

Click and drag here (after
selecting the Text box
tool) to create a control
for the date

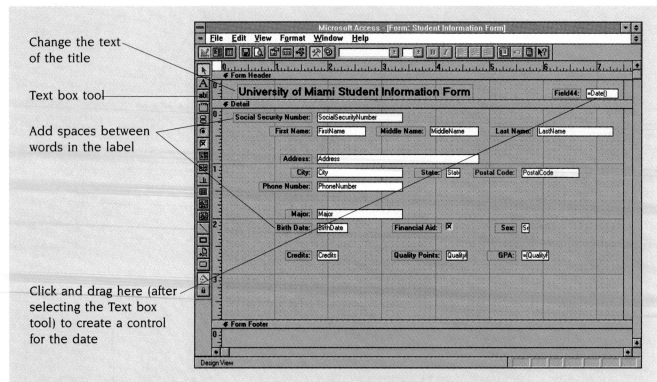

(a) Unbound Controls (step 2)

Categories list box

Click to select operation to
be assigned to the button

Command Button tool

Click and drag to create
the command button

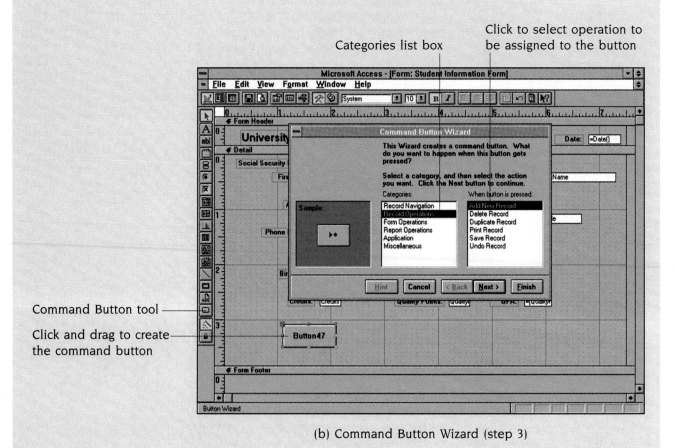

(b) Command Button Wizard (step 3)

FIGURE 2.8 Hands-on Exercise 3

- Click **Record Operations** in the Categories list box. Choose **Add New Record** as the operation. Click the **Next command button.**
- Click the **Text option button.** Click the **Next command button.**
- Type **Add Record** as the name of the button, then click the **Finish command button.** The completed command button should appear on your form.
- Save the form.

CUE CARDS

Cue Cards are always accessible and will coach you through a process as you work on your own database. Pull down the Help menu and click Cue Cards, or click the Cue Cards button on the toolbar. Follow the on-screen instructions to select the topic you need.

Step 4: Create the additional command buttons
- Click the **Command Button tool.** Click and drag on the form where you want the second button to go.
- Click **Record Navigation** in the Categories list box. Choose **Find Record** as the operation. Click the **Next command button.**
- Click the **Text option button.** Click the **Next command button.**
- Type **Find Record** as the name of the button, then click the **Finish command button.** The completed command button should appear on the monitor.
- Repeat these steps to add the command buttons to delete a record (Record Operations) and close the form (Form Operations).
- Save the form.

Step 5: Align the command buttons
- Select the four command buttons by pressing and holding the **Shift key** as you click each button. Release the Shift key when all of the buttons are selected.
- Pull down the **Format menu.** Click **Size** to display the cascade menu shown in Figure 2.8c. Click **to Widest** to set a uniform width for the selected buttons.
- Pull down the **Format menu** a second time, click **Horizontal Spacing,** then click **Make Equal.**
- Pull down the **Format menu** a third time, click **Align,** then click **Bottom** to complete the alignment.
- Save the form.

CHECK YOUR NUMBERS

The width of the form, plus the left and right margins, cannot exceed the width of the page. Thus increasing the the width of a form may require a corresponding decrease in the left and right margins or a change to landscape (rather than portrait) orientation. Pull down the File menu and choose the Print Setup command to modify the dimensions of the form prior to printing.

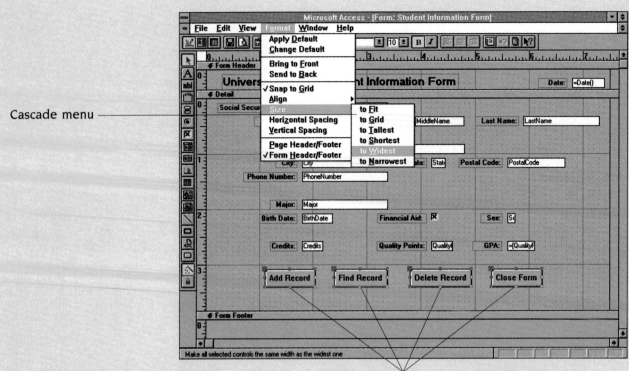

Cascade menu

Select multiple command buttons at one time by
pressing Shift as you click the additional buttons

(c) Align the Buttons (step 5)

FIGURE 2.8 Hands-on Exercise 3 (continued)

Step 6: Add a Combo box
➤ The Combo box that you create in this step will replace the existing text
box. Accordingly, click the text box for **Major,** then press the **Del key.** The
label and text box are deleted.
➤ Click the **Combo Box tool.** The mouse pointer changes to a tiny cross
attached to the image of a list box. Click and drag in the form where you
want the combo box, then release the mouse to open the Combo Box
Wizard.
➤ Click the **option button** indicating that you will type the values you want.
Click the **Next command button.**
➤ The **Number of Columns** box is selected as shown in Figure 2.8d. Type **1.**

Step 7: The Combo Box Wizard (continued)
➤ Click the first row under Col 1 heading (the second column will disappear).
Type **Undecided** as shown in Figure 2.8d. Press the **enter key** to move to the
row for the next major.
➤ Continue to enter majors as shown in Figure 2.8d. The Combo Box Wizard
follows the same convention with the record selector as with an ordinary
table.
➤ Click the **Next command button** when you have entered all the majors.
➤ Click the **option button** to store the selected value in a field as shown in Figure 2.8e. Click the arrow on the drop-down list box and select **Major.** Click
the **Next command button.**

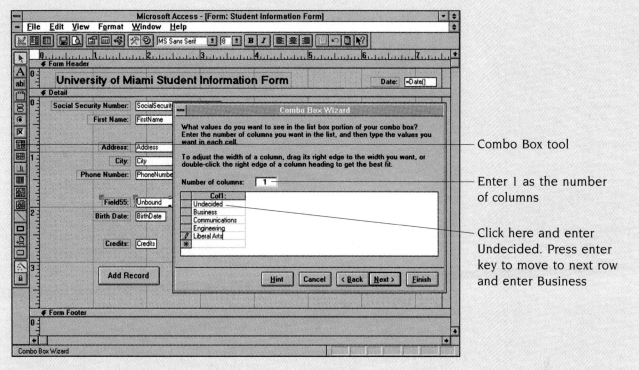

Combo Box tool

Enter 1 as the number of columns

Click here and enter Undecided. Press enter key to move to next row and enter Business

(d) The Combo Box Wizard (steps 6 and 7)

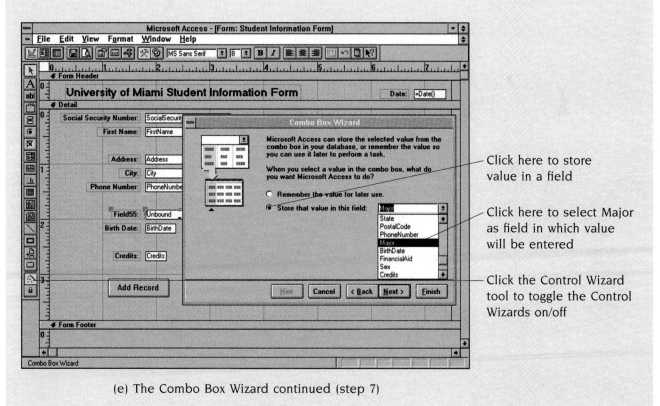

Click here to store value in a field

Click here to select Major as field in which value will be entered

Click the Control Wizard tool to toggle the Control Wizards on/off

(e) The Combo Box Wizard continued (step 7)

FIGURE 2.8 Hands-on Exercise 3 (continued)

➤ Type **Major** when asked for the label of the combo box and press **enter.** Click the **Finish command button.** Size and/or move the control so that it aligns properly on the form.

➤ Save the form.

LIST BOX VERSUS COMBO BOX

The toolbox enables you to create a list box or a **_combo box,_** both of which let you select a value from a displayed list. The difference is that a combo box lets you enter a value that is not on the list, whereas a list box does not. A combo box takes less room on the form as only the current selection is displayed; a list box displays all available choices.

Step 8: Change the Tab Order

➤ Point to the control for **Major,** click the **right mouse button** to display a short-cut menu, then click **Properties.** Click the drop-down list box and select **All Properties.**

➤ The property box for **Name,** which currently contains a field number, is selected. Type **Major.**

➤ Double click the **control-menu box** to close the dialog box.

➤ Pull down the **Edit menu.** Click **Tab Order** to display the dialog box in Figure 2.8f.

Drag Major to new position below Phone Number in the Custom Order list

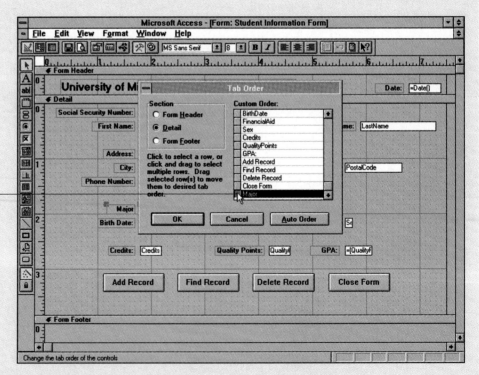

(f) Change the Tab Order (step 8)

FIGURE 2.8   Hands-on Exercise 3 (continued)

- ➤ Click the **down arrow** in the Custom Order list box to scroll to Major, the last control in the form.
- ➤ Click the row selector for **Major.** Move the pointer so that it changes to a white arrow, then drag until Major is immediately under PhoneNumber. Click **OK.**
- ➤ Save the form.

Step 9: Add color
- ➤ Click the **Palette icon** on the toolbar to display the Palette toolbar as shown in Figure 2.8g.
- ➤ Select all of the text boxes by pressing and holding the **Shift key** as you click each text box. Release the Shift key when all of the text boxes are selected.
- ➤ Click **Dark Blue** as the foreground color. The text changes to dark blue in the selected text boxes.
- ➤ Click in the form to deselect the text boxes.
- ➤ Save the form.

MORE IS NOT BETTER

More is not better, especially in the case of too many colors that detract from a form rather than enhance it. Access makes it almost too easy to switch foreground, background, and border colors and/or to change fonts and styles. Use restraint. A simple form is far more effective than one that uses too many fonts and colors simply because they are there.

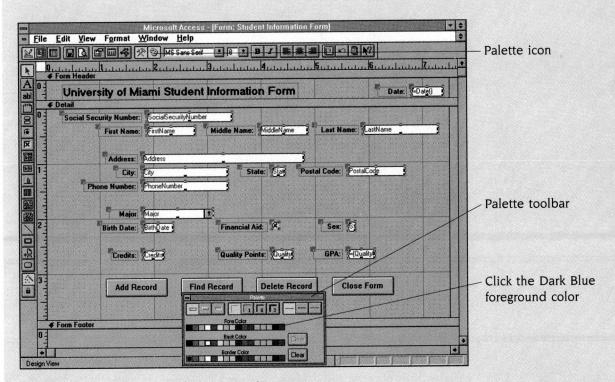

(g) Changing Colors (step 9)

FIGURE 2.8 Hands-on Exercise 3 (continued)

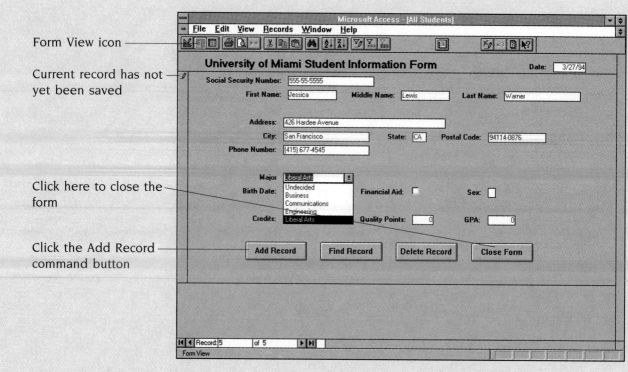

Form View icon

Current record has not yet been saved

Click here to close the form

Click the Add Record command button

(h) The Completed Form (step 10)

FIGURE 2.8   Hands-on Exercise 3 (continued)

Step 10: The completed form

➤ Click the **Form view icon** to switch to the form view. You will see the first record in the table.

➤ Click the **Add Record command button.** Click the text box for Social Security Number, then begin to add the record as shown in Figure 2.8h. The record selector changes to a pencil to indicate the record has not been saved.

➤ Press the **Tab key** or the **enter key** to move from field to field within the record.

➤ Click the **arrow** on the drop-down list box to display the list of majors.

➤ Click the **Close Form command button** when you have completed the record.

➤ Pull down the **File menu.** Click **Exit** to leave Access.

SUMMARY

Data should be stored in its smallest parts and should be sufficient to produce all required information. Calculated fields should not be stored in a table.

The Table Wizard is the easiest way to create a table. It lets you choose from a series of business or personal tables, asks you questions about the fields you want in the selected table, then creates the table for you.

A table has two views—the Design view and the Datasheet view. The Design view is used to create the table and display the fields within the table, as well as the data type and properties of each field. The Datasheet view is used after the table has been created to add, edit, and delete records.

A form provides an easy way to enter and display data in that it can be made to resemble the paper form on which a table is based. The Form Wizard is the easiest way to create a form. The Form Design view enables you to modify a form after it has been created.

A form consists of objects called controls. A bound control has a data source such as a field in the underlying table. An unbound control has no data source. A calculated control contains an expression. Controls are selected, moved, and sized the same way as any other Windows object. Forms may be further customized through the Toolbox and Palette.

 ## Key Words and Concepts

Bound control	Field	Memo field
Calculated control	Field name	Number field
Calculated field	Field property	OLE field
Check box	Field size	Palette toolbar
Combo box	Field type	Primary key
Control	Form	Table Wizard
Counter field	Form Design View	Text box
Cue Cards	Form View	Text field
Currency field	Form Wizard	Toolbox toolbar
Data type	Format property	Unbound control
Datasheet view	Index	Validation rule
Date/Time field	Inheritance	Validation text
Default value	Input mask	Yes/No field
Design view	Input mask wizard	
Expression	Label	

 ## Multiple Choice

1. Which of the following is true?
   (a) The Table Wizard must be used to create a table
   (b) The Form Wizard must be used to create a form
   (c) Both (a) and (b)
   (d) Neither (a) nor (b)

2. Which of the following validation checks is implemented automatically by Access?
   (a) Rejection of a record with a duplicate value of the primary key
   (b) Rejection of numbers in a text field
   (c) Both (a) and (b)
   (d) Neither (a) nor (b)

3. Social security number, phone number, and zip code should be designated as:
   (a) Number fields
   (b) Text fields
   (c) Yes/No fields
   (d) Any of the above, depending on the application

4. Which of the following is true of the primary key?
   (a) Its values must be unique
   (b) It must be defined as a text field
   (c) It must be the first field in a table
   (d) It can never be changed

5. Social security number is used as a primary key rather than name because:
   (a) The social security number is numeric, whereas the name is not
   (b) The social security number is unique, whereas the name is not
   (c) The social security number is a shorter field
   (d) All of the above

6. Which of the following is true regarding buttons within the Form Wizard?
   (a) The > button copies a selected field from a table onto a form
   (b) The < button removes a selected field from a form
   (c) Both (a) and (b)
   (d) Neither (a) nor (b)

7. Which of the following was *not* a suggested guideline for designing a table?
   (a) Include all necessary data
   (b) Store data in its smallest parts
   (c) Avoid calculated fields
   (d) Designate at least two primary keys

8. Which of the following are valid parameters for use with a form?
   (a) Portrait orientation, a form width of 6 inches, left and right margins of 1¼ inch
   (b) Landscape orientation, a form width of 9 inches, left and right margins of 1 inch
   (c) Both (a) and (b)
   (d) Neither (a) nor (b)

9. Which view is used to add, edit, or delete records in a table?
   (a) The Datasheet view
   (b) The Form view
   (c) Both (a) and (b)
   (d) Neither (a) nor (b)

10. Which of the following is true regarding toolbars in the Form view and Form Design view?
   (a) The toolbars are identical
   (b) The icon to add a new record is on the Form Design toolbar
   (c) The icon to display the Palette toolbar is on the Form View toolbar
   (d) Both toolbars contain the icon to switch to the Datasheet view

11. In which view will you see the record selector symbols of a pencil and a triangle?
   (a) Only the Datasheet view
   (b) Only the Form view
   (c) The Datasheet view and the Form view
   (d) The Form view, the Form Design view, and the Datasheet view

12. To move a control (in the Form Design view), you select the control, then:
   (a) Point to a border (the pointer changes to an arrow) and click and drag the border to the new position
   (b) Point to a border (the pointer changes to a hand) and click and drag the border to the new position
   (c) Point to a sizing handle (the pointer changes to an arrow) and click and drag the sizing handle to the new position
   (d) Point to a sizing handle (the pointer changes to a hand) and click and drag the sizing handle to the new position

13. Which fields are commonly defined with an input mask?
   (a) Social security number and phone number
   (b) First name, middle name, and last name
   (c) City, state, and zip code
   (d) All of the above

14. Which field type appears as a check box in a form?
   (a) Text field
   (b) Number field
   (c) Yes/No field
   (d) All of the above

15. Which properties would you use to limit a user's response to two characters, and automatically convert the response to uppercase?
   (a) Field Size and Format
   (b) Input Mask, Validation Rule, and Default Value
   (c) Input Mask and Required
   (d) Field Size, Validation Rule, Validation Text, and Required

ANSWERS

1. d	**6.** c	**11.** c
2. a	**7.** d	**12.** b
3. b	**8.** c	**13.** a
4. a	**9.** c	**14.** c
5. b	**10.** d	**15.** a

EXPLORING ACCESS

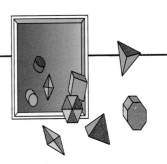

1. Use Figure 2.9 to match each action with its result. A given action may be used more than once or not at all.

Action	Result
a. Click at 1	___ Create a command button
b. Click at 2	___ Move the selected control
c. Click at 3	___ Save the form design
d. Click at 4	___ Create an unbound control
e. Click at 5	___ Suppress the display of the tool-box

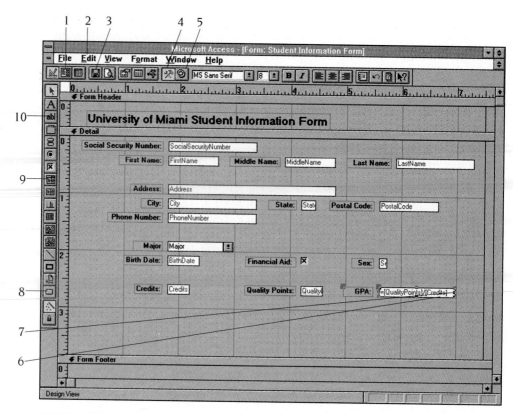

FIGURE 2.9 Screen for Problem 1

Action	Result
f. Click and drag at 6	___ Size the selected control
g. Click and drag at 7	___ Change to the Form view
h. Click at 8, click in the form, and drag to size control	___ Create a combo box
i. Click at 9, click in the form, and drag to size control	___ Change the tab order
j. Click at 10, click in the form, and drag to size control	___ Display the palette

2. Careful attention must be given to designing a table or else the resulting system will not perform as desired. Consider the following:

   a. An individual's age may be calculated from his or her birth date, which in turn can be stored as a field within a record. An alternate technique would be to store age directly in the record and thereby avoid the calculation. Which field, age or birth date, would you use? Why?

   b. Social security number is typically chosen as the primary key instead of a person's name. What attribute does the social security number possess that makes it the superior choice?

   c. Zip code is normally stored as a separate field to save money at the post office in connection with a mass mailing. Why?

   d. An individual's name is normally divided into two (or three) fields corresponding to the last name and first name (and middle initial). Why is this done; that is, what would be wrong with using a single field consisting of the first name, middle initial, and last name, in that order?

3. The error messages in Figure 2.10 appeared or could have appeared in conjunction with the hands-on exercises in the chapter. Indicate a potential cause of each error and a suggested course of action to correct the problem.

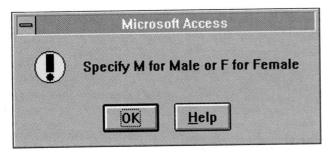

(a) Error Message 1

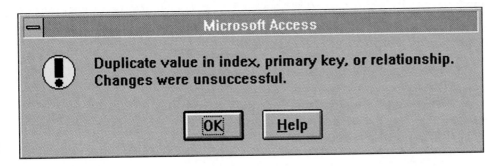

(b) Error Message 2

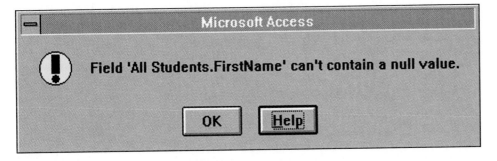

(c) Error Message 3

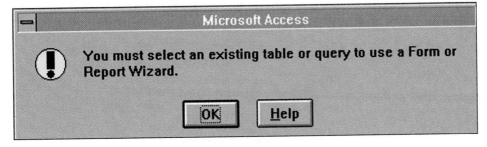

(d) Error Message 4

FIGURE 2.10   Error Messages for Problem 3

4. Field Properties: The Help screen in Figure 2.11 was produced by searching on *Field Size*.

a. What is the default setting of the Field Size property for a text field? What is the maximum field size for a text field?

b. What is the default setting of the Field Size property for a number field? Which setting should be used for fields such as QualityPoints or Credits in the Student table that was developed in the chapter?

c. What is the difference between the Byte, Integer, and Long Integer field sizes?

d. What is to be gained (or lost) by changing the Field Size property in an existing table from Double to Integer?

e. What is to be gained (or lost) by changing the Field Size property in an existing table from Integer to Long Integer?

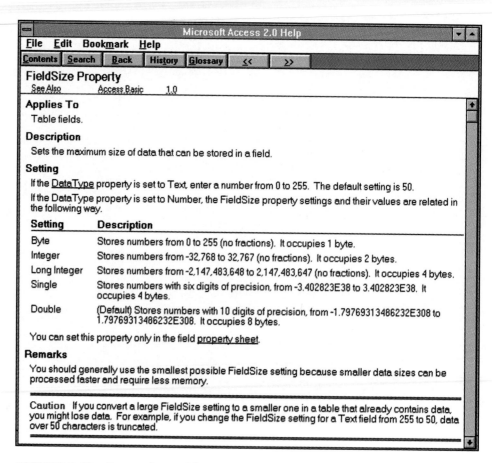

FIGURE 2.11 Screen for Problem 4

5. The Table Wizard: The Table Wizard anticipates several applications you might find useful on a personal basis and includes several tables to get you started. Select one of the personal tables of interest to you such as the Music Collection, Video Collection, or Exercise Log. Create the table and corresponding form, then enter at least 10 records. Use data validation as appropriate.

6. Open the EMPLOYEE.MDB database found on the data disk to create a form similar to the one in Figure 2.12.

   a. The form was created by using the Form Wizard and the Embossed style. The various controls were then moved and sized to match the arrangement in the figure.

   b. The date of execution, combo boxes, and command buttons were added after the form was created, using the techniques in the third hands-on exercise.

   c. To add lines to the form, click the Line tool in the toolbox, then click and drag on the form to draw the line. To draw a straight line, press and hold the Shift key as you draw the line.

   d. You need not match our form exactly, and we encourage you to experiment with a different design.

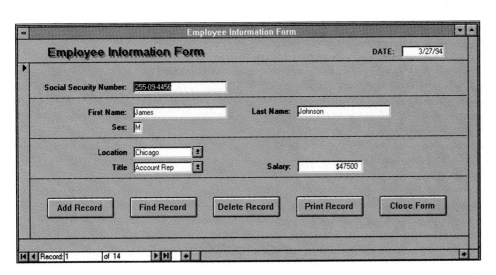

FIGURE 2.12 Screen for Problem 6

7. Open the USA.MDB database found on the data disk to create a form similar to the one in Figure 2.13.

   a. The form was created by using the Form Wizard and Standard style. The various controls were then moved and sized to match the arrangement in the figure.

   b. Population density is a calculated control and is computed by dividing the population by the area.

   c. You need not match our form exactly, and we encourage you to experiment with different designs.

   d. The Find command can be used after the form has been created to search through the table and answer questions about the United States, such as "Which state is nicknamed the Empire State?"

8. Modify the Student Information Form created in the hands-on exercises to match the form in Figure 2.14. (The form contains three additional controls that must be added to the All Students table.)

   a. Add DateAdmitted and EmailAddress as text fields in the All Students table. Add a Yes/No field to indicate whether or not the student is an International student.

   b. Add controls for the Date Admitted and Email address as shown in Figure 2.14. (Pull down the View menu, click Field list, then drag the fields from the Field list to the form.) Be sure to change the tab order after you

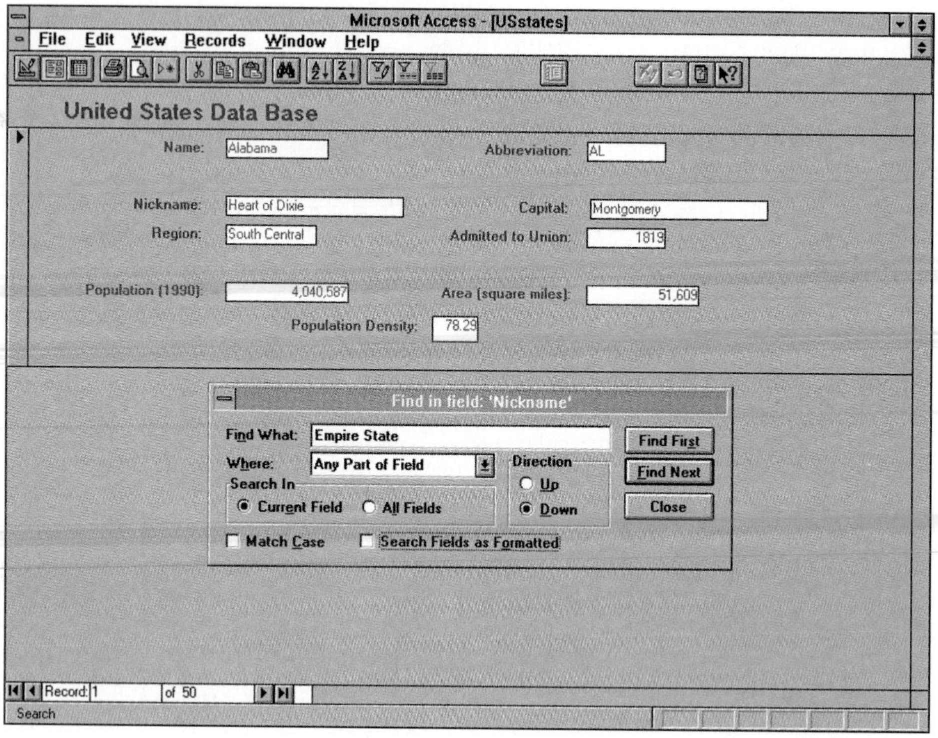

FIGURE 2.13 Screen for Problem 7

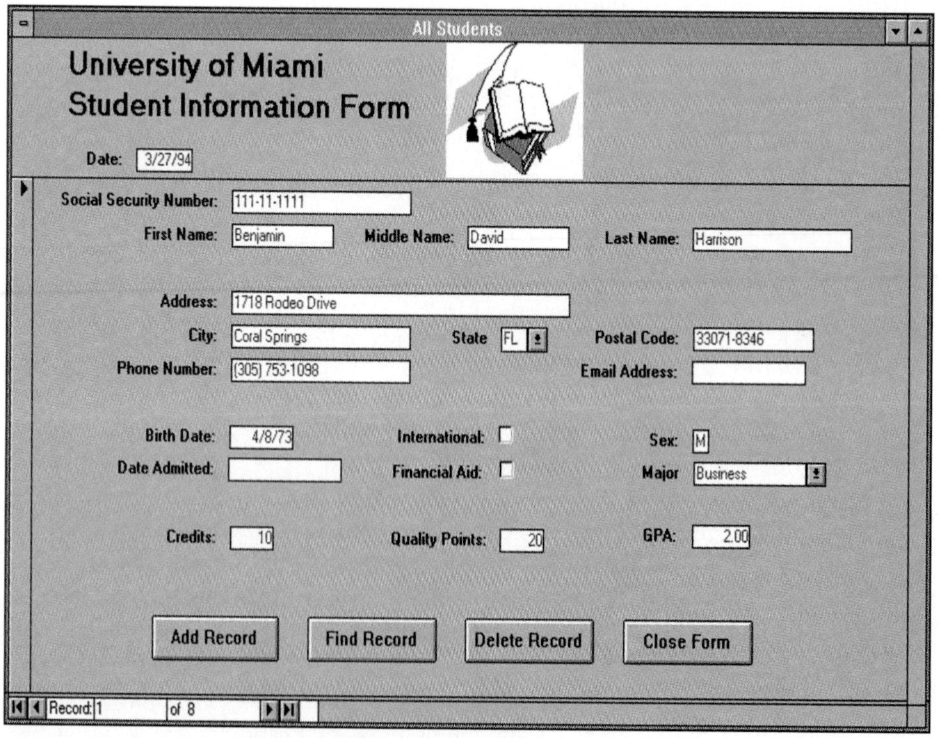

FIGURE 2.14 Screeen for Problems 8 and 9

have added the controls so that the user moves easily from one field to the next when entering data.

   c. Create a check box for the International field. (Click the Check box tool in the toolbox, then click and drag the International field from the field list to the form. You may have to pull down the View menu and click Field List to display the field list.)

   d. Delete the existing control for State and substitute a combo box instead. Use CA, FL, NJ, and NY as these are the most common states in the Student body. Modify the tab order to accommodate the new control.

   e. Resize the control in the Form Header so that *University of Miami Student Information Form* takes two lines. Press Ctrl+Enter to force a line break within the control.

   f. Add the graphic as described in problem 9.

9. Object Linking and Embedding: This exercise continues problem 8 (or it can be done immediately after the third hands-on exercise). The steps below describe how to insert a graphic created by another application as an object on an Access form. The exercise works as described, but you will be frustrated unless you have a fast 486 machine.

   a. Click the Object Frame tool on the toolbox. (If you are unsure as to which tool to click, just point to the tool to display the name of the tool.)

   b. Click and drag in the Form Header to size the frame, then release the mouse to display an Insert Object dialog box.

   c. Click the New option button. Scroll through the list box until you can select Microsoft Word 6.0 Picture, then click OK.

   d. Word for Windows will be opened automatically and a document window will be displayed with the insertion point in a rectangular frame. (The title bar of the Word document will reflect the Access Form.)

   e. Pull down the Insert menu, click Picture, then double click the graphic you want. (We chose BOOKS.WMF). Size the picture in Word so that it is the size you want on the Access form. Click the Close Picture command button.

   f. The status bar will display a message indicating that Word is updating the picture, after which you will be returned to Access. The graphic (from Word) appears on the form.

   g. You can move the frame containing the graphic in Access. You can also size the frame to display more (or less) of the picture but you *cannot* change its scale unless you double click the graphic and return to Word.

Case Studies

Personnel Management

You have been hired as the Personnel Director for a medium-sized firm (500 employees) and are expected to implement a system to track employee compensation. You want to be able to calculate the age of every employee as well as the length of service. You want to know each employee's most recent performance evaluation. You want to be able to calculate the amount of the most recent salary increase, in dollars as well as a percentage of the previous salary. You also want to know how long the employee had to wait for that increase—that is, how much time elapsed between the present and previous salary. Design a table capable of providing this information.

The Stockbroker

A good friend has come to you for help. He is a new stock broker whose firm provides computer support for existing clients, but does nothing in the way of data management for prospective clients. Your friend is determined to succeed and wants to use a PC to track the clients he is pursuing by telephone and through the mail. He wants to keep track of when he last contacted a person, how the contact was made (by phone or through the mail), and how interested the person was. He also wants to store the investment goals of each prospect, such as growth or income and whether a person is interested in stocks, bonds, and/or a retirement account. And finally, he wants to record the amount of money they have to invest. Design a table suitable for the information requirements of your friend.

Metro Zoo

Your job as Director of Special Programs at the Metro Zoo has put you in charge of this year's fund-raising effort. You have decided to run an "Adopt an Animal" campaign and are looking for contributions on three levels: $25 for a reptile, $50 for a bird, and $100 for a mammal. Adopting "parents" will receive a personalized adoption certificate, a picture of their animal, and educational information about the zoo. You already have a great mailing list—the guest book that is maintained at the zoo entrance. Your main job is to computerize that information and to store additional information about contributions that are received. Design a table that will be suitable for this project.

Form Design

Collect several examples of real forms such as a magazine subscription, auto registration, or employment application. Choose the form you like best and implement the system in Access. Start by creating the underlying table (with some degree of validation), then use the Form Wizard to create the form. How closely does the form you created resemble the paper form with which you began?

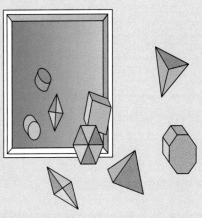

3

Information from the Database: Reports and Queries

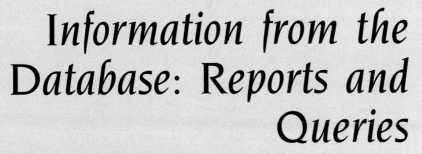

CHAPTER OBJECTIVES

After reading this chapter you will be able to:

1. Describe the different types of reports available through the Report Wizard.
2. Describe the different views in the Report Window and the purpose of each.
3. Describe the similarities between forms and reports with respect to bound, unbound, and calculated controls.
4. List the sections that may be present in a report and explain the purpose of each.
5. Differentiate between a query and a table; explain how the objects in an Access database (tables, forms, queries, and reports) interact with one another.
6. Use the Query By Example (QBE) grid to create and modify a select query.
7. Explain the use of multiple criteria rows within the QBE grid to implement And and Or conditions in a query.
8. Describe the different views in the Query window and the purpose of each.

OVERVIEW

Data and information are not synonymous. Data refers to a fact or facts about a specific record, such as a student's name, major, quality points, or number of completed credits. Information is data that has been rearranged into a more useful format. The fields within an individual student record are considered data. A list of students on the Dean's List is information produced from the data about individual students.

Chapters 1 and 2 described how to enter and maintain data through the use of tables and forms. This chapter shows how to convert the data to information through queries and reports. Queries enable you to ask questions about the database. Reports provide presentation quality output and display summary information about groups of records.

As you read the chapter, you will see that the objects in an Access database (tables, forms, reports, and queries) have many similar characteristics. We use these similarities to build on what you already know. You understand the concept of inheritance and recognize how fields in a form inherit their properties from the corresponding fields in a table. The same applies to the fields in a report. You have worked with the Design views of a table and a form, so you already appreciate the Design views for reports and queries. In similar fashion, since you already know how to move and size controls within a form, you also know how to move and size them in a report.

The chapter contains three hands-on exercises that give you the opportunity to practice what you have learned. All of the examples use an expanded version of the All Students table from Chapter 2.

REPORTS

A *report* is a printed document that displays information from a database. Figure 3.1 shows several sample reports. The reports were created with the Report Wizard and are based on the All Students table that was presented in Chapter 2. (The table has been expanded to 24 records and will be used in the hands-on exercises.) As you view each report, ask yourself how the data in the table was rearranged to produce the information in the report.

The *AutoReport* in Figure 3.1a is the simplest type of report. It lists every field for every record in a single column and typically runs for many pages.

The *Tabular report* in Figure 3.1b displays fields for a given record in a row rather than in a column. Each record in the underlying table is printed on its own row. Only selected fields are displayed, so the tabular report is more concise than the columnar report of Figure 3.1a. The records in Figure 3.1b are listed in alphabetical order by last name.

The report in Figure 3.1c is also a tabular report, but it contains very different information from the first two reports. It displays only the students with a GPA of 3.50 or higher. The Dean's List contains *selected records* from the All Students table, as opposed to the other two reports, which displayed every record.

The *Group/Total report* in Figure 3.1d displays summary calculations for groups of students. It groups students according to their major, then lists them alphabetically within each major. The report displays summary information for each group of students (the number of students in that major). It also contains summary information (not visible in Figure 3.1d) for the report as a whole, which shows the total number of students.

The letters in Figure 3.1e illustrate a *mail merge* in which the same letter is sent to many different people. (See problem 8 at the end of the chapter.) The mail merge uses selected fields (a student's name and address) for selected students (those who qualify for the Dean's List). The form letter is written in Word for Windows (or another word processor), but the data is taken from Access. The *mailing labels* in Figure 3.1f were created in support of the mail merge.

DATA VERSUS INFORMATION

Data and information are not synonymous although the terms are often interchanged. **Data** is the raw material and consists of the table (or tables) that constitutes a database. **Information** is the finished product. Data is converted to information by selecting records, performing calculations on those records, and/or changing the sequence in which the records are displayed. Decisions in an organization are made on the basis of information rather than raw data.

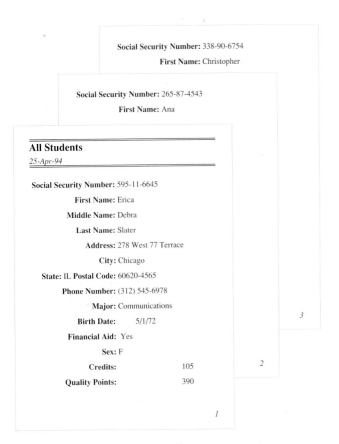

Social Security Number: 338-90-6754
First Name: Christopher

Social Security Number: 265-87-4543
First Name: Ana

All Students
25-Apr-94

Social Security Number: 595-11-6645
First Name: Erica
Middle Name: Debra
Last Name: Slater
Address: 278 West 77 Terrace
City: Chicago
State: IL **Postal Code:** 60620-4565
Phone Number: (312) 545-6978
Major: Communications
Birth Date: 5/1/72
Financial Aid: Yes
Sex: F
Credits: 105
Quality Points: 390

1

(a) AutoReport (columnar report)

Student Master List
24-Apr-94

Last Name	First Name	Phone Number	Major	Credits
Adili	Ronnie	(612) 445-7654	Business	60
Berlin	Jared	(803) 223-7868	Engineering	100
Camejo	Oscar	(716) 433-3321	Liberal Arts	100
Coe	Bradley	(415) 235-6543	Undecided	52
Cornell	Ryan	(404) 755-4490	Undecided	45
DiGiacomo	Kevin	(305) 531-7652	Business	105
Faulkner	Eileen	(305) 489-8876	Communications	30
Frazier	Steven	(410) 995-8755	Undecided	35
Gibson	Christopher	(305) 235-4563	Business	35
Heltzer	Peter	(305) 753-4533	Engineering	25
Huerta	Carlos	(212) 344-5654	Undecided	15
Joseph	Cedric	(404) 667-8955	Communications	45
Korba	Nickolas	(415) 664-0900	Engineering	100
Ortiz	Frances	(303) 575-3211	Communications	28
Parulis	Christa	(410) 877-6565	Liberal Arts	50
Price	Lori	(310) 961-2323	Communications	24
Ramsay	Robert	(212) 223-9889	Business	50
Slater	Erica	(312) 545-6978	Communications	105
Solomon	Wendy	(305) 666-4532	Engineering	50
Watson	Ana	(305) 595-7877	Liberal Arts	70
Watson	Ana	(305) 561-2334	Business	30
Weissman	Kimberly	(904) 388-8605	Liberal Arts	63
Zacco	Michelle	(617) 884-3434	Undecided	21
Zimmerman	Kimberly	(713) 225-3434	Business	120

Prepared by: Marita Morales

1

(b) Tabular Report

Dean's List
24-Apr-94

First Name	Last Name	Major	Credits	Quality Points	GPA
Peter	Heltzer	Engineering	25	100	4.00
Cedric	Joseph	Communications	45	170	3.78
Erica	Slater	Communications	105	390	3.71
Kevin	DiGiacomo	Business	105	375	3.57
Wendy	Solomon	Engineering	50	175	3.50

1

(c) The Dean's List

Major	Last Name	First Name		GPA
Liberal Arts				
	Camejo	Oscar		2.80
				1.80
				2.79
				2.63
				4

GPA by Major
25-Apr-94

Major	Last Name	First Name	GPA
Business			
	Adili	Ronnie	2.58
	DiGiacomo	Kevin	3.57
	Gibson	Christopher	1.71
	Ramsay	Robert	3.24
	Watson	Ana	2.50
	Zimmerman	Kimberly	3.29
	Total Students in Major:		6
Communications			
	Faulkner	Eileen	2.67
	Joseph	Cedric	3.78
	Ortiz	Frances	2.14
	Price	Lori	1.75
	Slater	Erica	3.71
	Total Students in Major:		5
Engineering			
	Berlin	Jared	2.50
	Heltzer	Peter	4.00
	Korba	Nickolas	1.66
	Soomon	Wendy	3.50
	Total Students in Major:		4

2.75
1.78
1.29
2.67
3.24
5

24

2

1

(d) Group/Total Report

FIGURE 3.1 Report Types

(e) Mail Merge

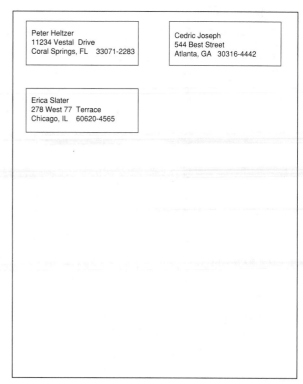

(f) Mailing Labels

FIGURE 3.1   Report Types (continued)

Anatomy of a Report

The ***Report Wizard*** is the easiest way to create a report, just as the Form Wizard is the easiest way to create a form. The Report Wizard asks you questions about the report you want, then builds the report for you. You can accept the report as it is created, or you can customize it to better suit your needs.

The best way to understand the structure of a report is to compare the printed version to the underlying design. Accordingly, Figure 3.2 shows the Design view of the tabular report from Figure 3.1b. (This is the report you will create in the first hands-on exercise.)

Every report is divided into sections, which appear at designated places when the report is printed. There are seven different sections, but a report need not contain all seven.

The ***report header*** appears once at the beginning of a report. It contains information describing the report, such as its title and the date the report was printed. (The report header appears before the page header on the first page of the report.) The ***report footer*** appears before the page footer on the last page of the report and displays summary information.

The ***page header*** appears at the top of every page in a report and can be used to display page numbers, column headings, and other descriptive information. The ***page footer*** appears at the bottom of every page and may contain page numbers (when they are not in the page header) or other descriptive information.

A ***group header*** appears at the beginning of a group of records and usually displays the name of the group. A ***group footer*** appears after the last record in a group and normally shows the group totals. (These sections appear only in a

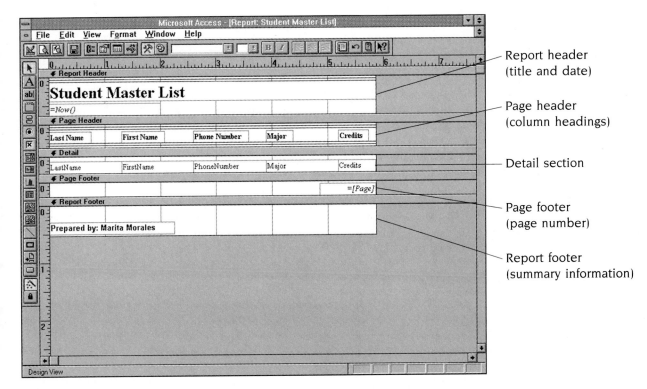

FIGURE 3.2 The Design View

Group/Total report and thus are not found in Figure 3.2. They are shown later in the chapter in Figure 3.8.)

The ***detail section*** makes up the main body of a report and is printed once for every record in the underlying table (or query). It displays one or more fields for each record in columnar or tabular fashion, according to the design of the report.

THE PRINTED DOCUMENT

The design of a report is a blueprint for the printed document. The Print command merges the design with the current data in the underlying table (or query) so that the printed document always reflects the most recent data in the database.

APPLY WHAT YOU KNOW

The following exercise has you create the report in Figure 3.1b. As you do the exercise, try to apply what you already know. Look for similarities between forms and reports. Knowledge of one is helpful in understanding the other. Both forms and reports are created initially with Wizards, then modified as necessary in the respective Design view. Controls appear in a report just as they do in a form.

Controls

A report is made up of controls that are bound, unbound, or calculated. A **bound control** has as its data source a field in the underlying table. An **unbound control** has no data source. Unbound controls are used to display titles, labels, lines, or rectangles. A **calculated control** has as its data source an expression rather than a field. A student's Grade Point Average is an example of a calculated control since it is computed by dividing the number of quality points by the number of credits.

The means for selecting, sizing, moving, aligning, and deleting controls are the same, regardless of whether you are working on a form or a report. Thus:

To select a control—	Click anywhere on a control.
To size a control—	Click the control to select it, then drag the sizing handles. Drag the top or bottom handles to size the box vertically. Drag the left or right handles to size the box horizontally. Drag the corner handles to size both horizontally and vertically.
To move a control—	Point to any border, but *not* to a sizing handle (the mouse pointer changes to a hand), then click the mouse and drag the control to its new position.

INHERITANCE

The *inheritance* feature of forms applies also to reports. A bound control inherits the same property settings as the associated field in the underlying table. Changing the property setting for a field after the report has been created does *not*, however, change the property of the control. In similar fashion, changing the property setting of a control does *not* change the property setting of the field in the underlying table.

HANDS-ON EXERCISE 1:

The Report Wizard

Objective To use the Report Wizard to create a tabular report; to modify a report by deleting an existing control and adding a new control; to change the properties of a control. Use Figure 3.3 as a guide in the exercise.

Step1: Open the OURDATA database

➤ Use Windows' File Manager to copy OURDATA.MDB from the data disk to a working disk if you are using a floppy disk for the exercise.
➤ Load Microsoft Access. Pull down the **File menu** and click **Open Database** to display the Open Database dialog box (or click the **Open Database icon**).
➤ If you haven't changed the default directory:
— Click the arrow on the Drives list box to select the appropriate drive—for example, drive C or drive A.
— Double click the root directory (a:\ or c:\) in the Directories list box to display the subdirectories on the selected drive.

— Double click the **ACCSDATA** directory to make it the active directory.
➤ Double click **OURDATA.MDB** to open the database for this exercise.

Step 2: Create a new report
➤ Click the **Report button.** Click **New** to produce the New Report dialog box in Figure 3.3a.
➤ Click the **arrow** in the Select a Table/Query text box. Click **All Students** to select the All Students table.
➤ Click the **Report Wizards button** to use the Report Wizard.

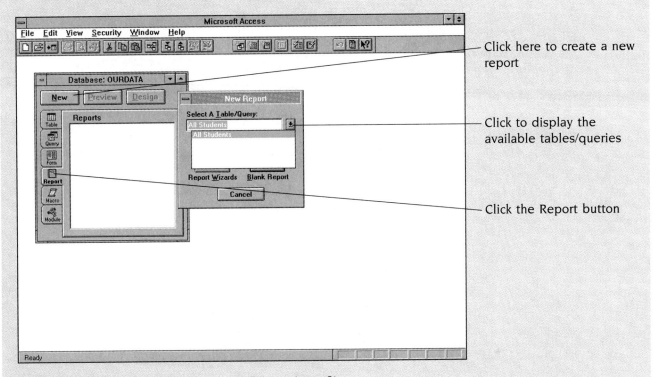

(a) Create a New Report (step 2)

FIGURE 3.3 Hands-on Exercise 1

Step 3: The Report Wizard
➤ Click **Tabular** as the type of report. Click **OK.**
➤ Click the **LastName field** in the Available Fields list box, then click the **> button** to enter this field in the report as shown in Figure 3.3b.
➤ Enter the remaining fields **(FirstName, PhoneNumber, Major,** and **Credits)** one at a time, by selecting the field name, then clicking the **> button.** Click the **Next command button** when you have entered all fields.

WHAT THE REPORT WIZARD DOESN'T TELL YOU

The fastest way to select a field is by double clicking; that is, double click a field in the Available fields list box, and it is automatically moved to the Field order list for inclusion in the report. The process also works in reverse; that is, you can double click a field in the Field order list and remove it from the report.

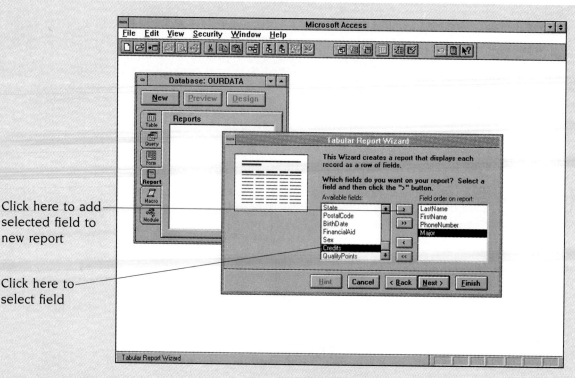

Click here to add selected field to new report

Click here to select field

(b) The Report Wizard (step 3)

FIGURE 3.3   Hands-on Exercise 1 (continued)

Step 4: The Report Wizard (continued)
➤ The Report Wizard next asks which field(s) you want to sort by. **LastName** is already selected. Click the **> button** to move LastName from the Available fields list box to the Sort order list box. Click the **Next command button.**
➤ Click the **Executive option button** as the style of the report. Click the **Portrait option button** under orientation. Click the **Next command button.**
➤ Type **Student Master List** as the title for your report.
➤ Check the box to **See all the fields on one page.**
➤ Click the option button to **See the report with data in it.**
➤ Click the **Finish command button.**

Step 5: The Save command
➤ Click the **Maximize button** so the report takes the entire window as shown in Figure 3.3c.
➤ Click the **Zoom icon** to see the whole page. Click the **Zoom icon** a second time to see a magnified portion of the page.
➤ Pull down the **File menu** and click **Save.**
➤ Type **Student Master List** in the Report Name text box as shown in Figure 3.3c. Click **OK.**
➤ Click the **down arrow** on the vertical scroll bar to move to the end of the report. You will see a double line under the credits for the last student (Zimmerman), followed by a total of all credits (1358). The total makes no sense conceptually and will be removed in the next step.

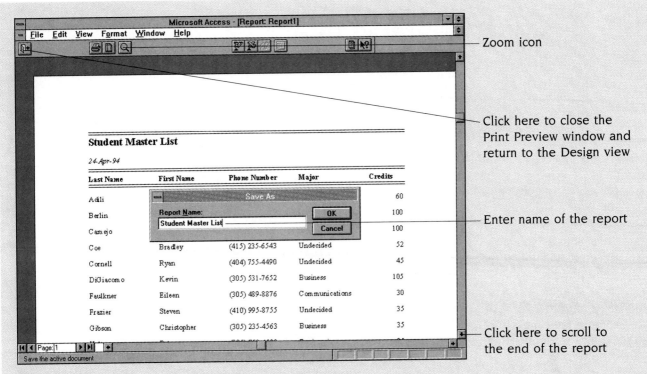

Zoom icon

Click here to close the Print Preview window and return to the Design view

Enter name of the report

Click here to scroll to the end of the report

(c) Save the Report (step 5)

FIGURE 3.3 Hands-on Exercise 1 (continued)

Step 6: The Design view

► Click the **Close Window icon** to close the Print Preview window and display the report in the Design view.

► Click the control in the Report Footer, which sums the Credits field. (You may not see the entire entry.) The field is selected as indicated by the sizing handles in Figure 3.3d. Press the **Del key** to delete the control.

► Click (select) the line immediately above the summation (the control you just deleted). Press and hold the **Shift key** to select the second line. Press the **Del key** to delete both lines.

► Pull down the **File menu** and click **Save** (or click the **Save icon**) to save the report.

ADDING AND REMOVING SECTIONS

Headers and footers, whether for the report as a whole, a page, or a group, are added and removed as a pair. To add or remove a section pair, pull down the Format menu and select (deselect) the desired Header/Footer combination. To suppress a section footer (while displaying the header), delete all of the controls in the footer, then set its height to zero by dragging the bottom edge of the section to meet the top.

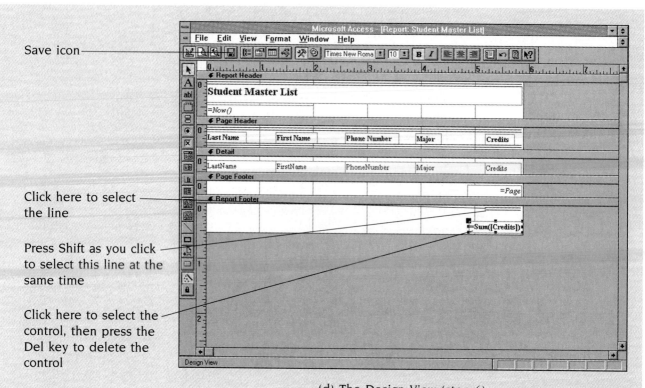

Save icon

Click here to select the line

Press Shift as you click to select this line at the same time

Click here to select the control, then press the Del key to delete the control

(d) The Design View (step 6)

FIGURE 3.3 Hands-on Exercise 1 (continued)

Step 7: Control Properties

➤ Click the control for the Report Title in the Report Header. The title of the report (Student Master List) is selected as shown by the sizing handles in Figure 3.3e.

➤ Pull down the **View menu** (or click the **right mouse button** to produce a shortcut menu). Click **Properties** to display the Properties box in Figure 3.3e.

➤ Scroll through the properties until you can click the **Font Size property.** Click the **arrow** to display the point sizes. Click **20.** Double click the **control-menu box** to close the Properties dialog box.

➤ Save the report.

SECTION PROPERTIES

Each section in a report has properties that control its appearance and behavior. Double click the section header (or double click the section background area) to display the property sheet and set the properties. You can hide the section by changing the Visible property to No. You can also change the Special Effect property to Raised or Sunken.

Step 8: Add an unbound control

➤ The Report Design toolbar is displayed immediately under the menu bar.

➤ If necessary click the **Toolbox icon** to display the Toolbox as shown in Figure 3.3f. The Toolbox may be fixed or floating according to its position the last time it was used.

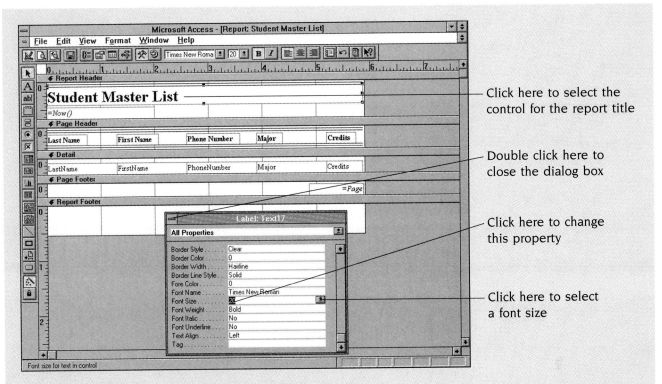

Click here to select the control for the report title

Double click here to close the dialog box

Click here to change this property

Click here to select a font size

(e) Properties (step 7)

Print Preview icon

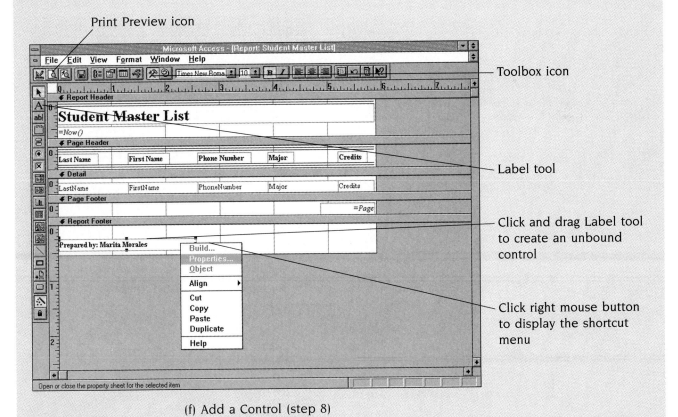

Toolbox icon

Label tool

Click and drag Label tool to create an unbound control

Click right mouse button to display the shortcut menu

(f) Add a Control (step 8)

FIGURE 3.3 Hands-on Exercise 1 (continued)

➤ Click the **Label tool,** then click and drag in the Report Footer where you want the label to go, and release the mouse. You should see a flashing insertion point inside the label control. (If you see the word *Unbound* instead of the insertion point, it means you selected the Text box tool rather than the Label tool; delete the text box and begin again.)

➤ Type **Prepared By** followed by your name as shown in Figure 3.3f. Press **enter** to complete the entry and also select the control. Point to the control and click the **right mouse button** to produce the shortcut menu shown in Figure 3.3f. Click **Properties** to display the Properties dialog box.

➤ Click the **down arrow** on the scroll box until you see the Font Name property. Click the box for the **Font Name property,** then click the **arrow** to display available fonts. Click **Arial.**

➤ Double click the **control-menu box** to close the Properties dialog box. Save the report.

Step 9: Print the completed report

➤ Click the **Print Preview icon** to exit the Design view. Click the **Zoom icon** to see the whole page as shown in Figure 3.3g.

➤ Click the **Print icon** to produce the Print dialog box. Click **OK** to print the report.

➤ Pull down the **File menu** and click **Close** (or double click the **control-menu box**) to close the report and return to the Database window.

➤ Close the **OURDATA** database and exit Access if you do not wish to continue with the next hands-on exercise.

Double click the control-menu box to close the Print Preview window

Print icon

Zoom icon

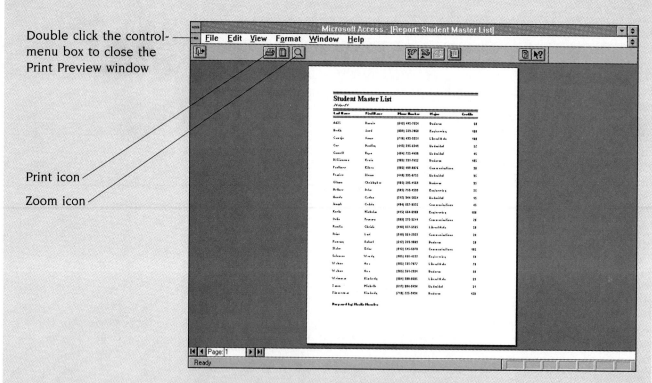

(g) Print Preview (step 9)

FIGURE 3.3 Hands-on Exercise 1 (continued)

CHANGE THE SORT ORDER

The Report Wizard gives you the opportunity to specify a field (or fields) on which to sort a report. What if, however, you have created a report, modified it extensively in the Design view, then changed your mind about the sort order? Fortunately, you don't have to go back to the Report Wizard and start over. Just pull down the View menu, choose Sorting and Grouping, then specify the new sort order in the Sorting and Grouping dialog box.

INTRODUCTION TO QUERIES

The report you just created displayed every student in the underlying table. What if, however, we wanted to see just the students who are majoring in Business? Or the students who are receiving financial aid? Or the students who are majoring in Business *and* receiving financial aid? The ability to ask questions such as these, and to see the answers to those questions, is provided through a query. Queries represent the real power of a database.

A *query* lets you see the data you want in the order you want it. It lets you select records from a table (or from several tables) and show some or all of the fields for the selected records. It also lets you perform calculations and display fields that are not present in the underlying table(s) such as a student's GPA.

A query represents a question and an answer. The question is developed by using a graphical tool known as the *Query By Example (QBE) grid.* The answer is displayed in a *dynaset,* which contains the records that satisfy the criteria specified in the query.

A dynaset looks and acts like a table, but it isn't a table; it is a *dyna*mic sub-*set* of a table that selects and sorts records as specified in the query. A dynaset is like a table in that you can enter a new record or modify an existing record. It is dynamic because the changes made to the dynaset are automatically reflected in the underlying table.

Figure 3.4a displays the All Students table we have been using throughout the chapter. (For ease of illustration, we do not show all of the fields.) Figure 3.4b contains the *QBE grid* used to select students whose major is "Undecided" and further, to list those students in alphabetical order. (The QBE grid is explained in the next section.) Figure 3.4c displays the answer to the query in a dynaset.

The table in Figure 3.4a contains 24 records. The dynaset in Figure 3.4c has only five records, corresponding to the students who are undecided about their major. The table in Figure 3.4a has 15 fields for each record (some of the fields are hidden). The dynaset in Figure 3.4c has only four fields. The records in the table are in social security order, whereas the records in the dynaset are in alphabetical order by last name.

The query in Figure 3.4 is an example of a *select query,* which is the most common type of query. A select query searches the underlying table (Figure 3.4a in the example) to retrieve the data that satisfies the query. The data is displayed in a dynaset (Figure 3.4c), which you can change to update the data in the underlying table(s). The specifications for selecting records, determining which fields to display for the selected records, and the sequence of the selected records are contained within the QBE grid of Figure 3.4b.

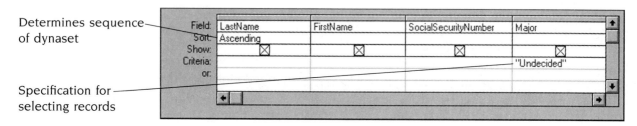

Records in order by
SocialSecurityNumber

(a) All Students Table

Determines sequence of dynaset

Specification for selecting records

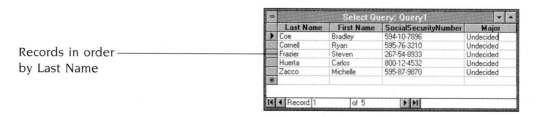

(b) Query By Example (QBE) Grid

Records in order by Last Name

Last Name	First Name	SocialSecurityNumber	Major
Coe	Bradley	594-10-7896	Undecided
Cornell	Ryan	595-76-3210	Undecided
Frazier	Steven	267-54-8933	Undecided
Huerta	Carlos	800-12-4532	Undecided
Zacco	Michelle	595-87-9870	Undecided

(c) Dynaset

FIGURE 3.4   Queries

REPORTS, QUERIES, AND TABLES

Every report is based on a table or a query. The design of the report may be the same with respect to the fields that are included, but the actual reports will be very different. A report based on a table contains every record in the table. A report based on a query contains only the records that satisfy the criteria in the query.

Query Window

The **Query window** has four views. The **Design view** is displayed by default and is shown in Figure 3.5. The Design view is used to create (or modify) a select query. The Datasheet view displays the resulting dynaset. The **Print Preview** shows how the dynaset will appear on the printed page. The **SQL view** enables you to use SQL statements to modify the query and is beyond the scope of the present discussion. The Query Design toolbar contains the icons to display all the views.

A select query is created in the Design view *without* the aid of a wizard. The Design view contains the **field list** for the table(s) on which the query is based (the All Students table in this example). It also displays the QBE grid, which is the essence of a select query.

The QBE grid consists of columns and rows. Each field in the query has its own column. A field is added to the query by dragging it from the field list to the QBE grid. There are several rows for each field. The **Field row** displays the field name. The **Sort row** enables you to sort in ascending or descending sequence. The **Show row** controls whether or not the field will be displayed in the dynaset. The **Criteria row(s)** determine the records that will be selected—for example, students with an undecided major as in Figure 3.5.

Data Type

The data type determines the way in which criteria appear in the QBE grid. A text field is enclosed in quotation marks. Number, currency, and counter fields are shown as digits with or without a decimal point. (Commas and dollar signs are not allowed.) Dates are enclosed in pound signs and are entered in the mm/dd/yy format. A Yes/No field is entered as Yes (or True) or No (or False).

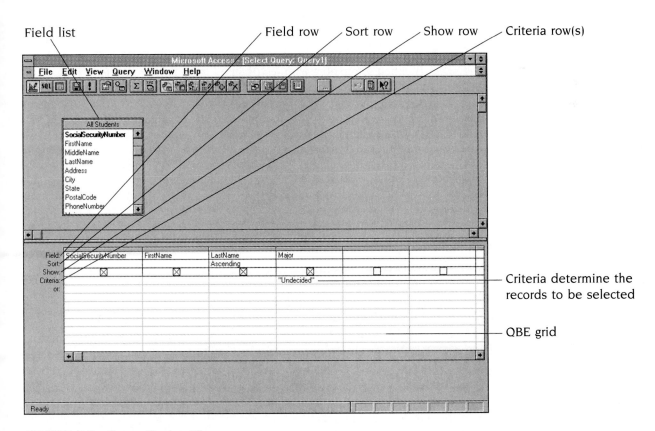

FIGURE 3.5 Query Design View

Selection Criteria

To specify selection criteria in the QBE grid, enter a value or expression in the Criteria row of the appropriate column. Figure 3.6 contains several examples of simple criteria and provides a basic introduction to select queries. Additional and more complex expressions are developed in Chapters 4 and 5.

The criteria in Figure 3.6a select the students majoring in Business. The criteria for text fields are case insensitive. Thus, *"Business"* is the same as *"business"* or *"BUSINESS"*.

Values entered in multiple columns of the same criteria row implement an **AND** condition in which the selected records must meet *all* of the specified criteria. The criteria in Figure 3.6b select students who are majoring in Business *and* who are from the state of Florida. The criteria in Figure 3.4c select Communications majors who are receiving financial aid. (The criterion for a Yes/No field is entered without quotation marks.)

Values entered in different criteria rows are connected by an **OR** condition in which the selected records satisfy *any* of the indicated criteria. The OR criteria in Figure 3.6d select students who are majoring in Business *or* who are from Florida.

Relational operators (>, <, >=, <=, =, and <>) are used with date or number fields to return records within a designated range. The criteria in Figure 3.6e select Engineering majors with less than 60 credits. The criteria in Figure 3.6f select Communications majors who were born after April 1, 1974.

Criteria can grow more complex by combining multiple And and Or conditions. The criteria in Figure 3.6g select Engineering majors with less than 60 credits *or* Communications majors who were born after April 1, 1974.

Other functions enable you to impose still other criteria. The ***Between function*** selects records that fall within a range of values. The criteria in Figure 3.6h select students who have between 60 and 90 credits. The Not function selects records that do not have the designated value. The criteria in Figure 3.6i select students with majors other than Liberal Arts.

Queries are discussed again in Chapters 4 and 5 where we show you how to develop more complex criteria.

(a) Business Majors

Field:	LastName	State	Major	BirthDate	FinancialAid	Credits
Sort:						
Show:	☒	☒	☒	☒	☒	☒
Criteria:			"Business"			
or:						

(b) Business Majors from Florida

Field:	LastName	State	Major	BirthDate	FinancialAid	Credits
Sort:						
Show:	☒	☒	☒	☒	☒	☒
Criteria:		"FL"	"Business"			
or:						

(c) Communications Majors Receiving Financial Aid

Field:	LastName	State	Major	BirthDate	FinancialAid	Credits
Sort:						
Show:	☒	☒	☒	☒	☒	☒
Criteria:			"Communications"		Yes	
or:						

(d) Business Majors or Students from Florida

Field:	LastName	State	Major	BirthDate	FinancialAid	Credits
Sort:						
Show:	☒	☒	☒	☒	☒	☒
Criteria:		"FL"				
or:			"Business"			

(e) Engineering Majors with Less than 60 Credits

Field:	LastName	State	Major	BirthDate	FinancialAid	Credits
Sort:						
Show:	☒	☒	☒	☒	☒	☒
Criteria:			"Engineering"			<60
or:						

(f) Communications Majors Born after April 1, 1974

Field:	LastName	State	Major	BirthDate	FinancialAid	Credits
Sort:						
Show:	☒	☒	☒	☒	☒	☒
Criteria:			"Communications"	>#4/1/74#		
or:						

FIGURE 3.6 Criteria

Field:	LastName	State	Major	BirthDate	FinancialAid	Credits
Sort:						
Show:	☒	☒	☒	☒	☒	☒
Criteria:			"Engineering"	<60		
or:			"Communications"	>#4/1/74#		

(g) Engineering Majors with Less than 60 Credits or
Communications Majors Born after April 1, 1974

Field:	LastName	State	Major	BirthDate	FinancialAid	Credits
Sort:						
Show:	☒	☒	☒	☒	☒	☒
Criteria:						Between 60 And 90
or:						

(h) Students with between 60 and 90 Credits (juniors)

Field:	LastName	State	Major	BirthDate	FinancialAid	Credits
Sort:						
Show:	☒	☒	☒	☒	☒	☒
Criteria:			Not "Liberal Arts"			
or:						

(i) Students with Majors other than Liberal Arts

FIGURE 3.6   Criteria (continued)

HANDS-ON EXERCISE 2:

Creating a Select Query

Objective To create a select query using the Query By Example (QBE) grid; to show how changing values in a dynaset changes the values in the underlying table; to create a report based on a query. Use Figure 3.7 as a guide in the exercise.

Step 1: Open the Student Database
➤ Load Access. Open the **OURDATA** database from the first exercise.
➤ Click the **Query button** in the Database window.
➤ Click the **New command button** to produce the New Query dialog box shown in Figure 3.7a. You are going to create a select query and *cannot* use the *Query Wizard.* Click the **New Query button.**

Step 2: Add the All Students table
➤ An open list box will appear within the query windows as shown in Figure 3.7b. The All Students table is the only table in the OURDATA database and is already selected. Click the **Add command button** to add this table to the query.
➤ Click the **Close command button** to close the Add Table dialog box.
➤ Click the **maximize button** to begin working in the query.

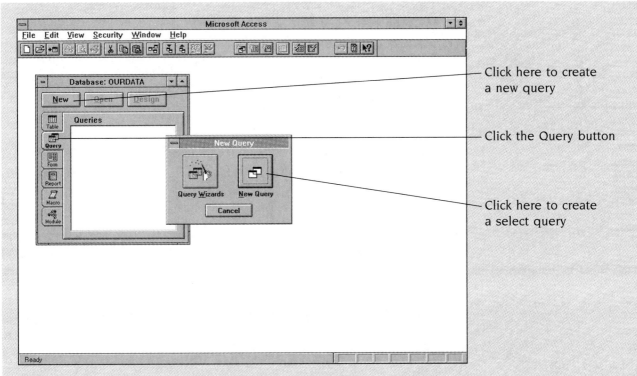

(a) Open the OURDATA Database (step 1)

Click here to create
a new query

Click the Query button

Click here to create
a select query

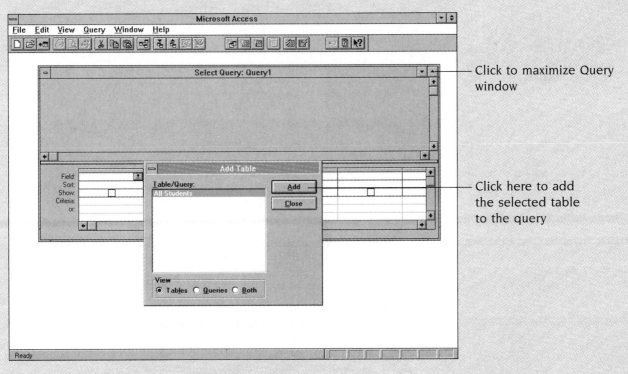

(b) Add the All Students Table (step 2)

Click to maximize Query
window

Click here to add
the selected table
to the query

FIGURE 3.7   Hands-on Exercise 2

CUSTOMIZE THE QUERY WINDOW

The Query window displays the field list and QBE grid in its upper and lower halves, respectively. To increase (decrease) the size of either portion of the window, drag the line dividing the upper and lower sections. Drag the title bar to move a field list. You can also size a field list by dragging a border just as you would size any other window.

Step 3: Create the query

➤ Click and drag the **LastName** field from the All Students field list to the Field row in the first column of the QBE grid in Figure 3.7c.

➤ Click and drag the **FirstName, PhoneNumber, Major,** and **Credits** fields in similar fashion, dragging each field to the next available column in the Field row. An X appears in the Show row under each field name to indicate the field will be displayed in the dynaset.

ADDING AND DELETING FIELDS

The fastest way to add a field to the QBE grid is to double click the field name in the field list. To add more than one field at a time, press and hold the Ctrl key as you click the fields within the field list, then drag the group to a cell in the Field row. To delete a field, click the column selector above the field name to select the column, then press the Del key.

Step 4: Specify the criteria

➤ Click the **Criteria row** for Major. Type **Undecided.**

➤ Click the **Sort row** under the LastName field. Click the **arrow** to open the drop-down list box. Click **Ascending.**

➤ Pull down the **File menu** and click **Save** to produce the dialog box in Figure 3.7c.

➤ Type **Undecided Major** as the Query Name. Click **OK.**

FLEXIBLE CRITERIA

Access offers a great deal of flexibility in the way you enter the criteria for a text field. You may or may not include quotation marks, and you may or may not precede the entry with an equal sign. "Undecided", Undecided, =Undecided, or ="Undecided" are all valid entries. Access converts your entry to standard format ("Undecided" in this example) after you have moved to the next cell.

Step 5: Run the query

➤ Pull down the **Query menu** and click **Run** (or click the **Run icon**) to run the query and change to the Datasheet view.

➤ You should see the five records in the dynaset of Figure 3.7d.

➤ Change Ryan Cornell's major to Business.

➤ Click the **Design view icon** to change the query.

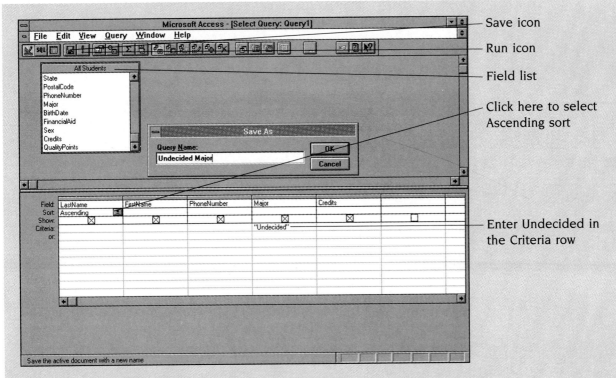

Save icon

Run icon

Field list

Click here to select
Ascending sort

Enter Undecided in
the Criteria row

(c) Create the Query (steps 3 and 4)

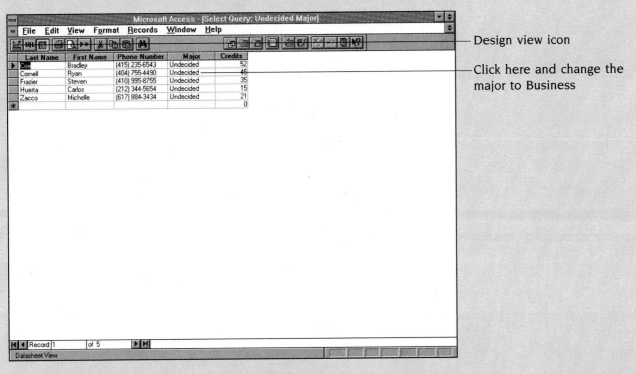

Design view icon

Click here and change the
major to Business

(d) Run the Query (step 5)

FIGURE 3.7   Hands-on Exercise 2 (continued)

Step 6: Modify the query

➤ Click the **Show check box** in the Major field to remove the X as shown in Figure 3.7e.

➤ Click the **Criteria row** under credits. Type **>30** to select only the Undecided majors with more than 30 credits.

➤ Click the **Save icon** to save the revised query.

➤ Click the **Run icon** to run the revised query. This time there are only two records in the dynaset, and the Major field does not appear.
  — Ryan Cornell does not appear because he has changed his major.
  — Carlos Huerta and Michelle Zacco do not appear because they do not have more than 30 credits.

Step 7: Create a report

➤ Pull down the **Window menu** and click **1 Database: OURDATA** (or click the **Database window icon** on the toolbar). You will see the Database window in Figure 3.7f.

➤ Click the **Report button.** Click the **New command button** to create a report based on the query you just created. Select **Undecided Major** from the Select a Table/Query drop-down list as shown in Figure 3.7f.

➤ Click the **Report Wizards command button** to use the Report Wizard to create the report.

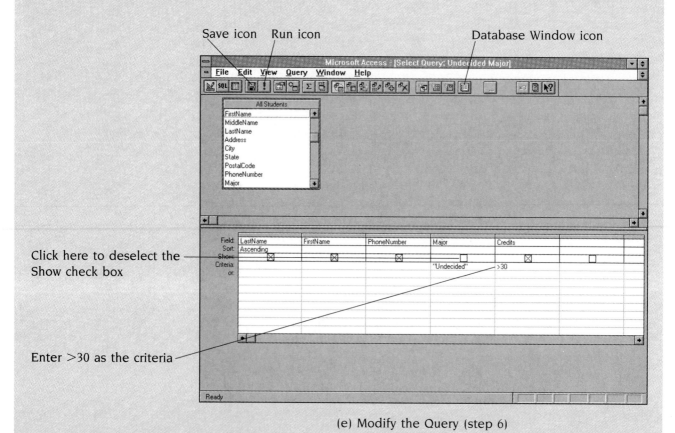

(e) Modify the Query (step 6)

FIGURE 3.7 Hands-on Exercise 2 (continued)

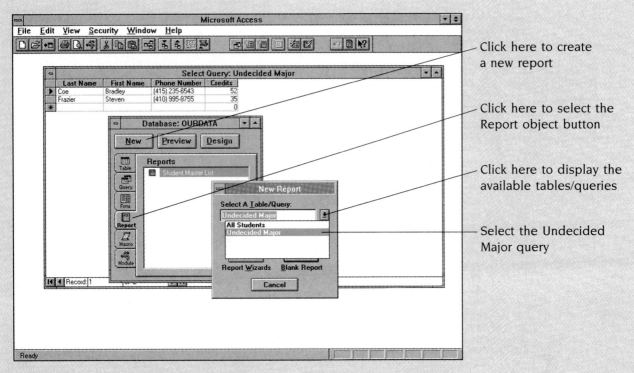

Click here to create a new report

Click here to select the Report object button

Click here to display the available tables/queries

Select the Undecided Major query

(f) Create a Report (step 7)

FIGURE 3.7 Hands-on Exercise 2 (continued)

Step 8: The Report Wizard

➤ Select **AutoReport** in the Report Wizard dialog box and click **OK.** You will see the message, Creating Report, on the status bar as the report is created.

➤ Click the **maximize button** to see the completed report as shown in Figure 3.7g. Click the **Zoom icon** to see the full page.

➤ Pull down the **File menu** and click **Save.** Type **Undecided Major** as the name of the report. Click **OK.**

➤ Click the **Close Window icon** to close the report.

Step 9: The Database Window

➤ If necessary click the **Database Window icon** on the toolbar to return to the Database window. Click the **maximize button.**

— Click the **Query button** to display the names of the queries in the OUR-DATA database. You should see the *Undecided Major* query created in this exercise.

— Click the **Report button.** You should see two reports: *Student Master List* (created in the previous exercise) and *Undecided Major* (created in this exercise).

— Click the **Form button.** You should see the *Student Information Form* corresponding to the form you created in Chapter 2.

— Click the **Table button.** You should see the *All Students table*, which is the basis of all other objects in the database.

➤ Close the **OURDATA** database and exit Access if you do not wish to continue with the next hands-on exercise.

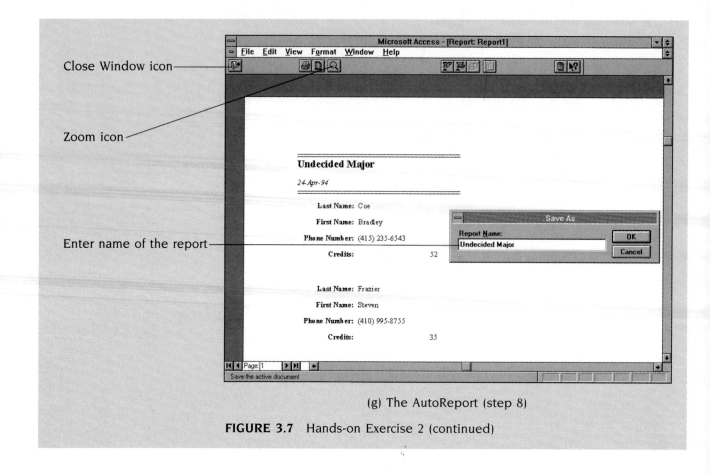

Close Window icon

Zoom icon

Enter name of the report

(g) The AutoReport (step 8)

FIGURE 3.7 Hands-on Exercise 2 (continued)

GROUP/TOTAL REPORTS

A Group/Total report displays summary information about groups of records. It is one of the most frequently used reports and the type you will create in the next exercise. Figure 3.8a shows the first page of the printed report. Figure 3.8b displays the corresponding Design view.

The report in Figure 3.8 groups students by major and then lists them alphabetically within major. A group header appears before each group of students to identify the group and display the major. A group footer appears at the end of each group and displays the average GPA for students in that major.

The report in Figure 3.8 uses the Avg function, but other types of summary calculations are possible:

     Sum— The total of all values in a specified field
     Avg— The average of values in a field
     Min— The minimum value in a field
     Max— The maximum value in a field
     Count—The number of records with an entry in the specified field

A Group/Total report (like any other report) is based on either a table or a query. We chose to base the report on a query to give you additional practice in creating a select query. The query you will create contains a calculated control, GPA, which is computed by dividing the QualityPoints field by the Credits field. The Criteria row is left empty since the Group/Total report is to contain every record in the All Students table.

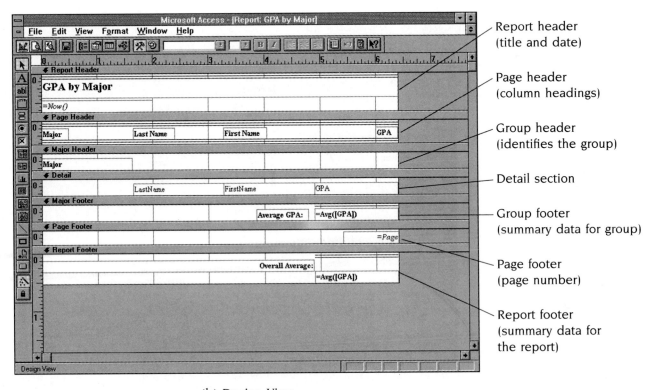

(a) Printed Report

(b) Design View

FIGURE 3.8 Group/Total Report

Creating a Group/Total Report

Objective Create a query containing a calculated field, then use the Report Wizard to create a Group/Totals report based on that query. Use Figure 3.9 as a guide in the exercise.

Step 1: Create the GPA Query

➤ Load Access. Open the **OURDATA** database.

➤ Click the **Query button** in the Database window. Click the **New command** button. Click the **New Query command button** as opposed to the Query Wizard button.

➤ The Add Table dialog box appears with the All Students table already selected. Click the **Add command button** to add this table to the query. Click the **Close command button** to close the Add Table dialog box.

➤ Click the **maximize button** to begin working on the query as shown in Figure 3.9a.

➤ Click and drag the **Major field** from the All Students field list to the query. Click and drag the **LastName, FirstName, QualityPoints,** and **Credits** fields in similar fashion.

➤ Click the **Sort row** for the Major field. Click the **arrow** to open the drop-down list box. Click **Ascending.**

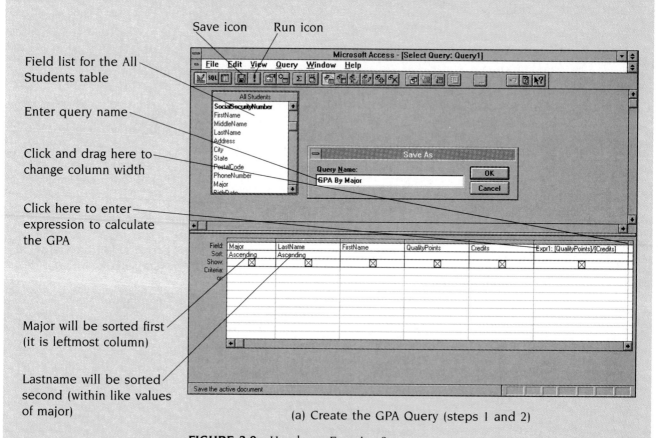

Save icon   Run icon

Field list for the All Students table

Enter query name

Click and drag here to change column width

Click here to enter expression to calculate the GPA

Major will be sorted first (it is leftmost column)

Lastname will be sorted second (within like values of major)

(a) Create the GPA Query (steps 1 and 2)

FIGURE 3.9 Hands-on Exercise 3

➤ Click the **Sort row** for the LastName field. Click the **arrow** to open the drop-down list box. Click **Ascending.**

SORTING ON MULTIPLE FIELDS

You can sort a query on more than one field, but you must be certain that the fields are in the proper order within the QBE grid. Access sorts from left to right (the leftmost field is the *primary key*), so the fields must be arranged in the desired sort sequence. To move a field within the QBE grid, click the column selector above the field name to select the column, then drag the column to its new position.

Step 2: Add a Calculated control
➤ Click the first empty cell in the Field row. Type **=[QualityPoints]/[Credits].** Do not be concerned if you cannot see the entire expression, but be sure you put **square brackets** around both field names.
➤ Press **enter.** Access has substituted Expr1: for the equal sign you typed initially. Drag the column boundary so that the entire expression is visible as in Figure 3.9a. (You may have to make some of the columns narrower to see all of the fields in the QBE grid.)
➤ Pull down the **File menu** and click **Save** (or click the **Save icon**) to produce the dialog box in Figure 3.9a.
➤ Type **GPA By Major** for the Query Name as shown in Figure 3.9a. Click **OK.**

USE DESCRIPTIVE NAMES

An Access database contains multiple objects—tables, forms, queries, and reports. It is important, therefore, that the name assigned to each object be descriptive of its function so that you can select the proper object from the Database window. The name of an object can contain up to 64 characters (letters and numbers) and may include spaces.

Step 3: Run the Query
➤ Pull down the **Query menu** and click **Run** (or click the **Run icon** on the Query Design toolbar). You will see the dynaset in Figure 3.9b:
  — Students are listed by major and alphabetically by last name within major.
  — The GPA is calculated to several places and appears in the Expr1 field.
➤ Click the **QualityPoints** field for Christopher Gibson. Replace 60 with **70.** Press **enter.** The GPA changes automatically to 2.
➤ Pull down the **Edit menu** and click **Undo Current Record** (or click the **Undo Current Field/Record icon** on the Query toolbar). The GPA returns to its previous value.
➤ Click the **Expr1 (GPA) field** for Christopher Gibson. Type **2.** Access will beep and prevent you from changing the GPA because it is a calculated field.
➤ Click the **Design view icon** to change the query.

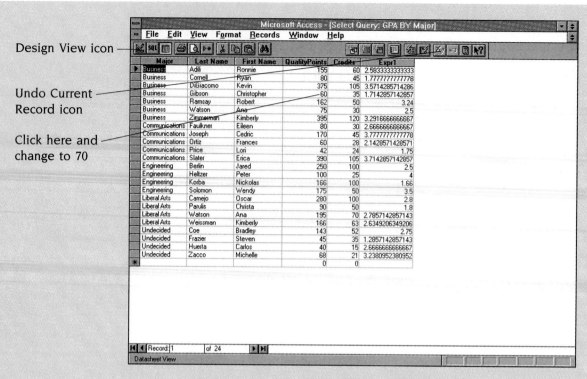

Design View icon

Undo Current Record icon

Click here and change to 70

(b) Run the Query (step 3)

FIGURE 3.9   Hands-on Exercise 3 (continued)

ADJUST THE COLUMN WIDTH

Point to the right edge of the column you want to resize, then drag the mouse in the direction you want to go. Alternatively, you can double click the column selector line to fit the longest entry in that column. Adjusting the column width in the Design view does not affect the column width in the Datasheet view, but you can use the same technique in both views.

Step 4: Modify the Query
➤ Click and drag to select **Expr1** in the Field row for the calculated field. (Do not select the colon.) Type **GPA** to substitute a more meaningful field name.
➤ Point to the GPA and click the **right mouse button** to display a shortcut menu. Click **Properties** to display the dialog box in Figure 3.9c.
➤ Click the box for the **Format property.** Click the **down arrow** to display the available formats. Click **Fixed.** Double click the **control-menu box** to close the Field Properties dialog box. Save the query.

Step 5: Rerun the query
➤ Pull down the **Query menu** and click **Run** (or click the **Run icon** on the Query Design toolbar). You will see a new dynaset corresponding to the modified query as shown in Figure 3.9d.
— Students are still listed by major and alphabetically within major.
— The GPA is calculated to two places and appears under the GPA field.
➤ Click the **Database window icon.**

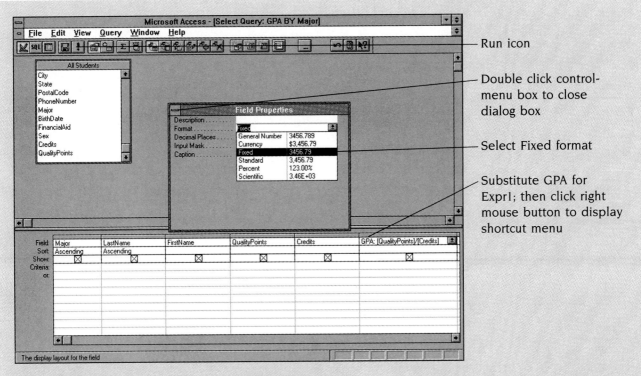

Run icon

Double click control-
menu box to close
dialog box

Select Fixed format

Substitute GPA for
Expr1; then click right
mouse button to display
shortcut menu

(c) Modify the Query (step 4)

Click New to create
a new report

Click the Report
object button

Database Window icon

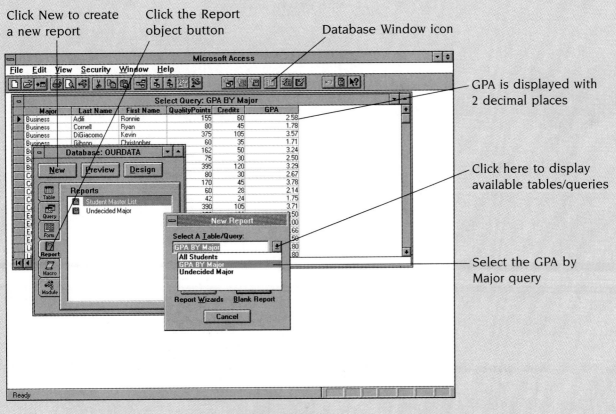

GPA is displayed with
2 decimal places

Click here to display
available tables/queries

Select the GPA by
Major query

(d) Create a New Report (step 6)

FIGURE 3.9   Hands-on Exercise 3 (continued)

THE TOP VALUES PROPERTY

Can you create a query that lists only the five students with the highest GPA? It's easy, if you know about the *Top Values property* to limit the number of displayed records. Click the Sort row in the QBE grid for the GPA field and choose *descending* as the sort *sequence.* Click the right mouse button *outside* the QBE grid to display a shortcut menu, click Properties, then click the box for Top Values. Enter the number of records, then double click the control-menu box to close the Properties dialog box. When you run the query, you will see only the top five students. (You can see the bottom five instead if you specify *ascending sequence* rather than descending as the sort sequence.)

Step 6: Create the report
➤ Click the **Report button.** Click the **New command button.** Select **GPA by Major** from the Select a Table/Query list as the query on which to base the report.
➤ Click the **Report Wizards button** to begin creating the report. Click **Group/Totals.** Click **OK.**

USE THE SAME NAME

Help yourself to select the proper object from the Database window by using the same name for a report and its underlying query. You can also use the same name for a form and its underlying table. A query cannot, however, have the same name as a table. If, when naming a query, you choose the name of an existing table, Access displays a warning message asking whether you want to replace the table. If you respond yes, Access replaces the table with the query and the data in the table is lost!

Step 7: The Report Wizard
➤ Click the **Major field** in the Available fields list box. Click the **> button** to include this field in the report.
➤ Add the **LastName, FirstName,** and **GPA** fields one at a time. Do not include the QualityPoints or Credits fields. Click the **Next command button.**
➤ Select **Major** as the field to group records by and click the **> button.** Click the **Next command button.**
➤ The next dialog box prompts you about how to group the data. Normal is already selected. Click the **Next command button.**
➤ Select **LastName** as the field to sort by and click the **> button.** Click the **Next command button.**
➤ Click the option buttons for the **Executive style** and **Portrait orientation.** Click the **Next command button.**
➤ Check the box to **See all the fields on one page.** Remove the check from the box to calculate percentages.

➤ Click the option button to **Modify the report's design.** Click the **Finish command button.** You should see the Report Design view as shown in Figure 3.9e. Maximize the Report window.

➤ Save the report as **GPA By Major.**

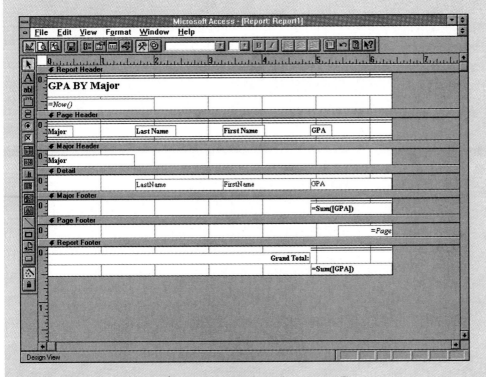

(e) The Report Design View (step 7)

FIGURE 3.9 Hands-on Exercise 3 (continued)

Step 8: Modify the Report

➤ Click the control in the Major footer, which displays sizing handles to indicate the control has been selected as shown in Figure 3.9f.

➤ Click immediately to the left of the word Sum. Type **Avg,** then press the Del key **three times** to delete the word **Sum.**

➤ Click the **Label tool** on the Toolbox to select the tool, then click and drag to the left of the =Avg([GPA]) control in the Major footer to enter a label.

➤ You should see a flashing insertion point inside the label control. (If you see the word Unbound instead of the insertion point, it means you selected the Text box tool rather than the Label tool; delete the text box and begin again.)

➤ Type **Average GPA:** as shown in Figure 3.9f. Click the control to select it and click the **right justification icon** on the Report Design toolbar.

➤ Press and hold the **Shift key** as you click the Average GPA control. Pull down the **Format menu.** Click **Align.** Click **Bottom.**

➤ Change the Sum function in the Report Footer to the Average function. Change the label Grand Total to **Overall Average.**

➤ Save the report.

Print Preview icon

Label tool

Right justification icon

Replace the Sum function with Avg

Click and drag Label tool to create a label

Change to Overall Average

Replace Sum function with Avg

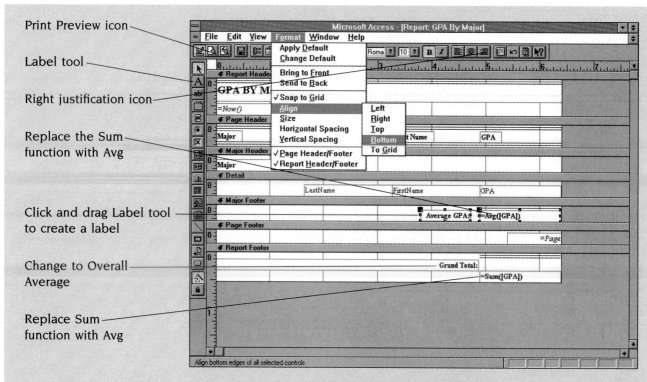

(f) Modify the Report (step 8)

FIGURE 3.9   Hands-on Exercise 3 (continued)

Step 9: View and print the report

➤ Click the **Print Preview icon** to view the completed report as shown in Figure 3.9g. The Status Bar shows you are on page 1 of the report.

➤ Click the **Zoom icon** to see the entire page. Click the **Zoom icon** a second time to return to the higher magnification that lets you read the report.

➤ Click the **Navigation button** to move to the next page (page 2). (If you do not move to the next page, it is because you selected Sample Preview instead of Print Preview. Click the icon to close the window and return to the Design view, then click the Print Preview icon.)

➤ Click the **Navigation button** to move back to page 1.

➤ Pull down the **File menu** and click **Print** (or click the **Printer icon**) to display the Print dialog box. The All option button is already selected under Print Range. Click **OK** to print the report.

PRINT PREVIEW VERSUS SAMPLE PREVIEW

Access provides two different ways to preview a report, each with its own icon on the Report Design toolbar. The *Sample Preview* displays every section in a report but contains only a few detail records; it is used to take a quick look at a report to check its overall layout and appearance. Note, too, that while the Sample Preview sorts and groups the data, it ignores any criteria in the underlying query and thus may contain records that do not appear in the actual report. *Print Preview,* on the other hand, displays the entire report exactly as it will be printed and thus can extend to several pages.

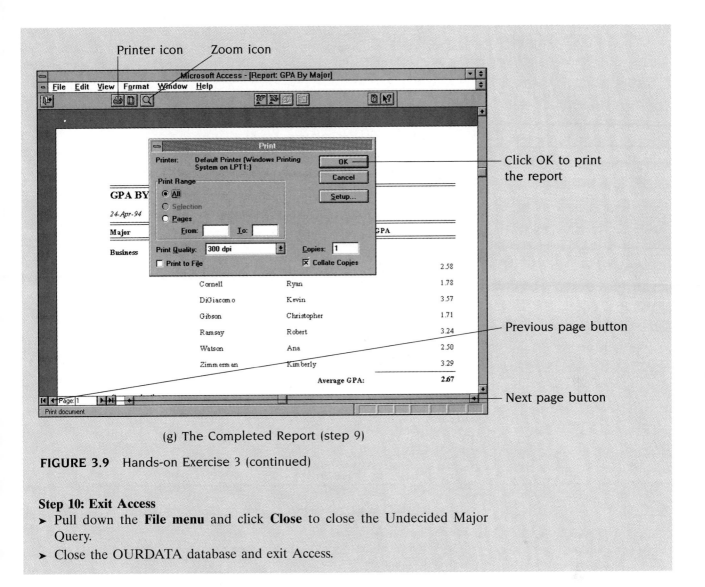

(g) The Completed Report (step 9)

FIGURE 3.9 Hands-on Exercise 3 (continued)

Step 10: Exit Access
➤ Pull down the **File menu** and click **Close** to close the Undecided Major Query.
➤ Close the OURDATA database and exit Access.

SUMMARY

Data and information are not synonymous. Data refers to a fact or facts about a specific record. Information is data that has been rearranged into a more useful format. Data may be viewed as the raw material, whereas information is the finished product.

A report is a printed document that displays information from the database. Reports are created through the Report Wizard, then modified as necessary in the Design view of the Report window. A report is made up of sections. Every section contains controls that are bound, unbound, or calculated, according to their data source.

Every report is based on either a table or a query. A report based on a table contains every record in that table. A report based on a query will contain only the records satisfying the criteria in the query.

A query enables you to select records from a table (or from several tables), display the selected records in any order, and perform calculations on fields within the query. A select query is the most common type of query and is created by using the Query By Example grid. A select query displays its output in a dynaset, which can be used to update the data in the underlying table(s).

All objects (tables, forms, queries, and reports) in an Access database are named according to the same rules. The name can contain up to 64 characters (letters or numbers) and can include spaces. A report can have the same name as the table or query on which it is based to emphasize the relationship between the two.

 # Key Words and Concepts

AND criteria
Ascending sequence
Asterisk
AutoReport
Bound control
Calculated control
Criteria row
Data
Datasheet view
Descending sequence
Design view
Detail section
Dynaset
Field row

Group footer
Group header
Group/Total report
Information
Inheritance
OR criteria
Page footer
Page header
Primary key
Print Preview
QBE grid
Query
Query By Example
Query window

Query Wizard
Relational operators
Report
Report footer
Report header
Report Wizard
Sample Preview
Select query
Sort row
Show row
Tabular report
Top Values property
Unbound control
Wild card

 # Multiple Choice

1. Which of the following is a reason for basing a report on a query rather than a table?
   (a) To limit the report to selected records
   (b) To include a calculated field in the report
   (c) Both (a) and (b)
   (d) Neither (a) nor (b)

2. An Access database may contain:
   (a) One or more tables
   (b) One or more queries
   (c) One or more reports
   (d) All of the above

3. Which of the following is true regarding the names of objects within an Access database?
   (a) A query and a table may have the same name
   (b) A query and a report may have the same name
   (c) Both (a) and (b)
   (d) Neither (a) nor (b)

4. The dynaset created by a query may contain:
   (a) A subset of records from the associated table but must contain all of the fields for the selected records
   (b) A subset of fields from the associated table but must contain all of the records

(c) Both (a) and (b)

(d) Neither (a) nor (b)

5. Which toolbar contains an icon to display the properties of a selected object?

(a) The Query Design toolbar

(b) The Report Design toolbar

(c) Both (a) and (b)

(d) Neither (a) nor (b)

6. Which of the following does *not* have both a Design view and a Datasheet view?

(a) Tables

(b) Forms

(c) Queries

(d) Reports

7. Which of the following is true regarding the wild card character within Access?

(a) A question mark stands for a single character in the same position as the question mark

(b) An asterisk stands for any number of characters in the same position as the asterisk

(c) Both (a) and (b)

(d) Neither (a) nor (b)

8. Which of the following will print at the top of every page?

(a) Report header

(b) Control header

(c) Both (a) and (b)

(d) Neither (a) nor (b)

9. A query, based on the OURDATA.MDB database within the chapter, contains two fields from the Student table (QualityPoints and Credits) as well as a calculated field (GPA). Which of the following is true?

(a) Changing the value of Credits or QualityPoints in the query's dynaset automatically changes these values in the underlying table

(b) Changing the value of GPA automatically changes its value in the underlying table

(c) Both (a) and (b)

(d) Neither (a) nor (b)

10. Which of the following must be present in every report?

(a) A report header and a report footer

(b) A page header and a page footer

(c) Both (a) and (b)

(d) Neither (a) nor (b)

11. Which of the following may be included in a report as well as a form?

(a) Bound control

(b) Unbound control

(c) Calculated control

(d) All of the above

12. The navigation buttons ► and ◄ will:
   (a) Move to the next or previous record in a table
   (b) Move to the next or previous page in a report
   (c) Both (a) and (b)
   (d) Neither (a) nor (b)

13. Assume that you are creating a query based on an Employee table, and that the query contains fields for Location and Title. Assume further that there is a single criteria row and that New York and Manager have been entered under the Location and Title fields, respectively. The dynaset will contain:
   (a) All employees in New York
   (b) All managers
   (c) Only the managers in New York
   (d) All employees in New York and all managers

14. You have decided to modify the query from the previous question to include a second criteria row. The Location and Title fields are still in the query, but this time New York and Manager appear in *different* criteria rows. The dynaset will contain:
   (a) All employees in New York
   (b) All managers
   (c) Only the managers in New York
   (d) All employees in New York and all managers

15. Which of the following is true about a query that lists employees by city and alphabetically within city?
   (a) The QBE grid should specify a descending sort on both city and employee name
   (b) The City field should appear to the left of the employee name in the QBE grid
   (c) Both (a) and (b)
   (d) Neither (a) nor (b)

ANSWERS

1. c	**6.** d	**11.** d
2. d	**7.** c	**12.** c
3. b	**8.** d	**13.** c
4. d	**9.** a	**14.** d
5. d	**10.** d	**15.** b

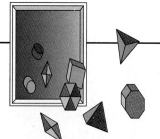

EXPLORING ACCESS

1. Use Figure 3.10 to match each action with its result. A given action may be used more than once or not at all.

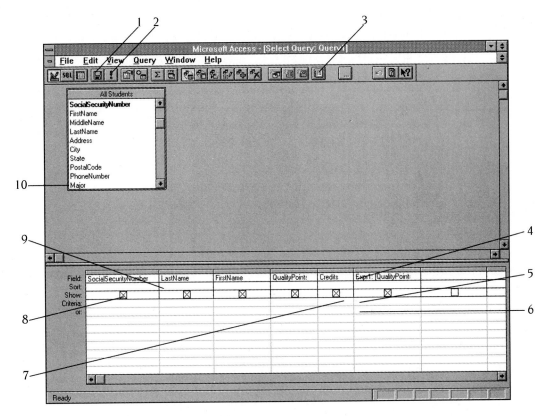

FIGURE 3.10 Screen for Problem 1

Action	Result
a. Click at 1	___ Sort the query by LastName
b. Click at 2	___ Limit the dynaset to students with more than 30 credits *and* a GPA higher than 3.0
c. Click at 3	___ Display the Database window
d. Click at 5, enter GPA, then press the Del key four times	___ Rename the calculated field
e. Click at 7 and enter > 30	___ Suppress the display of the Social Security Number
f. Click at 7 and enter >30, then click at 5 and enter >3.0	___ Add Major to the QBE grid
g. Click at 7 and enter >30, then click at 6 and enter >3.0	___ Limit the dynaset to students with more than 30 credits
h. Click at 8	___ Run the query
i. Click at 9	___ Limit the dynaset to students with more than 30 credits *or* students with a GPA higher than 3.0
j. Double click at 10	___ Save the query

2. Use what you learned in Chapters 2 and 3 to answer the following questions about the objects (tables, forms, queries, and reports) in an Access database.
   a. Which objects have a Design view? a Datasheet view?
   b. Which object has two different types of previews?
   c. Which objects are based on a table or query?
   d. Which objects enable you to change data in the underlying table?
   e. Which objects inherit properties from a table?
   f. Which objects are associated with controls?
   g. Which objects may have the same name?

3. Answer the following with respect to the query in Figure 3.11.
   a. What are the selection criteria?
   b. In which sequence will the selected records be displayed?
   c. Which fields (if any) are calculated fields?
   d. What is the difference between checking or not checking the Show box for Credits?

   How would you modify the query to:
   e. List all students in alphabetical order
   f. List all students by major and alphabetically within major
   g. List in alphabetical order students who are women *and* who are Business majors
   h. List in alphabetical order students who are women *or* who are Business majors
   i. List in alphabetical order all women who are Business majors, with at least 60 credits, a GPA higher than 3.00, and who are not receiving financial aid
   Use the AutoReport feature of the Report Wizard and the OURDATA database to create and print reports for parts (g), (h), and (i).

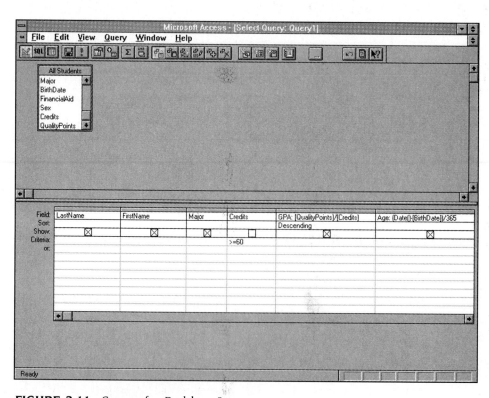

FIGURE 3.11 Screen for Problem 3

4. Query By Example: Answer the following with respect to the query in Figure 3.12.
   a. What are the selection criteria?
   b. In which sequence will the selected records be displayed?
   c. Which fields (if any) are calculated fields?
   d. What is the difference between checking or not checking the Show box for ISBN number?

   How would you modify the query to:
   e. List all books in alphabetical order?
   f. List all books by publisher and alphabetically within publisher?
   g. List the books published by Prentice Hall in 1994 in ascending sequence by ISBN number?
   h. List the books published by Prentice Hall *or* books published in 1994 in ascending sequence by ISBN number?
   i. List in alphabetical order the books published by Prentice Hall in 1994 that have a list price of more than $50?

   Use the AutoReport feature of the Report Wizard and the BKSTORE.MDB database to create and print reports for parts (g), (h), and (i).

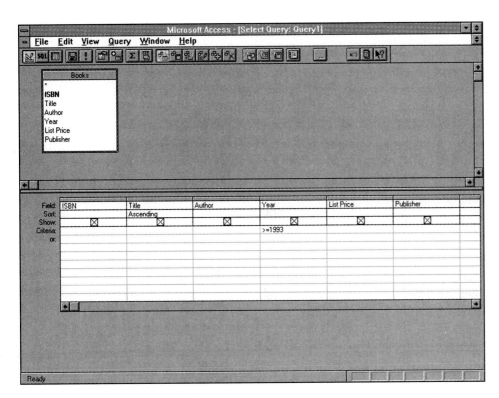

FIGURE 3.12 Screen for Problem 4

5. Use the OURDATA.MDB database as the basis for the following queries and reports:

   a. Create a select query for students on the Dean's List (GPA >= 3.600). Include the student's name, major, quality points, credits, and GPA. List the students alphabetically.

b. Use the Report Wizard to prepare a tabular report based on the query in part a. Include your name in the Report header as the academic advisor.

c. Create a select query for students on Academic probation (GPA < 2.00). Include the same fields as the query in part a. List the students in alphabetical order.

d. Use the Report Wizard to prepare a tabular report based on the query in part (c).

6. Use the Group/Total Report Wizard and the EMPLOYEE.MDB database to create the following reports:

a. A report containing all employees in sequence by location and alphabetically within location. Show the employee's last name, first name, location, title, and salary. Include summary statistics to display the total salaries in each location as well as the company as a whole.

b. A report containing all employees in sequence by title and alphabetically within title. Show the employee's last name, first name, location, title, and salary. Include summary statistics to display the average salary for each title as well as the average salary in the company.

7. Object linking and embedding: Use the Group/Total Report Wizard and the USA.MDB database to create the report shown in Figure 3.13. (Only the first page is shown.) The report lists states by geographic region, and alphabetically within region. Summary statistics on population and area are displayed for each group together with the percentage each group contributes to the country as a whole. The report header includes a map of the United States that was imported into Access from PowerPoint. To bring in the clip art:

a. Switch to the Design view of the report. Click the Object Frame tool to create an unbound frame control.

United States
by Region
25-Apr-94

Region	Name	Capital	Population	Area
Middle Atlantic				
	Delaware	Dover	666,168	2,057
	Maryland	Annapolis	4,781,468	10,577
	New Jersey	Trenton	7,730,188	7,836
	New York	Albany	17,990,455	49,576
	Pennsylvania	Harrisburg	11,881,643	45,333
	Totals for Region:		**43,049,922**	**115,379**
	Percent of US:		**17.35%**	**3.19%**
Mountain				
	Arizona	Phoenix	3,665,228	113,909
	Colorado	Denver	3,294,394	104,247
	Idaho	Boise	1,006,749	83,557
	Montana	Helena	799,065	147,138
	Nevada	Carson City	1,201,833	110,540
	New Mexico	Sante Fe	1,515,069	121,666
	Utah	Salt Lake City	1,722,850	84,916
	Wyoming	Madison	453,588	97,914
	Totals for Region:		**13,658,776**	**863,887**
	Percent of US:		**5.51%**	**23.87%**
New England				
	Connecticut	Hartford	3,287,116	5,009
	Maine	Augusta	1,227,928	33,215

1

FIGURE 3.13 Report for Problem 7

b. Select MS PowerPoint 4.0 Slide from the resulting dialog box. Click OK.

c. PowerPoint is now the active application. Pull down the Format menu and select Slide Layout. Choose a blank page as the layout. Click Apply. Click the Insert Clip Art icon on the PowerPoint toolbar.

d. Choose the desired clip art, then double click the control-menu box to return to Access. Respond Yes when asked if you want to Update.

e. You can move the embedded object (the PowerPoint clip art) just as you would any other Windows object. Double click the object to return to PowerPoint if you want to size it, change its position within the frame, or choose a different clip art image.

f. Add your name to the report header and submit the completed report to your instructor.

8. **Exploring Mail Merge:** A mail merge takes the tedium out of sending form letters, as it creates the same letter many times, changing the name, address, and other information as appropriate from letter to letter. The form letter is created in Word for Windows, but the data file is taken from an Access table or query.

Figure 3.14 shows how Word for Windows is used to create a series of form lettters that will be sent to students on the Dean's List. Proceed as follows:

a. Open the OURDATA.MDB database used in the chapter. Modify the query created in problem 5 to contain the student's address, city, state, and postal code.

b. Click the Report button in the Database window. Click New. Choose the query from part (a) containing the students on the Dean's List as the Table/Query on which to base the report.

c. Click the Report Wizard button. Scroll to MS Word Mail Merge and select it as the Wizard you want. Click OK.

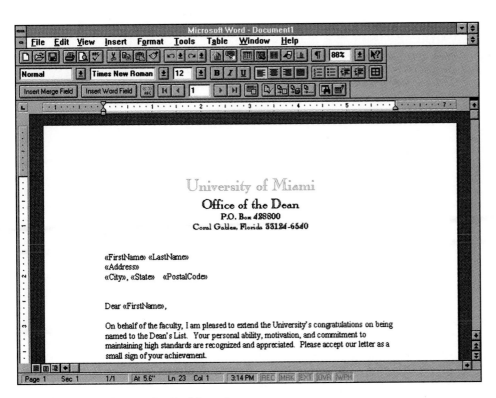

FIGURE 3.14 Screen for Problem 8

d. You should see a dialog box for the Mail Merge Wizard. Click the option button to Create a new document and link the data. Word opens automatically. (Check the box to open Microsoft Word Help if you want to display the Help information.)

e. Create the letter shown in Figure 3.14. To enter a merge field (an entry in angled brackets) click the Insert Merge Field button and choose the appropriate field. Click the Merge to New Document icon (use Tool Tips to identify the icon), then print the letters and submit them to your instructor.

f. Additional information on how to create a mail merge can be obtained by searching on *Mail Merge* in the Word Help menu. You can also refer to *Exploring Word for Windows*, Grauer and Barber, Prentice Hall, 1994, pages 118–128.

Case Studies

The Fortune 500

Research the Fortune 500 (or a similar list) to obtain the gross revenue and net income for the present and previous year for the twenty largest corporations. Create an Access database to hold a table for this data and an associated form to enter the data. Validate your data carefully, then produce at least three reports based on the data.

The United States of America

What is the total population of the United States? What is its area? Can you name the 13 original states or the last five states admitted to the Union? Do you know the 10 states with the highest population or the five largest states in terms of area? Which states have the highest population density (people per square mile)?

The answers to these and other questions can be obtained from the USA.MDB database that is available on the data disk. The key to the assignment is to use the Top Values property within a query that limits the number of records returned in the dynaset. Use the database to create several reports that you think will be of interest to the class.

The Super Bowl

How many times has the NFC won the Super Bowl? When was the last time the AFC won? What was the largest margin of victory? What was the closest game? What is the most points scored by two teams in one game? How many times have the Miami Dolphins appeared? How many times did they win? Use the data in the SUPERBWL.MDB database to create a trivia sheet on the Super Bowl, then incorporate your analysis into a letter addressed to NBC Sports. Convince them you are a super fan and that you merit two tickets to next year's game.

4

One-to-many Relationships: Subforms and Multiple Table Queries

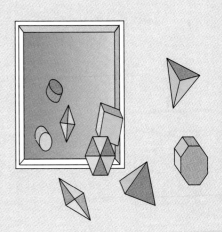

CHAPTER OBJECTIVES

After reading this chapter you will be able to:

1. Explain how a one-to-many relationship is essential in the design of a database; differentiate between a primary key and a foreign key.

2. Create a one-to-many relationship within Access; distinguish between the main table and the related table.

3. Define referential integrity; explain how the enforcement of referential integrity maintains consistency within a database.

4. Explain how a subform is used in conjunction with a one-to-many relationship; use the Form Wizard to create a subform.

5. Create a query based on multiple tables; display the table names within the QBE grid.

6. Create a report based on a query.

7. Create a main form containing two subforms linked to one another; display a subform in Form view or Datasheet view.

OVERVIEW

The Student database in Chapters 2 and 3 presented the different types of objects in an Access database: tables, forms, queries, and reports. It was, however, a simple database because it contained only one table. The real power of Access is derived from a relational database, which contains multiple tables.

This chapter presents a new case study, which focuses on a relational database. The case is that of a consumer loan system within a bank. The database contains two tables, one for customers and one for loans. There is a one-to-many relationship between the tables in that one customer can have many loans.

The case solution includes a discussion of database concepts. It reviews the definition of a primary key and explains how the primary key of one table exists as a foreign key in a related table. It also introduces the concept of referential integrity, which ensures that the tables within the database are consistent with one another. And most important, it shows how to implement these concepts in an Access database.

The chapter builds on what you already know by expanding the earlier material on forms, queries, and reports. It describes how to create a main form and a corresponding subform that contains data from a related table. It develops a query that contains data from multiple tables, then creates a report based on that query.

Suffice it to say that this is a critically important chapter because it is built around a relational database as opposed to a single table. Thus, when you complete the chapter, you will have a much better appreciation of what can be accomplished within Access. As always, the hands-on exercises are essential to your understanding of the material.

CASE STUDY: CONSUMER LOANS

Let us assume that you are in the Information Systems department of a commercial bank and are assigned the task of implementing a system for consumer loans. The bank needs complete data about every loan (the amount, interest rate, term, and so on). It also needs data about the customers holding those loans (name, address, telephone, etc.).

The problem is how to structure the data so that the bank will be able to obtain all of the information it needs from its database. The system must be able to supply the name and address of the person associated with a loan. The system must also be able to retrieve all of the loans for a specific individual.

The solution calls for a database with two tables, one for loans and one for customers. To appreciate the elegance of this approach, consider first a single table containing a combination of loan and customer data as shown in Figure 4.1. At first glance, this solution appears to be satisfactory. You can, for example, search for a specific loan (e.g., L022) and determine that Lori Sangastiano is the customer associated with that loan. You can also search for a particular customer (e.g., Michelle Zacco) and find all of her loans (L028, L030, and L060).

There is a problem, however, in that the table duplicates customer data throughout the database. Thus, when one customer has multiple loans, the cus-

Loan ID	Loan Data (Date, Amount, Interest Rate...)	Customer Data (First Name, Last Name, Address...)
L001	Loan data for Loan L001	Customer data for Wendy Solomon
L004	Loan data for Loan L004	Customer data for Wendy Solomon
L010	Loan data for Loan L010	Customer data for Alex Rey
L014	Loan data for Loan L014	Customer data for Wendy Solomon
L020	Loan data for Loan L020	Customer data for Ted Myerson
L022	Loan data for Loan L022	Customer data for Lori Sangastiano
L026	Loan data for Loan L026	Customer data for Matt Hirsch
L028	Loan data for Loan L028	Customer data for Michelle Zacco
L030	Loan data for Loan L030	Customer data for Michelle Zacco
L031	Loan data for Loan L031	Customer data for Eileen Faulkner
L032	Loan data for Loan L032	Customer data for Scott Wit
L033	Loan data for Loan L033	Customer data for Alex Rey
L039	Loan data for Loan L039	Customer data for David Powell
L040	Loan data for Loan L040	Customer data for Matt Hirsch
L047	Loan data for Loan L047	Customer data for Benjamin Grauer
L049	Loan data for Loan L049	Customer data for Eileen Faulkner
L052	Loan data for Loan L052	Customer data for Eileen Faulkner
L053	Loan data for Loan L053	Customer data for Benjamin Grauer
L054	Loan data for Loan L054	Customer data for Scott Wit
L057	Loan data for Loan L057	Customer data for Benjamin Grauer
L060	Loan data for Loan L060	Customer data for Michelle Zacco
L062	Loan data for Loan L062	Customer data for Matt Hirsch
L100	Loan data for Loan L100	Customer data for Benjamin Grauer
L109	Loan data for Loan L109	Customer data for Wendy Solomon
L120	Loan data for Loan L120	Customer data for Lori Sangastiano

FIGURE 4.1 Single Table Solution

tomer's name, address, and other data is stored multiple times. Maintaining the data in this form is a time-consuming and error-prone procedure, because any change to the customer's data has to be made in many places.

A second problem arises if you attempt to add a new customer before the customer takes out a loan. The bank requires its customers to qualify for a loan before lending the money. Adding a customer to the database before the loan is granted is difficult, however, because it requires the creation of an empty loan record to hold the customer data.

The deletion (payoff) of a loan creates a third type of problem. What happens, for example, when Ted Myerson pays off loan L020? The loan record would be deleted, but so too would Ted's data as he has no other outstanding loans. The bank might want to grant Mr. Myerson another loan in the future, but it would lose his data with the deletion of the existing loan.

The database in Figure 4.2 represents a much better design because it eliminates all three problems. It eliminates the *redundancy* by using two different tables, a Loans table and a Customers table. Each record in the Loans table has

LoanID	Date	Amount	InterestRate	Term	Type	CustomerID
L001	15-Jan-94	$475,000	6.90%	15	M	C04
L004	23-Jan-94	$35,000	7.20%	5	C	C04
L010	25-Jan-94	$10,000	5.50%	3	C	C05
L014	31-Jan-94	$12,000	9.50%	10	O	C04
L020	08-Feb-94	$525,000	6.50%	30	M	C06
L022	12-Feb-94	$10,000	7.50%	5	O	C07
L026	15-Feb-94	$35,000	6.50%	5	O	C10
L028	20-Feb-94	$250,000	8.80%	30	M	C08
L030	21-Feb-94	$5,000	10.00%	3	O	C08
L031	28-Feb-94	$200,000	7.00%	15	M	C01
L032	01-Mar-94	$25,000	10.00%	3	C	C02
L033	01-Mar-94	$20,000	9.50%	5	O	C05
L039	03-Mar-94	$56,000	7.50%	5	C	C09
L040	10-Mar-94	$129,000	8.50%	15	M	C10
L047	11-Mar-94	$200,000	7.25%	15	M	C03
L049	21-Mar-94	$150,000	7.50%	15	M	C01
L052	22-Mar-94	$100,000	7.00%	30	M	C01
L053	31-Mar-94	$15,000	6.50%	3	O	C03
L054	01-Apr-94	$10,000	8.00%	5	C	C02
L057	15-Apr-94	$25,000	9.50%	4	C	C03
L060	18-Apr-94	$41,000	9.90%	4	C	C08
L062	22-Apr-94	$350,000	7.50%	15	M	C10
L100	01-May-94	$150,000	6.00%	15	M	C03
L109	03-May-94	$350,000	8.20%	30	M	C04
L120	08-May-94	$275,000	9.20%	15	M	C07

(a) Loans Table

CustomerID	First Name	Last Name	Address	City	State	Zip Code	Phone Number
C01	Eileen	Faulkner	7245 NW 8 Street	Minneapolis	MN	55346	(612) 894-1511
C02	Scott	Wit	5660 NW 175 Terrace	Baltimore	MD	21224	(410) 753-0345
C03	Benjamin	Grauer	10000 Sample Road	Coral Springs	FL	33073	(305) 444-5555
C04	Wendy	Solomon	7500 Reno Rod	Houston	TX	77090	(713) 427-3104
C05	Alex	Rey	3456 Main Highway	Denver	CO	80228	(303) 555-6666
C06	Ted	Myerson	6545 Stone Street	Chapel Hill	NC	27515	(919) 942-7654
C07	Lori	Sangastiano	4533 Aero Drive	Santa Rosa	CA	95403	(707) 542-3411
C08	Michelle	Zacco	488 Gold Street	Gainesville	FL	32601	(904) 374-5660
C09	David	Powell	5070 Battle Road	Decatur	GA	30034	(301) 345-6556
C10	Matt	Hirsch	777 NW 67 Avenue	Fort Lee	NJ	07624	(201) 664-3211

(b) Customers Table

FIGURE 4.2 Multiple Table Solution

data about a specific loan (LoanID, Date, Amount, Interest Rate, Term, Type, and CustomerID). Each record in the Customers table has data about a specific customer (CustomerID, First Name, Last Name, Address, City, State, Zip Code, and Phone Number). In addition, each record in the Loans table is associated with a matching record in the Customers table through the CustomerID field common to both tables. This solution may seem complicated, but it is really quite elegant.

Consider, for example, how easy it is to change a customer's address. If Michelle Zacco were to move, you would go into the Customers table, find her record (Customer C08), and make the necessary change. You would not have to change any of the records in the Loans table, because they do not contain customer data, but only an indication of who the customer is. In other words, you would change Michelle's address in only one place, and the change would be automatically reflected for every associated loan.

The addition of a new customer is done immediately in the Customers table. This is much easier than the approach of Figure 4.1, which required an existing loan in order to add a new customer. And finally, the deletion of an existing loan is also easier than with the single-table organization. A loan can be deleted from the Loans table without losing the corresponding customer data.

The database in Figure 4.2 is composed of two tables in which there is a ***one-to-many relationship*** between customers and loans. One customer (Michelle Zacco) can have many loans (loan numbers L028, L030, and L060), but a specific loan (L028) can have only one customer (Michelle Zacco). The tables are related to one another by a common field (CustomerID) that is present in both the Customers and the Loans table.

Access enables you to create the one-to-many relationship between the tables, then uses that relationship to answer questions about the database. It can retrieve information about a specific loan such as the name of the customer holding that loan. It can also find all of the loans for a particular customer. Consider:

Query: What is the name and address of the customer associated with loan number L010?
Answer: Alex Rey, at 3456 Main Highway in Denver.

To determine the answer, Access searches the Loans table for loan L010 to obtain the CustomerID (C05 in this example). It then searches the Customers table for the customer with the matching CustomerID and retrieves the name and address.

Query: Which loans are associated with Wendy Solomon?
Answer: Wendy Solomon has four loans. Loan L001 for $475,000, loan L004 for $35,000, loan L014 for $12,000, and loan L109 for $350,000.

This time Access begins in the Customers table and searches for Wendy Solomon to determine the CustomerID (C04). It then searches the Loans table for all records with a matching CustomerID.

PEDAGOGY VERSUS REALITY

Our database requires the CustomerID and LoanID to begin with the letters C and L, respectively, to emphasize the tables in which these fields are found. Our database also places artificial limits on the number of customers and loans at 100 and 1000, respectively. (CustomerID goes from C00 to C99 and LoanID goes from L000 to L999.)

Implementation in Access

An Access database contains multiple tables. Each table stores data about a specific subject such as customers or loans. Each table has a *primary key,* which is a field (or combination of fields) that uniquely identifies each record. CustomerID is the primary key in the Customers table. LoanID is the primary key in the Loans table.

A one-to-many relationship uses the primary key of the "one" table as a *foreign key* in the "many" table. (A foreign key is simply the primary key of another table.) The CustomerID appears in both the Customers table and the Loans table. It is the primary key in the Customers table where its values are unique. It is a foreign key in the Loans table where its values are not unique. Thus, multiple records in the Loans table can have the same CustomerID to implement the one-to-many relationship between customers and loans.

To create a one-to-many relationship, you open the *Relationships window* in Figure 4.3 and add the necessary tables. You then drag the field you want to relate from the field list of one table (CustomerID in the example) to the matching field in the other table. The field you drag (the primary key) belongs to the *primary table.* The matching field (the foreign key) belongs to the *related table.*

Referential Integrity

Referential integrity ensures that the records in related tables are consistent with one another. When enforcement of referential integrity is in effect, Access will prevent you from adding records to a related table when there is no associated record in the primary table. In other words, you cannot add a record to the Loans

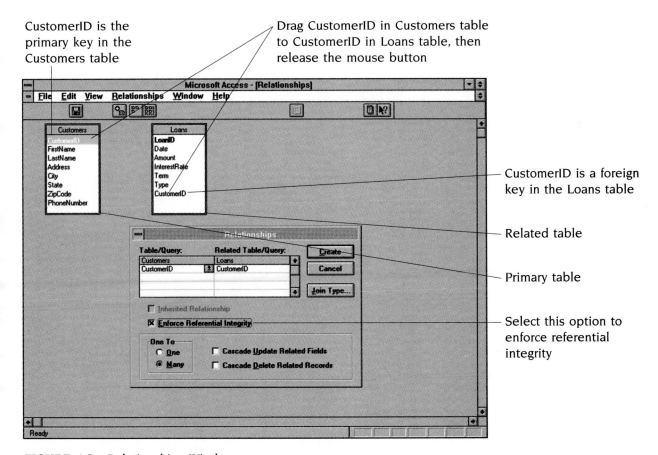

FIGURE 4.3 Relationships Window

table unless there is a corresponding Customer record. Or stated another way, you must add a Customer record before assigning a loan to that customer.

Enforcement of referential integrity will also prevent you from deleting a record in the primary (Customers) table if there is a corresponding record in the related (Loans) table. In similar fashion, you cannot change the primary key of a Customer record when there are matching Loan records. (These restrictions do not apply if you check the *Cascade Delete Related Records* or *Cascade Update Related Fields* option in the Relationships dialog box. The Cascading options are discussed further in Chapter 5.)

HANDS-ON EXERCISE 1:

One-to-many Relationships

Objective To create a one-to-many relationship between existing tables in a database; to demonstrate referential integrity between the tables in a one-to-many relationship. Use Figure 4.4 as a guide in the exercise.

Step 1: Open the NATLBANK database
➤ Load Access. If you are using a floppy disk (instead of the hard drive), you must copy **NATLBANK.MDB** and **NATLBANK.LDB** from the data disk to a working disk as you did in Chapter 1.

➤ Click the **Open Database icon.** Open the **NATLBANK.MDB** database in the ACCSDATA directory.

➤ Pull down the **Edit menu** and click **Relationships.** The Relationships window will open as shown in Figure 4.4a.

Relationships window —

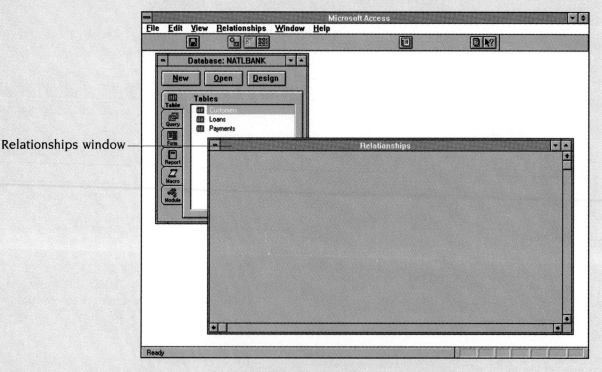

(a) The NATLBANK Database (step 1)

FIGURE 4.4 Hands-on Exercise 1

Step 2: Add the Customers and Loans tables

➤ Click the Database window to make it active, then click the **Minimize button** in the Database window to minimize the window and remove the clutter on the desktop.

➤ Pull down the **Relationships menu** and click **Add Table** (or click the **Add Table icon**).

➤ The **Customers table** is already selected. Click the **Add command button** to add the table to the Relationships window as shown in Figure 4.4b.

➤ Click the **Loans table** in the Table/Query list. Click the **Add command button** to add this table to the Relationships window as well.

➤ Do *not* add the Payments table at this time. Click the **Close command button** to close the Add Table dialog box.

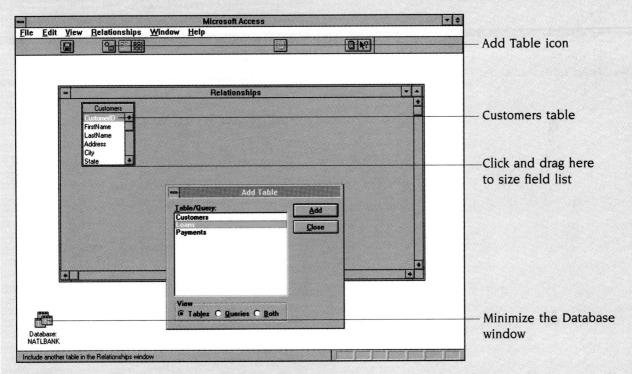

(b) Add the Tables (step 2)

FIGURE 4.4 Hands-on Exercise 1 (continued)

Step 3: Move and size the field list

➤ Point to the bottom border of the Customers field list (the mouse pointer changes to a double arrow), then click and drag the border until all of the fields are visible.

➤ Click and drag the bottom border of the Loans field list until all of the fields are visible.

➤ Click and drag the title bar of the Loans field list so that it is approximately one inch away from the Customers field list as shown in Figure 4.4c.

Step 4: Create the relationship

➤ Click and drag the **CustomerID field** in the Customers field list to the **CustomerID field** in the Loans field list. You will see the Relationships dialog box in Figure 4.4c when you release the mouse.

Click and drag
CustomerID in the
Customers table to
CustomerID in the
Loans table

Click here to create
the relationship

Click here to enforce
referential integrity

One-to-Many option is
automatically selected

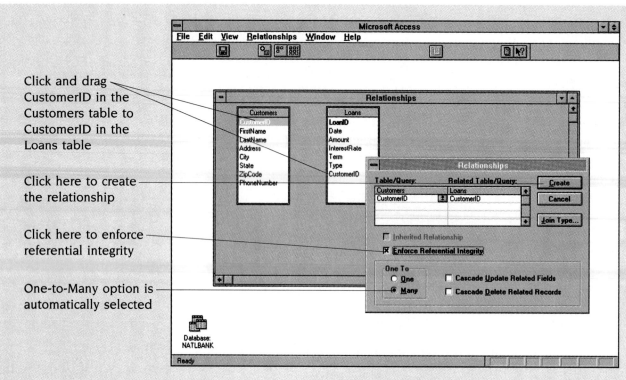

(c) Create the Relationship (step 4)

FIGURE 4.4   Hands-on Exercise 1 (continued)

➤ Check the **Enforce Referential Integrity** check box. The **One-to-many** option button is selected automatically.
➤ Be sure that the options selected on your screen match those in the Relationships dialog box in Figure 4.4c.
➤ Click the **Create command button** to establish the relationship and close the Relationships dialog box. You should see a line indicating a one-to-many relationship between the Customers and Loans tables as shown in Figure 4.4d.
➤ Click the **Save icon** to save the relationship.

WHAT YOU SEE IS WHAT YOU GET

Access uses the number 1 and the infinity symbol (∞) to indicate a one-to-many relationship in which referential integrity is enforced. The 1 appears at the end of the join line near the primary (one) table. The infinity symbol appears at the end nearest the related (many) table. Access shows the primary keys in each table in bold.

Step 5: Deleting a relationship
➤ Click the line indicating the relationship between the tables. The line turns bold, indicating it (the relationship) has been selected.
➤ Press the **Del key.** You will see the dialog box in Figure 4.4d asking whether

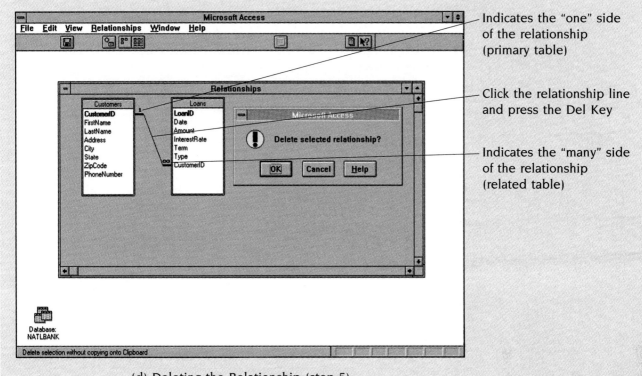

Indicates the "one" side of the relationship (primary table)

Click the relationship line and press the Del Key

Indicates the "many" side of the relationship (related table)

(d) Deleting the Relationship (step 5)

FIGURE 4.4 Hands-on Exercise I (continued)

you want to delete the relationship. Click the **Cancel command button** since you do *not* want to delete the relationship.

➤ Double click the **control-menu box** in the Relationships window to close the window.

Step 6: Add a customer record

➤ Click the **Database window icon** on the toolbar.

➤ Open the **Customers table.** Click the **Maximize button** to give yourself additional room when adding a record.

➤ Click the **New icon** on the toolbar as shown in Figure 4.4e. The record selector moves to the last record (record 11).

➤ Enter **C11** as the CustomerID as shown in Figure 4.4e. The record selector changes to a pencil as soon as you enter the first character.

➤ Enter data for yourself as the new customer. Data validation has been built into the Customers table, so you must enter the data correctly or it will not be accepted.

— The message, *Customer ID must begin with the letter C followed by a two digit number,* indicates that the CustomerID field is invalid.

— The message, *Field 'Customers.LastName' can't contain a null value,* indicates that you must enter a last name.

— A beep in either the ZipCode or PhoneNumber fields indicates that you are entering a nonnumeric character.

— If you encounter a data validation error, press Esc (or Click OK), then reenter the data.

➤ Remember your CustomerID (C11) because you will need to enter it in the corresponding loan records.

New icon   Last Name is blank

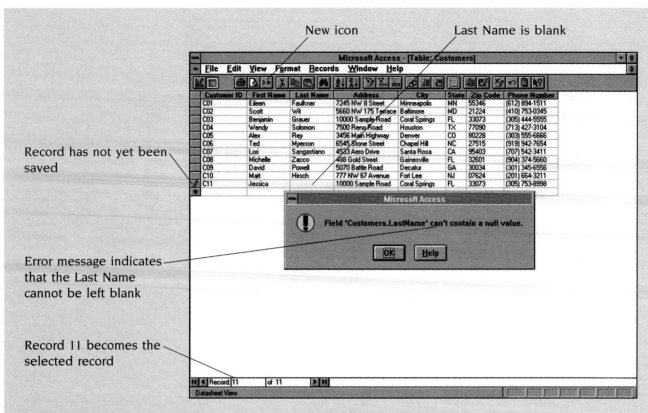

Record has not yet been saved

Error message indicates that the Last Name cannot be left blank

Record 11 becomes the selected record

(e) Add a Customer Record (step 6)

FIGURE 4.4   Hands-on Exercise 1 (continued)

THE RECORD SELECTOR

The record selector symbol indicates the status of the record. A triangle means the data in the current record has not changed. A pencil indicates you are in the process of entering (or changing) the data. An asterisk appears next to the blank record at the end of every table.

Step 7: Add a loan record

➤ Click the **Database Window icon** on the toolbar.

➤ Open the **Loans table.** Click the **Maximize button** to give yourself additional room when adding a record.

➤ Click the **New icon** on the toolbar. The record selector moves to the blank record at the end of the table (record 26).

➤ Add a new loan record. Use **L121** for the LoanID. Use other data of your own choosing.

➤ Data validation has been built into the Loans table so you will have to enter data correctly for it to be accepted.

➤ Be sure to enter **C11** in the CustomerID field. (This is the CustomerID you entered in step 6.)

ARRANGING THE DESKTOP

An Access database contains several objects that can be open at the same time. Pull down the Window menu, then click the Cascade or Tile command to arrange the open windows on the desktop. If you cascade the windows, you will most likely size and/or move them afterwards. To size a window, point to any border or corner and drag in the desired direction. To move a window, point to the title bar and drag the window to its new position.

Step 8: Referential integrity

➤ Click the **Database window icon** on the toolbar, then click the **Minimize button** to minimize the window. The Customers and Loans windows are the only open windows on the desktop.

➤ Pull down the **Window menu.** Click **Cascade** to cascade the Customers and Loans tables. Move and size the open windows so that your desktop matches ours in Figure 4.4f.

➤ Click the **CustomerID field** of your loan record and replace the CustomerID (C11) with **C88.** Press **enter.** You will see the dialog box in Figure 4.4f, indicating that referential integrity has been violated because there is no corresponding Customer record.

➤ Click **OK.** Re-enter **C11** as the valid CustomerID. Press **enter.**

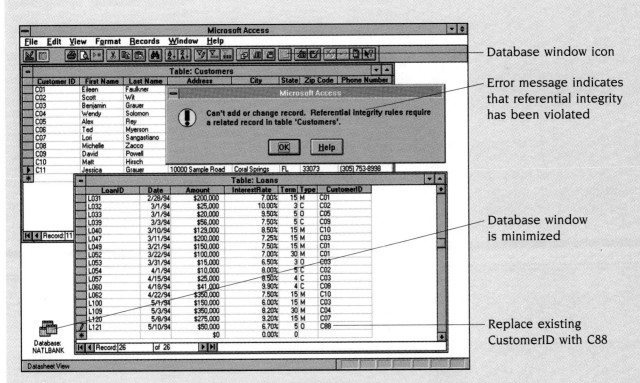

(f) Referential Integrity (step 8)

FIGURE 4.4 Hands-on Exercise 1 (continued)

➤ Click the window for the Customers table. Click the **row selector** to select the first record (Customer C01). Press the **Del key** (in an attempt) to delete this record.

➤ Access indicates that you cannot delete this record because related records exist and referential integrity rules would be violated. Click **OK.**

Step 9: Close the database

➤ Double click the control-menu box to close the Customers table.

➤ Double click the control-menu box to close the Loans table.

➤ Close the Database window if you do not want to continue with the next hands-on exercise at this time.

SUBFORMS

A *subform* is a form within a form. It appears inside a main form to display records from a related table. A main form and its associated subform to display the loans for one customer are shown in Figure 4.5. The *main form* (also known as the primary form) is based on the primary table (the Customers table). The subform is based on the related table (the Loans table).

The main form and the subform are linked to one another so that the subform displays only the records related to the record currently displayed in the main form. The main form shows the "one" side of the relationship (the customer). The subform shows the "many" side of the relationship (the loans). The main form displays the customer data for one record (Eileen Faulkner with CustomerID C01). The subform shows the loans for that customer. Note, too, that the main form is displayed in the *Form view,* whereas the subform is displayed in the *Datasheet view.*

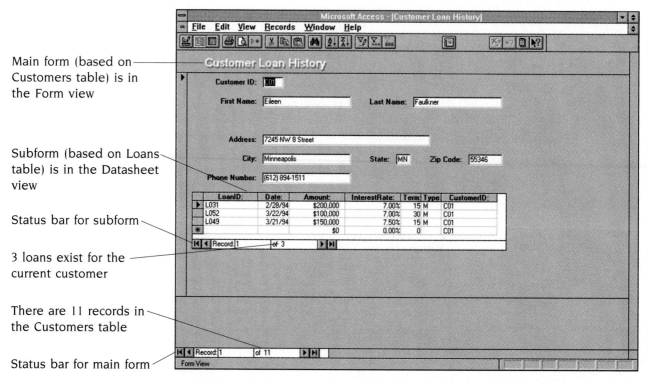

Main form (based on Customers table) is in the Form view

Subform (based on Loans table) is in the Datasheet view

Status bar for subform

3 loans exist for the current customer

There are 11 records in the Customers table

Status bar for main form

FIGURE 4.5 Main Form and Subform

Each form in Figure 4.5 has its own status bar and associated navigation buttons. The status bar for the main form indicates that the active record is record 1 of 11 records in the Customers table. The status bar for the subform indicates record 1 of 3 records. (The latter number shows the number of loans for this customer rather than the number of loans in the Loans table.)

The easiest way to create a main form and corresponding subform is through the *Main/Subform Wizard* as will be done in the following hands-on exercise. The Wizard creates both of the forms for you, then establishes the link between the forms automatically.

THE POWER OF SUBFORMS

A subform is a separate form that is designed and saved just as any other form. A main form can have any number of subforms. Subforms can also extend to two levels; that is, you can have a subform linked to a subform that exists within a main form. (See hands-on exercise 4, which begins on page 157.)

HANDS-ON EXERCISE 2:

Creating a Subform

Objective To use the Form Wizard to create a subform that displays the related records in a one-to-many relationship; to move and size controls in an existing form; to enter data in a subform. Use Figure 4.6 as a guide in the exercise.

Step 1: Create a new form
➤ Open the **NATLBANK.MDB** database from the previous exercise.
➤ Click the **Form button.** Click **New** to produce the New Form dialog box.
➤ Click the arrow in the **Select A Table/Query** text box. Click **Customers** to select the Customers table.
➤ Click the **Form Wizards button** to open the Form Wizard. Choose **Main/Subform** as shown in Figure 4.6a. Click **OK.**

Step 2: The Main/Subform Wizard
➤ The next several screens ask questions about the Main/Subform you want to create.
— Click **Loans** as the table containing the data for the subform as shown in Figure 4.6b. Click the **Next command button.**
— The Wizard indicates that data for the main form comes from Customers (the Customers table). Click the **>> button** to select all available fields. Click the **Next command button.**
— The Wizard indicates that data for the subform comes from Loans (the Loans table). Click the **>> button** to select all available fields. Click the **Next command button.**
— Click **Embossed** for the style of the form. Click the **Next command button.**

Click the Form button

Choose the Main/Subform Wizard

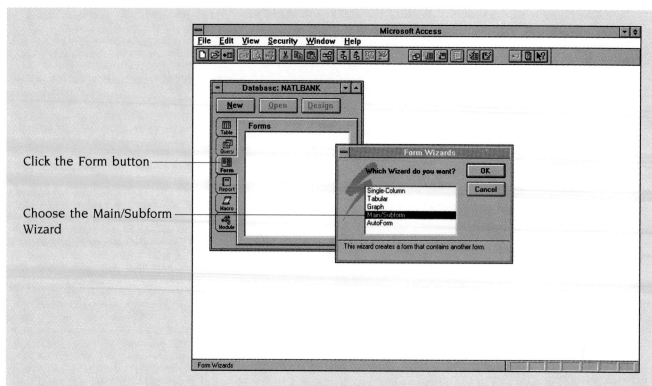

(a) The Form Wizard (step 1)

Data for main form will come from the Customers table

Select Loans as the data source for the subform

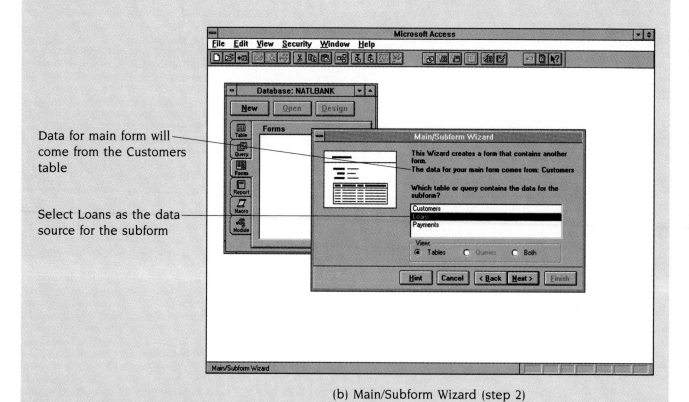

(b) Main/Subform Wizard (step 2)

FIGURE 4.6 Hands-on Exercise 2

- Type **Customer Loan History** as the title of the form. Click the option button to **Open the Form with data in it.** Click the **Finish command button.**

➤ You will see a message indicating that you must save the subform before the Main/Subform Wizard can proceed. Click **OK.** Type **Loans** in the Save As dialog box. Click **OK.**

Step 3: View the data

➤ Click the **Maximize button** so that the form takes the entire window as shown in Figure 4.6c.

➤ The customer information for the first customer (C01) is displayed in the main portion of the form. The loans for that customer are displayed in the subform.

➤ The status bar at the bottom of the window (corresponding to the main form) displays record 1 of 11 records (you are looking at the first record in the Customers table).

➤ The status bar for the subform displays record 1 of 3 records (you are on the first of three loan records for this customer).

➤ Click the ▶ **button** on the status bar for the main form to move to the next customer record. The subform is updated automatically to display the two loans belonging to this customer.

➤ Press the **PgDn key** to move through the customer records until you come to the last record in the customer file.

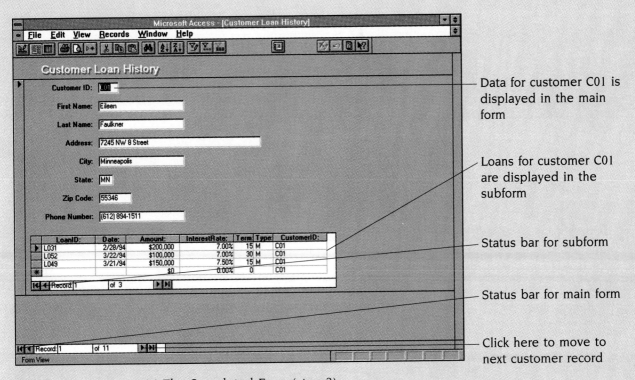

(c) The Completed Form (step 3)

FIGURE 4.6 Hands-on Exercise 2 (continued)

Step 4: Enter a new loan
➤ You should be at customer C11, which is the record you entered in the previous exercise. (Click the **PgUp key** if you are on a blank record.)
➤ Click the **LoanID field** next to the asterisk in the subform. The record selector changes to a triangle.
➤ Enter data for the new loan as shown in Figure 4.6d. (You do *not* have to enter the CustomerID since it appears automatically due to the relationship between the Customers and Loans tables.) The record selector changes to a pencil as soon as you begin to enter data.
➤ Click the **Design View icon** when you have completed the new loan record.

Step 5: Modify the main form
➤ We will improve the appearance of the main form by rearranging its controls as shown in Figure 4.6e.
➤ Click the control for **LastName** to select the control and display the sizing handles. Move the LastName control so that it is next to the FirstName control.
➤ Click and drag the other controls to complete the form:
— Place the controls for City, State, and ZipCode on the same line.
— Move the control for PhoneNumber under the control for City.
➤ Point to the border of the Loans subform, then click and drag to move the subform underneath the phone number.

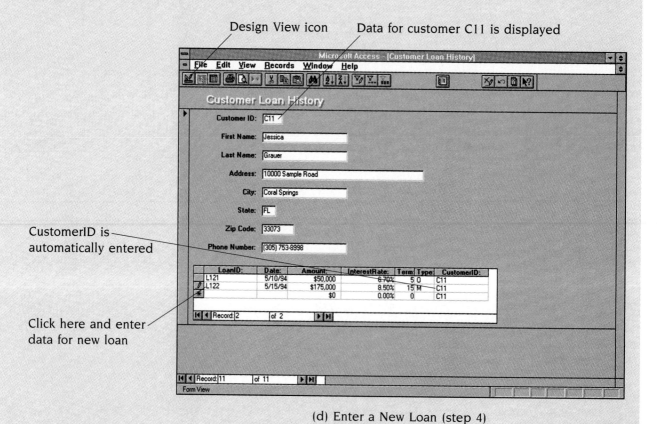

(d) Enter a New Loan (step 4)

FIGURE 4.6 Hands-on Exercise 2 (continued)

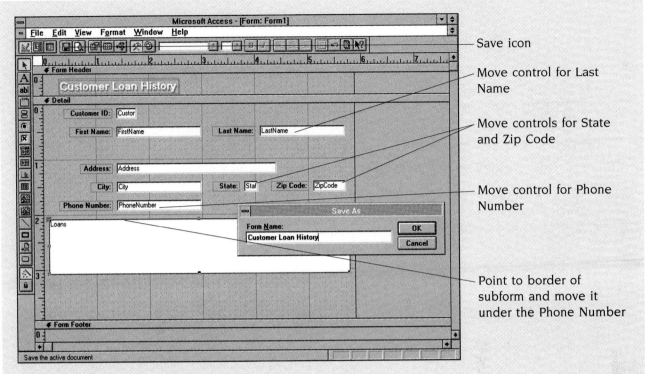

Save icon

Move control for Last Name

Move controls for State and Zip Code

Move control for Phone Number

Point to border of subform and move it under the Phone Number

(e) Modify the Main Form (step 5)

FIGURE 4.6   Hands-on Exercise 2 (continued)

➤ Click the **Save icon** to save the modified form. Type **Customer Loan History** as the name of the form in the Save As dialog box as shown in Figure 4.6e. Click **OK**.

ALIGN THE CONTROLS

To align controls in a straight line (horizontally or vertically), press and hold the Shift key as you click the labels of the controls to be aligned. Pull down the Format menu, click Align, and select the edge to align (Left, Right, Top, and Bottom). Click the Undo command if you are not satisfied with the result.

Step 6: The Subform
➤ Point anywhere inside the Loans subform, then click the **right mouse button** to display a shortcut menu.
➤ Click **Properties** to display the Subform/Subreport properties box shown in Figure 4.6f.
➤ Notice that the CustomerID field appears next to two properties (Link Child Fields and Link Master Fields), which is how the main and subforms are linked to one another.
➤ Double click the **control-menu box** to close the Subform/Subreport properties box.

Form View icon

Double click the control-
menu box to close the
Properties dialog box

Indicates the linking field
in the two tables

Point to the Loans
subform and click the
right mouse button for
shortcut menu

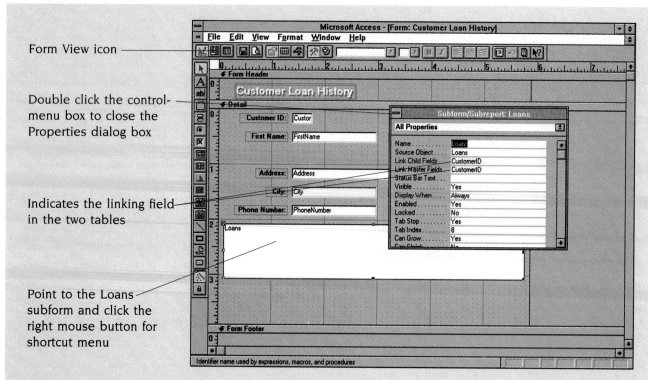

(f) The Subform (step 6)

Double click the control-
menu box to close the
form

Form View icon

Print icon

Data for customer C11 is
displayed

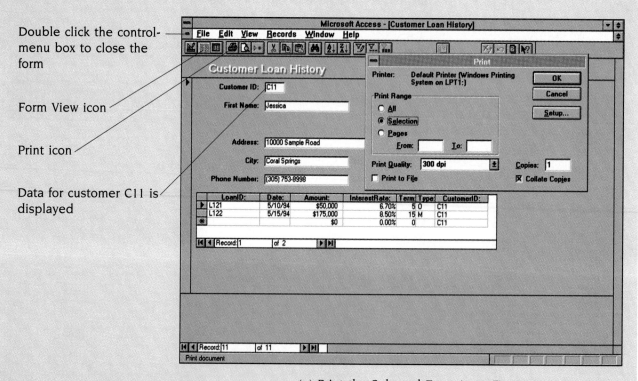

(g) Print the Selected Form (step 7)

FIGURE 4.6 Hands-on Exercise 2 (continued)

Step 7: Print the form

➤ Click the **Form View icon** to return to the Form view in Figure 4.6g. The record for customer C11 should still be in view.

➤ Pull down the **File menu** and click **Print** (or click the **Print icon**) to display the Print dialog box.

➤ Click the **Selection option button.** Click **OK** to print the selected form.

➤ Double click the **control-menu box** to close the form. Click **Yes** if asked to save the changes to the form.

➤ Exit Access if you do not want to continue with the next hands-on exercise at this time.

MULTIPLE TABLE QUERIES

A relational database consists of multiple tables, each dealing with a specific subject. The tables can be related to one another through a main form and a subform as was done in the preceding exercise. They can also be related through a select query that is developed from multiple tables.

The real power of a select query is its ability to include fields from several tables. If, for example, you wanted the name and address of all customers holding a certain type of loan, you would need data from both the Customers table and the Loans table. You would create the select query by using the QBE grid just as you did in Chapter 3; the only difference is that you would add both tables to the query. You would select the customer's name and address fields from the Customers table, and the various loan parameters from the Loans table.

Figure 4.7a shows the Design view of a query to select the 15-year mortgages (loan type "M") issued after April 1, 1994. Figure 4.7b displays the resulting dynaset. You should recognize the QBE grid and the Field, Sort, Show, and Criteria rows from our earlier discussion. The *Table row* is new and displays the name of the table containing the field name.

In Figure 4.7a the LastName and the FirstName fields are taken from the Customers table. All of the other fields are from the Loans table. The one-to-

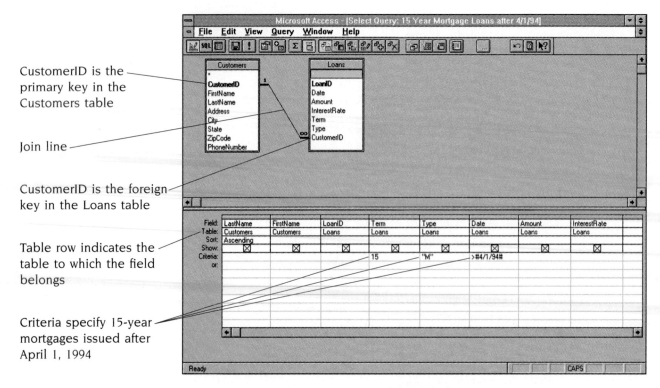

CustomerID is the primary key in the Customers table

Join line

CustomerID is the foreign key in the Loans table

Table row indicates the table to which the field belongs

Criteria specify 15-year mortgages issued after April 1, 1994

(a) Query Window

Last Name	First Name	LoanID	Term	Type	Date	Amount	InterestRate
Grauer	Jessica	L122	15	M	5/15/94	$175,000	8.50%
Grauer	Benjamin	L100	15	M	5/1/94	$150,000	6.00%
Hirsch	Matt	L062	15	M	4/22/94	$350,000	7.50%
Sangastiano	Lori	L120	15	M	5/8/94	$275,000	9.20%

Record: 1   of 4

(b) Dynaset

FIGURE 4.7 A Multitable Query

many relationship between the Customers table and the Loans table is shown graphically within the Query window. The tables are related through the CustomerID field, which is the primary key in the Customers table and a foreign key in the Loans table. The line between the two field lists is called a *join line* and tells Access how to relate the data in the tables.

Return for a moment to the discussion at the beginning of the chapter where we asked the name and address of the customer holding loan L010 (Alex Rey at 3456 Main Highway). Look at the data in Figure 4.2 at the beginning of the chapter and see how you have to consult both tables to answer the query. You do it intuitively; Access does it by using a query containing fields from both tables.

Forms and reports become more interesting and contain more information when they are based on multiple table queries. The following exercise has you create a query similar to the one in Figure 4.7, then create a report based on that query.

THE JOIN LINE

Access joins the tables in a query automatically if a relationship exists between the tables. Access will also join the tables (even with no previous relationship) if both tables have a field with the same name and data type, and if one of the fields is a primary key. You can also create the join yourself by dragging a field from one table to the other, but this type of join applies only to the query in which it was created.

HANDS-ON EXERCISE 3:

Queries and Reports

Objective Create a query that relates two tables to one another, then create a report based on that query. Use Figure 4.8 as a guide in the exercise.

Step 1: Create a select query
- ➤ Open the **NATLBANK** database from the previous exercise.
- ➤ Click the **Query button** in the Database window. Click the **New button** to produce the New Query dialog box.
- ➤ Click the **New Query button** to produce the Add Table dialog box in Figure 4.8a. (The tables have not yet been added.)

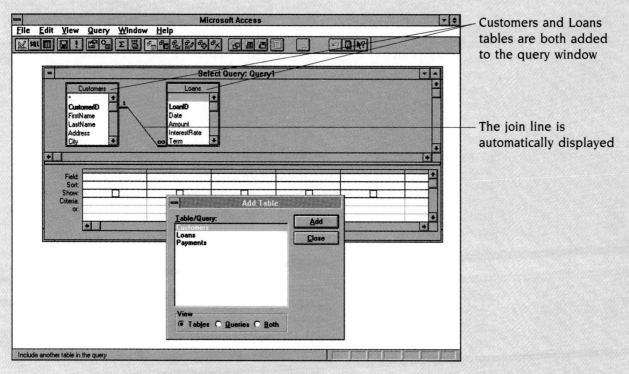

Customers and Loans tables are both added to the query window

The join line is automatically displayed

(a) Add the Tables (step 2)

FIGURE 4.8 Hands-on Exercise 3

Step 2: Add the tables

➤ Click the Customers table in the Table/Query list, then click the **Add command button** to add the Customers table to the query.

➤ Click the Loans table in the Table/Query list, then click the **Add command button** to add the Loans table to the query. The relationship between the tables is shown automatically.

➤ Click the **Close command button** to close the Add Table dialog box.

ADDING AND DELETING TABLES

To add a table to an existing query, pull down the Query menu, click Add Table, then double click the name of the table from the Table/Query list. To delete a table, click anywhere in its field list and press the Del key, or pull down the Query menu and click Remove Table.

Step 3: Move and size the field lists

➤ Click the **maximize button** so that the Query Design window takes the entire desktop.

➤ Point to the line separating the field lists from the QBE grid (the mouse pointer changes to a cross), then click and drag in a downward direction. This gives you more space to display the field lists for the tables in the query as shown in Figure 4.8b.

➤ Click and drag the bottom of the Customers table field list until you see all of the fields in the Customers table.

➤ Click and drag the bottom of the Loans table field list until you see all of the fields in the Loans table.

➤ Click and drag the title bar of the Loans table to the right until you are satisfied with the appearance of the line connecting the tables.

Step 4: Create the query

➤ Pull down the **View menu.** Click **Table Names** to include the Tables row in the QBE grid as shown in Figure 4.8c.

➤ Double click the **LastName** and **FirstName** fields in the Customers table to add these fields to the QBE grid. Double click the **title bar** of the Loans table to select all of the fields, then drag the selected group of fields to the QBE grid. Check that you have the necessary fields to complete the query as shown in Figure 4.8c.

➤ Enter the selection criteria as follows:
 — Click the **Criteria row** under the **Date field.** Type **Between 1/1/94 and 3/31/94.** (You do not have to type the pound signs.)
 — Click the **Criteria row** for the **Amount field.** Type **>200000.**
 — Type **M** in the Criteria row for the **Type field.** (You do not have to type the quotation marks.)

➤ Select all of the columns in the QBE grid by clicking the column selector in the first column, then pressing and holding the Shift key as you scroll to the last column and click its column selector. Double click the right edge of any column selector in the Field row to adjust the column width of all the columns simultaneously.

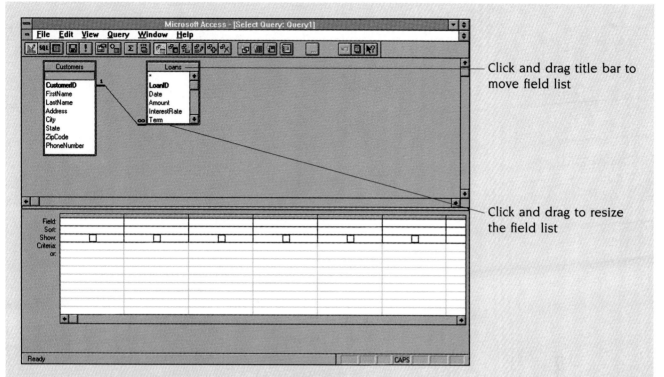

Click and drag title bar to move field list

Click and drag to resize the field list

(b) Move and Size the Field Lists (step 3)

Double click field name to add it to the QBE grid

Run icon

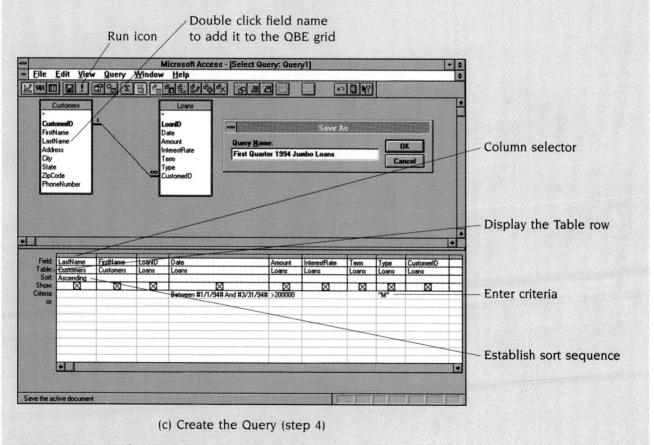

Column selector

Display the Table row

Enter criteria

Establish sort sequence

(c) Create the Query (step 4)

FIGURE 4.8 Hands-on Exercise 3 (continued)

➤ Click the **Sort row** under the LastName field, then click the arrow to open the drop-down list box. Click **Ascending.**

➤ Click the **Save icon** on the Query Design toolbar. Save the query as **First Quarter 1994 Jumbo Loans.**

CONVERSION TO STANDARD FORMAT

Access is flexible in accepting text and date expressions in the Criteria row of a select query. A text entry can be entered with or without quotation marks (e.g., M or "M"). A date entry can be entered with or without pound signs (you can enter 1/1/94 or #1/1/94#). Access does, however, convert your entries to standard format as soon you move to the next cell in the QBE grid. Thus, text entries are always displayed in quotation marks, and dates are always enclosed in pound signs.

Step 5: Run the query

➤ Click the **Run icon** (the exclamation point) to run the query and create the dynaset in Figure 4.8d. Three jumbo loans are listed.

➤ Click the **Amount field** for loan L028. Type **100000** as the corrected amount and press **enter.** (This will reduce the number of jumbo loans in subsequent reports to two.)

➤ Double click the **control-menu box** to close the query.

Double click the control-menu box to close the query

Enter 100000 as the corrected amount

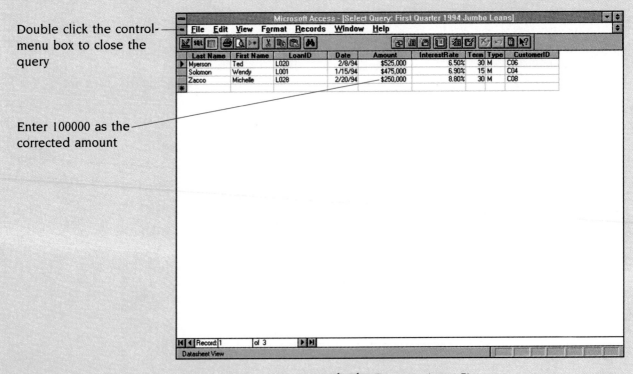

(d) The Dynaset (step 5)

FIGURE 4.8 Hands-on Exercise 3 (continued)

TYPE MISMATCH

The data type determines the way in which criteria appear in the QBE grid. A text field is enclosed in quotation marks. Number, currency, and counter fields are shown as digits with or without a decimal point. Dates are enclosed in pound signs. A Yes/No field is entered as Yes or No without quotation marks. Entering criteria in the wrong form produces a *Data Type Mismatch* error when attempting to run the query.

Step 6: Create a report
➤ The NATLBANK database should be open as shown in Figure 4.8e (although the size of your window may be different from the figure).
➤ Click the **Report button.** Click the **New command button.** Select **First Quarter 1994 Jumbo Loans** (the query you just created) from the Select A Table/Query list.
➤ Click the **Report Wizards button.** Click **Tabular.** Click **OK.**

Step 7: The Report Wizard
➤ Double click **LoanID** from the Available fields list box to add this field to the report. Add the **LastName, FirstName, Date,** and **Amount** fields as shown in Figure 4.8f. Click the **Next command button.**

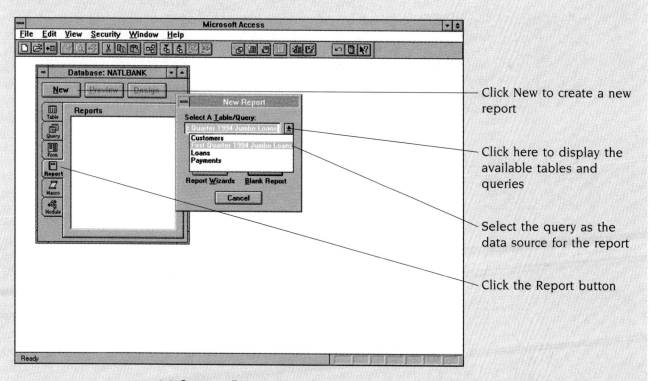

(e) Create a Report (step 6)

FIGURE 4.8 Hands-on Exercise 3 (continued)

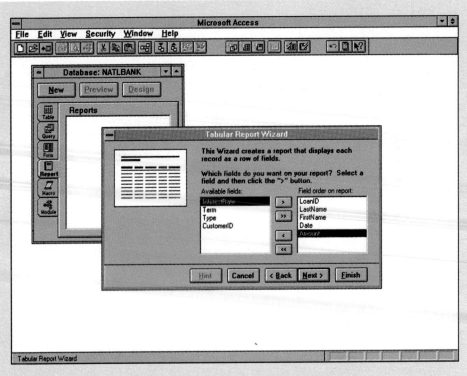

(f) The Report Wizard (step 7)

FIGURE 4.8 Hands-on Exercise 3 (continued)

➤ The Report Wizard asks which field(s) you want to sort by. Double click the **LoanID** field. Click the **Next command button.**

➤ Click the **Executive option button** as the style of the report. Click the **Portrait option button** under Orientation. Click the **Next command button.**

➤ Check the box to **See all the fields on one page.**

➤ Click the option button to **See the report with data in it.** Click the **Finish command button.**

Step 8: Print the completed report.

➤ Click the **maximize button.** If necessary, click the **Zoom icon** in the Print Preview window so that you can see the whole report as in Figure 4.8g.

➤ The report is based on the query created earlier. Michelle Zacco is *not* in the report because the amount of her loan was updated in the query's dynaset in step 5.

➤ Click the **Print icon** to produce the Print dialog box. Click **OK** to print the report.

➤ Double click the report's **control-menu box** to close the report. You will be asked whether to save the report. Click **Yes.** Save the report as **First Quarter 1994 Jumbo Loans,** which is the same name as the query on which the report is based.

➤ Close the NATLBANK database and exit Access.

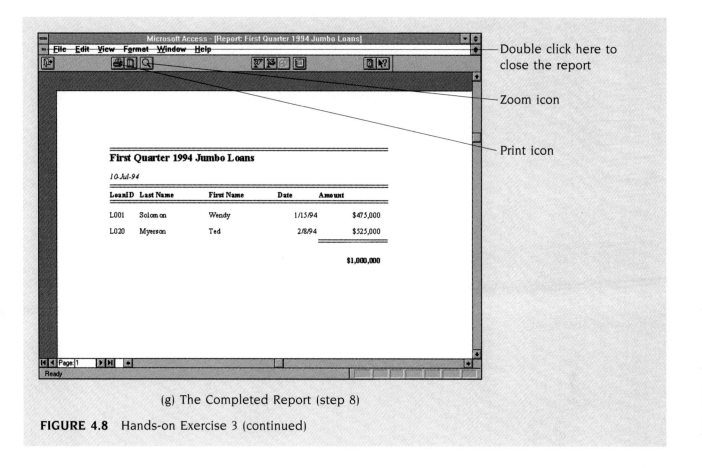

Microsoft Access - [Report: First Quarter 1994 Jumbo Loans]

File   Edit   View   Format   Window   Help

First Quarter 1994 Jumbo Loans

10-Jul-94

LoanID	Last Name	First Name	Date	Amount
L001	Solomon	Wendy	1/15/94	$475,000
L020	Myerson	Ted	2/8/94	$525,000
				$1,000,000

Page: 1

Ready

(g) The Completed Report (step 8)

FIGURE 4.8   Hands-on Exercise 3 (continued)

EXPANDING THE DATABASE

One of the advantages of a relational database is that it can be easily expanded to include additional data without disturbing the existing tables. The database used throughout the chapter consisted of two tables: a Customers table and a Loans table. Figure 4.9 extends the database to include a Payments table containing the payments received by the bank.

The original database had a one-to-many relationship between customers and loans. One customer may have many loans, but a given loan is associated with only one customer. The expanded database contains a second one-to-many relationship between loans and payments. One loan has many payments, but a specific payment is associated with only one loan. The primary key of the Loans table (LoanID) appears as a foreign key in the Payments table.

The Payments table in Figure 4.9c includes one record for every payment received by the bank. Each record in the Payments table has three fields: LoanID, Date (the date the payment was received), and Payment (the amount of the payment, which may include extra principal). The primary key in the Payments table is the *combination* of the LoanID and the PaymentDate. Neither field is unique, but the combination of the two fields is unique.

There are, for example, five payments for loan L001, but each was made on a different date. In similar fashion, two payments were received on April 15th, but each was for a different loan (L001 and L026). There is only one payment for loan L001 on April 15th because the combination of LoanID and PaymentDate is unique. (We are assuming only one payment per loan at a time; if a customer were to send in multiple payments for the same loan on the same date, they would be added together and recorded as a single payment.)

(a) Customers Table

CustomerID	First Name	Last Name	Address	City	State	Zip Code
C01	Eileen	Faulkner	7245 NW 8 Street	Minneapolis	MN	55346
C02	Scott	Wit	5660 NW 175 Terrace	Baltimore	MD	21224
C03	Benjamin	Grauer	10000 Sample Road	Coral Springs	FL	33073
C04	Wendy	Solomon	7500 Reno Road	Houston	TX	77090
C05	Alex	Rey	3456 Main Highway	Denver	CO	80228
C06	Ted	Myerson	6545 Stone Street	Chapel Hill	NC	27515
C07	Lori	Sangastiano	4533 Aero Drive	Santa Rosa	CA	95403
C08	Michelle	Zacco	488 Gold Street	Gainesville	FL	32601
C09	David	Powell	5070 Battle Road	Decatur	GA	30034

(b) Loans Table

LoanID	Date	Amount	InterestRate	Term	Type	CustomerID
L001	15-Jan-94	$475,000	6.90%	15	M	C04
L004	23-Jan-94	$35,000	7.20%	5	C	C04
L010	25-Jan-94	$10,000	5.50%	3	C	C05
L014	31-Jan-94	$12,000	9.50%	10	O	C04
L020	08-Feb-94	$525,000	6.50%	30	M	C06
L022	12-Feb-94	$10,000	7.50%	5	O	C07
L026	15-Feb-94	$35,000	6.50%	5	O	C10
L028	20-Feb-94	$250,000	8.80%	30	M	C08
L030	21-Feb-94	$5,000	10.00%	3	O	C08
L031	28-Feb-94	$200,000	7.00%	15	M	C01
L032	01-Mar-94	$25,000	10.00%	3	C	C02
L033	01-Mar-94	$20,000	9.50%	5	O	C05
L039	03-Mar-94	$56,000	7.50%	5	C	C09
L040	10-Mar-94	$129,000	8.50%	15	M	C10
L047	11-Mar-94	$200,000	7.25%	15	M	C03
L049	21-Mar-94	$150,000	7.50%	15	M	C01
L052	22-Mar-94	$100,000	7.00%	30	M	C01
L053	31-Mar-94	$15,000	6.50%	3	O	C03
L054	01-Apr-94	$10,000	8.00%	5	C	C02
L057	15-Apr-94	$25,000	9.50%	4	C	C03
L060	18-Apr-94	$41,000	9.90%	4	C	C08
L062	22-Apr-94	$350,000	7.50%	15	M	C10
L100	01-May-94	$150,000	6.00%	15	M	C03
L109	03-May-94	$350,000	8.20%	30	M	C04
L120	08-May-94	$275,000	9.20%	15	M	C07

(c) Payments Table (partial list)

LoanID	Date	Payment
L001	2/15/94	$4,242.92
L001	3/15/94	$4,242.92
L001	4/15/94	$4,242.92
L001	5/15/94	$4,242.92
L001	6/15/94	$4,242.92
L004	2/23/94	$696.35
L004	3/23/94	$696.35
L004	4/23/94	$696.35
L004	5/23/94	$696.35
L004	6/23/94	$696.35
L010	2/25/94	$301.96
L010	3/25/94	$301.96
L010	4/25/94	$301.96
L010	5/25/94	$301.96
L010	6/25/94	$301.96
L014	2/28/94	$155.28
L014	3/31/94	$155.28
L014	4/30/94	$155.28
L014	5/30/94	$155.28
L014	6/30/94	$155.28
L020	3/8/94	$3,318.36
L020	4/8/94	$3,318.36
L020	5/8/94	$3,318.36
L020	6/8/94	$3,318.36
L022	3/12/94	$210.40
L022	4/12/94	$210.40
L022	5/12/94	$210.40
L022	6/12/94	$210.40
L026	3/15/94	$684.82
L026	4/15/94	$684.82
L026	5/15/94	$684.82
L026	6/15/94	$684.82
L028	3/20/94	$1,975.69
L028	4/20/94	$1,975.69
L028	5/20/94	$1,975.69
L028	6/20/94	$1,975.69
L030	3/21/94	$161.34
L030	4/21/94	$161.34
L030	5/21/94	$161.34
L030	6/21/94	$161.34
L031	3/28/94	$1,797.66
L031	4/28/94	$1,797.66
L031	5/28/94	$1,797.66
L031	6/28/94	$1,797.66

FIGURE 4.9 Expanding the Database

We began the chapter by showing you hypothetical records in the database and asking you to answer queries based on that data. We end the chapter the same way by asking you to reference one or more tables in Figure 4.9. As you consider each query, think of how it would appear in the QBE grid.

Query: How many payments have been received for loan L022? What was the date of the last payment?

Answer: Four payments have been received for loan L022. The last payment was received on 6/12/94.

The query can be answered with reference to just the Payments table by finding all payments for loan L022. To determine the last payment, you would retrieve the records in descending order by Date and retrieve the last record.

Query: How many payments have been received from Michelle Zacco since May 1, 1994?

Answer: Four payments have been received. Two of the payments were for loan L028 on May 20th and June 20th. Two were for loan L030 on May 21st and June 21st.

To answer this query, you would look in the Customers table to determine the CustomerID for Ms. Zacco, search the Loans table for all loans for this customer, then retrieve the corresponding payments from the Payments table. The exercises at the end of the chapter ask you to create queries such as these, then use those queries as the basis of a form or a report.

Figure 4.10 displays a query and associated report based on the expanded database. The Query window in Figure 4.10a shows the relationships in the expanded database. One join line indicates the one-to-many relationship between customers and loans. A second join line depicts the relationship between loans and payments. (Note how the LoanID and Date fields are both shown in bold in the Payments field list to indicate that the primary key consists of both fields.)

The QBE grid contains fields from all three tables to produce the dynaset used as the basis of the report in Figure 4.10b. The LastName and FirstName fields are taken from the Customers table, the LoanID from the Loans table, and the Date and Payment from the Payments table. The report lists payments by customer, by LoanID within customer, and by date within LoanId. The most recent payment (for each customer) is shown first because of the descending sort on the Date field.

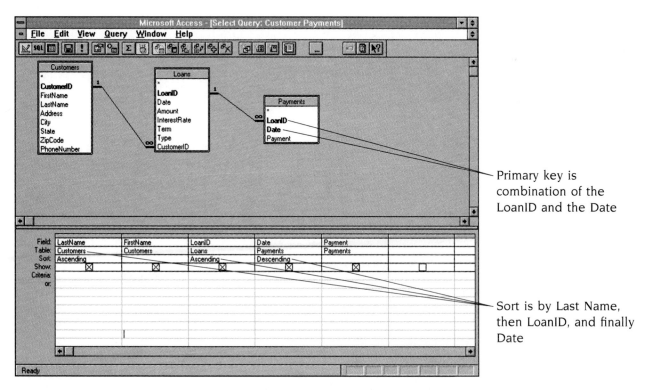

(a) Multiple Table Query

FIGURE 4.10 Queries and Reports

Customer Payments

09-Jul-94

Last Name	First Name	LoanID	Date	Payment
Faulkner	Eileen			
		L031	6/28/94	$1,797.66
		L031	5/28/94	$1,797.66
		L031	4/28/94	$1,797.66
		L031	3/28/94	$1,797.66
		L049	6/21/94	$1,390.52
		L049	5/21/94	$1,390.52
		L049	4/21/94	$1,390.52
		L052	6/22/94	$665.30
		L052	5/22/94	$665.30
		L052	4/22/94	$665.30
				$13,358.10
Grauer	Benjamin			
		L047	6/11/94	$1,825.73
		L047	5/11/94	$1,825.73
		L047	4/11/94	$1,825.73
		L053	6/30/94	$459.74
		L053	5/30/94	$459.74
		L053	4/30/94	$459.74
		L057	6/15/94	$616.21
		L057	5/15/94	$616.21
		L100	6/1/94	$1,265.79
				$9,354.62
Hirsch	Matt			
		L026	6/15/94	$684.82
		L026	5/15/94	$684.82

1

(b) Group/Totals Report

FIGURE 4.10 Queries and Reports (continued)

Linked Subforms

Subforms were introduced earlier in the chapter as a means of displaying data from related tables. Figure 4.11 continues the discussion by showing a main form with linked subforms. The main (Customers) form and the Loans subform are the forms you developed in the second hands-on exercise. The Payments subform is new and will be developed in the next exercise.

The records displayed in the three forms are linked to one another according to the relationships within the database. There is a one-to-many relationship between customers and loans so that the first subform displays all of the loans for one customer. The Loans subform is in the Form view rather than the Datasheet view, and so the loans are displayed one at a time. There is also a one-to-many relationship between loans and payments. The second (Payments) subform is linked to the Loans subform and displays all of the payments for one loan.

The Status bar for the main form indicates record 5 of 11, meaning that you are viewing the fifth of 11 Customer records. The Status bar for the Loans subform indicates record 2 of 2, corresponding to the second of two loans for the fifth customer. And finally, the Status bar for the Payments subform indicates record 1 of 5, corresponding to the first of five payment records for this customer.

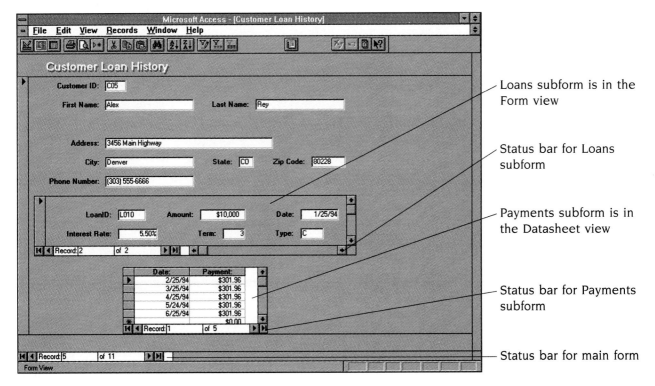

FIGURE 4.11   Linked Subforms

The three sets of navigation buttons enable you to advance to the next record(s) in any of the forms. The records move in conjunction with one another. Thus, if you advance to the next record in the Customers form, you will automatically display a different record in the Loans subform, as well as a different set of payment records in the Payments subform.

HANDS-ON EXERCISE 4:

Linked Subforms

Objective To create a main form with two levels of subforms; to display a subform in Form view or Datasheet view. Use Figure 4.12 as a guide.

Step 1: Add a relationship
➤ Open the NATLBANK database.
➤ Pull down the **Edit menu.** Click **Relationships** to open the Relationships window as shown in Figure 4.12a. Maximize the window.
➤ Pull down the **Relationships menu.** Click **Add table.** Click the **Payments table** from the Table/Query list. Click the **Add command button** to add the Payments table to the Relationships window. Click **the Close command button** to close the Add table dialog box.
➤ Drag the title bar of the Payments table to position the table as shown in Figure 4.12a.
➤ Drag the **LoanID field** from the Loans table to the **LoanID field** in the Payments table. You will see the Relationships dialog box.

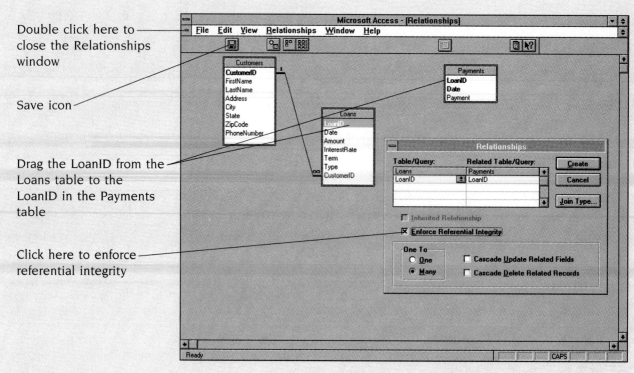

Double click here to close the Relationships window

Save icon

Drag the LoanID from the Loans table to the LoanID in the Payments table

Click here to enforce referential integrity

(a) Edit Relationships (step 1)

FIGURE 4.12 Hands-on Exercise 4

➤ Check the box to **Enforce Referential integrity.** Click the **Create command button** to create the relationship.

➤ Click the **Save icon** to save the Relationships window. Double click the **control-menu box** to close the Relationships window.

Step 2: Create the Payments form

➤ Click the **Form button.** Click **New** to produce the New Form dialog box. Scroll to select **Payments** as the table on which to base the form, then click the **Form Wizards button** to use the Form Wizard.

➤ Click **Single Column** as the type of form. Click **OK.**

➤ Double click the **Date** and **Payment fields** to add these fields to the form. Choose **Embossed,** then follow the remaining steps in the Form Wizard. Click the option button to **Modify the form's design** before clicking the **Finish command button.**

➤ Delete the title of the form in the Form Header, then drag the bottom of the Form Header toward the top to hide this section as shown in Figure 4.12b.

➤ Drag the right margin to increase the width of the form, then move the Payment control next to the control for the date. Drag the bottom border to make the Detail section smaller.

➤ Save the form as **Payments** as shown in Figure 4.12b. Double click the **control-menu box** to close the form and return to the Database window.

Step 3: Add the Second Subform

➤ Open the **Customer Loan History Form** (created in the second hands-on exercise) in Design view. Move and size the Form Design window so that you can see the Database window as shown in Figure 4.12c.

Double click here to close the form

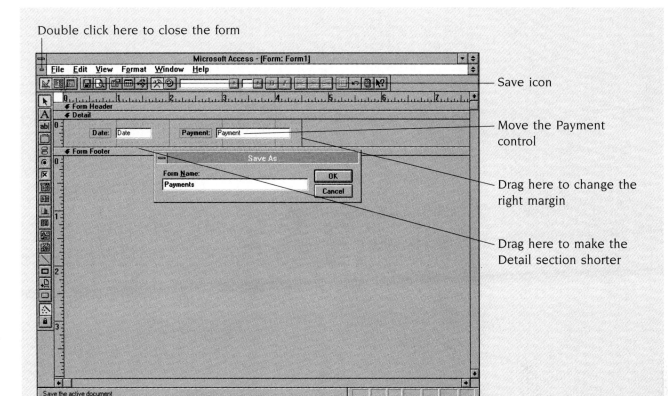

Save icon

Move the Payment control

Drag here to change the right margin

Drag here to make the Detail section shorter

(b) Create the Payments Form (step 2)

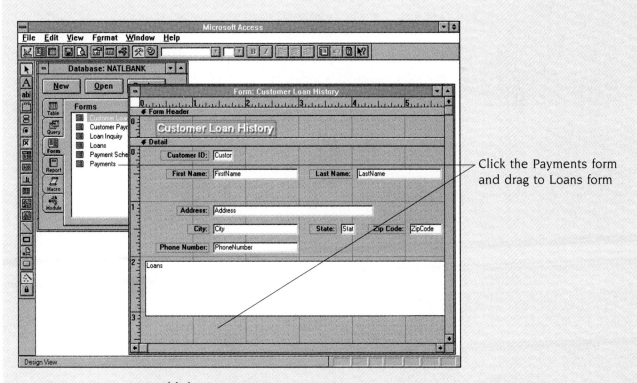

Click the Payments form and drag to Loans form

(c) Add the Payments Form (step 3)

FIGURE 4.12 Hands-on Exercise 4 (continued)

➤ Click and drag the icon next to the Payments Form in the Database window underneath the Loans form in the Customer Loan History Form.
➤ Click in the Form Design window. You should see a second white rectangular box corresponding to the Payments form.

Step 4: Create an Unbound control
➤ Maximize the Form Design window. Size the Payments subform to make it smaller. Delete the Payments label next to the subform.
➤ Click the **Text Box icon** and drag it on the form to create an Unbound control as shown in Figure 4.12d. You will see an Unbound control and an attached label containing a field number (e.g., Field32).
➤ Click in the text box of the control (Unbound will disappear). Type **=[Loans].Form![LoanID]**, where Loans and LoanID correspond to the name of the first subform and the name of the linking field, respectively.
➤ Point to the Unbound control and click the right mouse button to display a shortcut menu. Click **Properties.**
➤ Change the **Name property** to **LoanID** as shown in Figure 4.12d. Change the **Visible property** to **No.**
➤ Save the form. Double click the **control-menu box** to close the Properties dialog box.

Step 5: Establish the Link field
➤ Point to the Payments subform and click the right mouse button to display a shortcut menu. Click **Properties** to display the Subform properties box shown in Figure 4.12e.

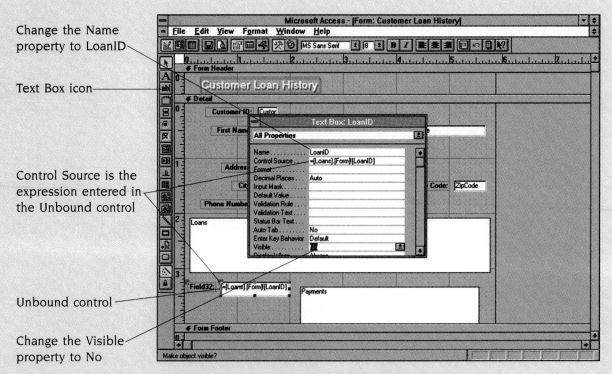

(d) Create an Unbound Control (step 4)

FIGURE 4.12 Hands-on Exercise 4 (continued)

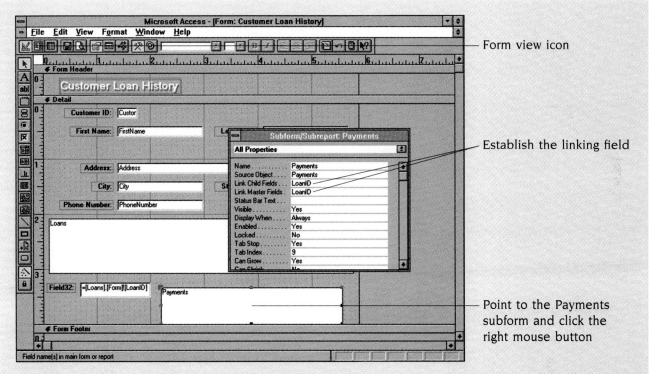

Form view icon

Establish the linking field

Point to the Payments subform and click the right mouse button

(e) Establish the Link Fields (step 5)

FIGURE 4.12 Hands-on Exercise 4 (continued)

➤ Click the **Link Child Fields property.** Type **LoanID.** Click the **Link Master Fields property. Type LoanID** to link the Loans and Payments subforms by the value of the LoanID field.
➤ Double click the **control-menu box** to close the Subform properties box.
➤ Save the form.

LINKING FORMS AND SUBFORMS

Linking fields do not have to appear in the main and subform but must be included in the underlying table or query. LoanID, for example, is used to link the Loans form and the Payments form; the field appears in the Loans form but does not appear in the Payments form.

Step 6: The Form view
➤ Click the **Form View icon** switch to the Form view. You should see a main form and two subforms as shown in Figure 4.12f. (You may want to return to the Design view to move and size the subforms.) Do not be concerned if the size of your form is different from ours. Click anywhere in the main form.
— The Status bar of the main form indicates record 1 of 11, meaning that you are positioned on the first of 11 records in the Customers table.
— The Status bar for the Loans subform indicates record 1 of 3, corresponding to the first of three records for this customer
— The Status bar for the Payments subform indicates record 1 of 4, corresponding to the first of four payments for this loan.

Loans subform

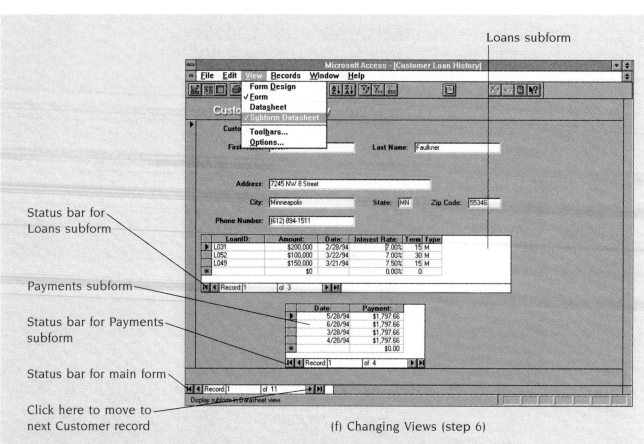

Status bar for Loans subform

Payments subform

Status bar for Payments subform

Status bar for main form

Click here to move to next Customer record

(f) Changing Views (step 6)

FIGURE 4.12 Hands-on Exercise 4 (continued)

> Click the ▶ symbol on the Status bar of the main (Customer) form to move to the second record. The records displayed in the other forms change automatically. Click the ◀ symbol to return to record 1.
> Click in the **Loans subform.** Pull down the **View menu.** Click **Subform Datasheet** to deselect it. The Loans form is now displayed in the Form view (although you cannot see all of the fields).

SEQUENCE THE RECORDS IN A FORM OR SUBFORM

A form (subform) should be based on a query rather than a table if the records are to be displayed in a specified sequence. If, for example, you wanted to display the records in the Payments subform by date, then the subform should be based on a query that specifies the desired sequence.

Step 7: Modify the Loans subform
> Click the **Design View icon** to switch to the Design view for the main form. The Loans and Payments subforms appear as white rectangular boxes within the main form.
> Click anywhere *outside* the Loans subform to deselect the form, then double click the Loans form to open it in Design view.

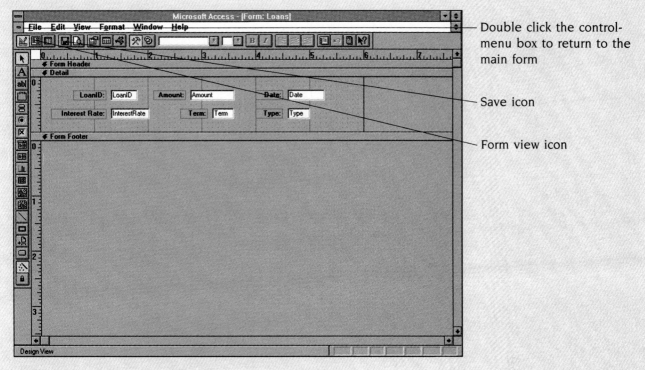

Double click the control-menu box to return to the main form

Save icon

Form view icon

(g) Modify the Loans Subform (step 7)

FIGURE 4.12 Hands-on Exercise 4 (continued)

➤ Move and size the controls in the Loans subform as shown in Figure 4.12g. Save the Loans subform.

➤ Double click the **control-menu box** to return to the Design view of the main form.

SET THE DEFAULT VIEW

Set the Default View property of the subform to open the form in the view you want. To set the property, open the subform in the Design view, point to the white box at the intersection of the rulers, and click the right mouse button to bring up the shortcut menu. Click Properties to set the Default View property to Datasheet or Single Form.

Step 8: The completed form

➤ Click the **Form view icon** to return to the Form view shown in Figure 4.12h.

➤ If necessary, click the **Loans subform,** pull down the **View menu,** and click Subform Datasheet (to remove the check), and display the Loans subform in Form view. You might want to return to the Design view to size the Loans and/or Payments subform. You might also want to return to the Loans subform to move and size its controls.

➤ Double click the **control-menu box** to close the form. Click **Yes** if asked to save any of the forms.

➤ Close the NATLBANK database and exit Access.

Double click the control-menu box to close the form

Loans subform in Form view

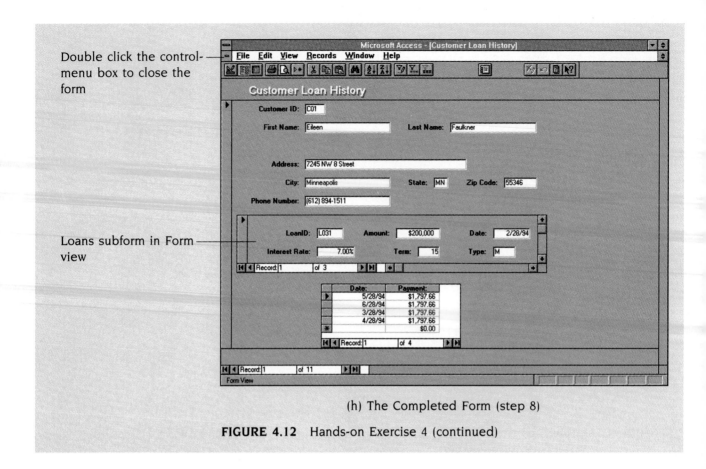

(h) The Completed Form (step 8)

FIGURE 4.12   Hands-on Exercise 4 (continued)

SUMMARY

An Access database contains multiple tables. Each table stores data about a specific subject. Each table has a primary key, which is a field (or combination of fields) that uniquely identifies each record.

A one-to-many relationship uses the primary key of the "one" table as a foreign key in the "many" table. (A foreign key is simply the primary key of another table.) The Relationships window enables you to graphically create a one-to-many relationship by dragging the join field from one table to the other.

Referential integrity ensures that the tables in a database are consistent with one another. When referential integrity is enforced, Access prevents you from adding records to a related table when there is no associated record in the primary table. It also prevents you from deleting a record in the primary table if there is a corresponding record in the related table.

A subform is a form within a form and is used to display data from a related table. It is created most easily with the Form Wizard, then modified in the Form Design view just as any other form. A main form can have any number of subforms. Subforms can extend to two levels, enabling a subform to be linked to another subform.

The power of a select query lies in its ability to include fields from several tables. The query shows the relationships that exist between the tables by drawing a join line that indicates how the tables are related. The Table row displays the name of the table containing the corresponding field. Once created, a multiple table query can be the basis for a form or report.

Tables can be added to a relational database without disturbing the data in existing tables. A database can have several one-to-many relationships.

Key Words and Concepts

Cascade Delete	Main form	Redundancy
Cascade Update	Main/Subform Wizard	Referential integrity
Data Type Mismatch	One-to-many	Related table
Datasheet view	relationship	Relationships window
Foreign key	Page Setup command	Subform
Form view	Primary key	Table row
Join line	Primary table	

Multiple Choice

1. Which of the following would cause a problem of referential integrity in a database in which there is a one-to-many relationship between customers and loans?
   (a) The deletion of a Customer record with a corresponding Loan record
   (b) The deletion of a Loan record with a corresponding Customer record
   (c) Both (a) and (b)
   (d) Neither (a) nor (b)

2. Which of the following is true about a database that monitors players and the teams to which those players are assigned?
   (a) The PlayerID will be defined as a primary key within the Teams table
   (b) The TeamID will be defined as a primary key within the Players table
   (c) The PlayerID will appear as a foreign key within the Teams table
   (d) The TeamID will appear as a foreign key within the Players table

3. Which of the following best expresses the relationships within the expanded NATLBANK database as it appeared at the end of the chapter?
   (a) There is a one-to-many relationship between customers and loans
   (b) There is a one-to-many relationship between loans and payments
   (c) Both (a) and (b)
   (d) Neither (a) nor (b)

4. A database has a one-to-many relationship between health plans and employees (one health plan can have many employees). Which of the following is true?
   (a) The Employee table is the main table; the Health Plan table is the related table
   (b) The Health Plan table is the main table; the Employee table is the related table
   (c) Both tables are related tables
   (d) Both tables are main tables

5. Every table in an Access database:
   (a) Must be related to every other table
   (b) Must have one or more foreign keys
   (c) Both (a) and (b)
   (d) Neither (a) nor (b)

6. Which of the following is true of the main and subform used in conjunction with the one-to-many relationship between customers and loans?
   (a) The main form was based on the Loans table
   (b) The subform was based on the Customers table
   (c) Both (a) and (b)
   (d) Neither (a) nor (b)

7. Which of the following is true regarding the navigation buttons (▶ and ◀) for a main form and its associated subform?
   (a) The navigation buttons pertain to just the main form
   (b) The navigation buttons pertain to just the subform
   (c) There are separate navigation buttons for each form
   (d) There are no navigation buttons at all

8. Which of the following is true about a main form and subform created through the Form Wizard?
   (a) The main form is displayed in the Form view; the subform is displayed in the Datasheet view
   (b) The main form is displayed in the Datasheet view; the subform is displayed in the Form view
   (c) Both forms are displayed in the Datasheet view
   (d) Both forms are displayed in the Form view

9. Which of the following is true?
   (a) A main form may contain multiple subforms
   (b) A subform may contain another subform
   (c) Both (a) and (b)
   (d) Neither (a) nor (b)

10. Which command displays the open tables in an Access database in equal-size windows with one window partially hiding the other?
    (a) The Tile command in the Window menu
    (b) The Cascade command in the Window menu
    (c) The Tile command in the Relationships menu
    (d) The Cascade command in the Relationships menu

11. Which of the following describes how to move and size a window?
    (a) Click and drag the title bar to size a window
    (b) Click and drag a border or corner to move the window
    (c) Both (a) and (b)
    (d) Neither (a) nor (b)

12. Which of the following can be created with a wizard?
    (a) A select query
    (b) A subform
    (c) Both (a) and (b)
    (d) Neither (a) nor (b)

13. Which of the following is true regarding entries in a Criteria row of a select query?
    (a) A text field may be entered with or without quotation marks
    (b) A date field may be entered with or without pound signs
    (c) Both (a) and (b)
    (d) Neither (a) nor (b)

14. Which of the following is true about a select query?
   (a) It may reference fields in one or more tables
   (b) It may have one or more criteria rows
   (c) It may sort on one or more fields
   (d) All of the above

15. A report may be based on:
   (a) A table
   (b) A query
   (c) Both (a) and (b)
   (d) Neither (a) nor (b)

ANSWERS

1. a	**6.** d	**11.** d
2. d	**7.** c	**12.** b
3. c	**8.** a	**13.** c
4. b	**9.** c	**14.** d
5. d	**10.** b	**15.** c

EXPLORING ACCESS

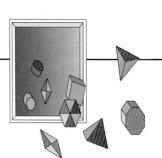

1. Use Figure 4.13 to match each action with its result. A given action may be used more than once or not at all.

Action	**Result**
a. Click at 1	___ Size the column
b. Click at 2	___ Add the Payment field to the QBE grid
c. Click at 3	___ Create an ascending sort by LoanID
d. Click and drag at 4	___ Save the query
e. Click and drag at 5	___ Display the table names in the QBE grid
f. Click at 6	___ Move the Loans field list
g. Double click at 7	___ Enter a CustomerID as criteria for the query
h. Click at 8	___ Size the Loans field list to display all field names
i. Click at 9 and enter the CustomerID	___ Run the query
j. Click and drag at 10	___ Display the Database window

2. The error messages in Figure 4.14 appeared or could have appeared in conjunction with the hands-on exercises in the chapter. Indicate a potential cause of each error and a suggested course of action to correct the problem.

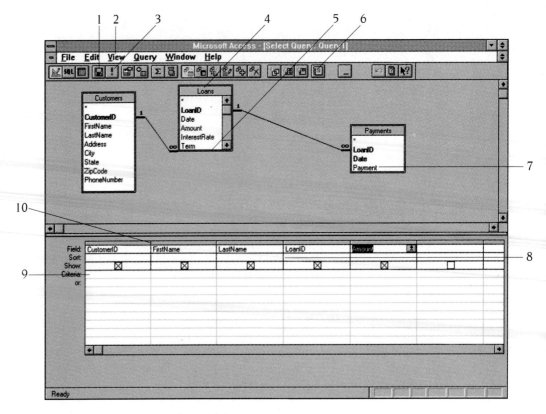

FIGURE 4.13 Screen for Problem 1

(a) Error Message 1

(b) Error Message 2

FIGURE 4.14 Error Messages for Problem 2

(c) Error Message 3

(d) Error Message 4

FIGURE 4.14 Error Messages for Problem 2 (continued)

3. Relationships and referential integrity: Answer the following with respect to the Relationships window in Figure 4.15.
   a. What are the relationships in Figure 4.15?
   b. What is the primary key of each table? How is this indicated?
   c. What foreign keys (if any) are in the Teams table? in the Players table? in the Coaches table?
   d. What is the main table in the Team-Player relationship? What is the related table?
   e. What is the main table in the Team-Coach relationship? What is the related table?
   f. Can you delete a Team record if there is a matching Player record? Can you delete a Player record if there is a matching Team record?
   g. Can you change the value of the TeamID field in the Teams table if there is a matching Coach record?

4. Relationships and referential integrity: Answer the following with respect to the Relationships window in Figure 4.16:
   a. What are the relationships in Figure 4.16?
   b. What is the primary key of each table? How is this indicated?
   c. What foreign keys (if any) are in the Offices table? in the Brokers table? in the Clients table?
   d. What is the main table in the Office-Broker relationship? What is the related table?
   e. What is the main table in the Broker-Client relationship? What is the related table?
   f. Can you delete a Broker record if there is a matching Client record? Can you delete a Client record if there is a matching Broker record?
   g. Can you change the value of the OfficeID field in the Offices table if there is a matching Broker record?

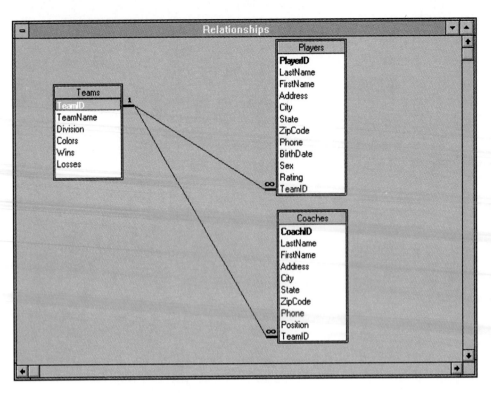

FIGURE 4.15   Screen for Problem 3

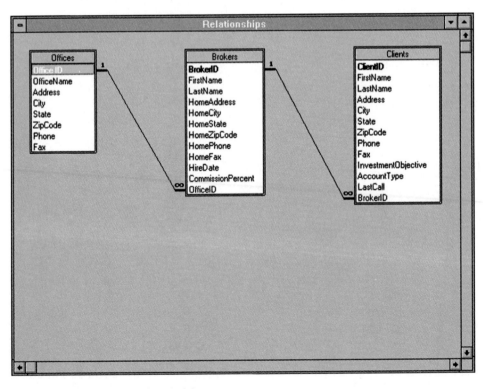

FIGURE 4.16   Screen for Problem 4

5. Answer the following with respect to the expanded NATLBANK database shown in Figure 4.9.

(a) Which payments were received by the bank during May 1994? What is the name of the customer who made each payment?

(b) What are the three largest loans currently held by the bank? (Use the Top Values property to display only the three required records in the query's dynaset.)

(c) What are the name and address of every customer who currently has a car loan (Loan type C)?

(d) The Payments table in the figure is in the NATLBANK database on the data disk. Create select queries for each of the queries in parts a through c, then print the dynaset for each query.

6. The Expression Builder: Figure 4.17 shows how the Expression Builder can be used to add the Pmt function to a query. (The Pmt function in Access is identical to the PMT function in Excel.)

a. Create the select query in Figure 4.17 by adding the indicated fields from the Loans table as shown in the figure.

b. Click the first available Field column, then click the Build icon on the Query Design toolbar to display the Expression Builder.

c. Double click Functions (if there is a plus sign in its icon), then click Built-In Functions. Click Financial in the second column, then double click Pmt to enter the Pmt function in the Expression Builder.

d. Click the Help command button to display information about each of the arguments in the Pmt function. Double click the control-menu box to exit from the Help window.

e. Replace each of the arguments in the Pmt function with the appropriate field names from the Loans table. One by one, select each argument and enter the replacement for that argument exactly as shown in Figure 4.17.

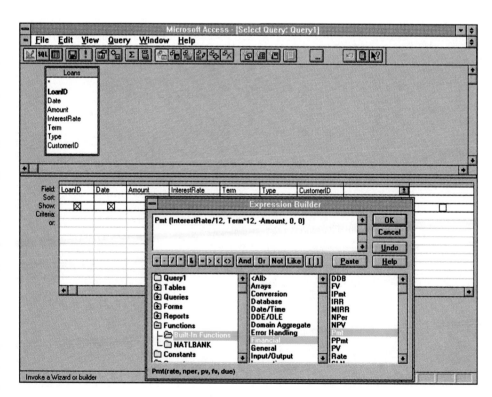

FIGURE 4.17 Screen for Problem 6

Click the OK command button to insert the Pmt function in the QBE grid. Save the query as Loan with Payment Information.

f. Click the icon to run the query and display the dynaset. You will see the calculated payment amount (to many decimal places) for each loan in the Loans table.

g. Return to the Query Design view. Change the name of the field containing the Pmt function from Expr1 to Payment Due. Change the Format property of this field to Currency. Save the query.

h. Run the query a second time to confirm that the changes in part g have taken effect.

7. Figure 4.18 is a modified version of the main and subform created in the second hands-on exercise. The subform contains the Payment Due and is based on the query created in problem 6.

a. Create a form based on the Loan with Payment Information query created in problem 6. Use the Form Wizard and choose Autoform as the type of form. Save the form as Loan with Payment Information.

b. Open Customer Loan History (the main form). Change to the Design View. Delete the Payments subform. Delete the unbound control that links the two subforms.

c. Point to the Loans subform and click the right mouse button to display a shortcut menu. Choose Properties.

d. Change the Name property to Loan with Payment Information (the name of the query created in part e of the previous problem. Change the Source Object property to Loan with Payment Information.

e. Double click the control-menu box to close the Properties dialog box.

f. Select the Form view to see the modified form, then return to the Design view if necessary to increase the width of the main form and/or subform.

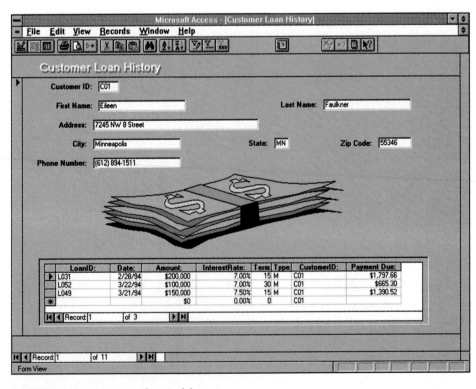

FIGURE 4.18 Screen for Problem 7

g. Use what you learned about forms in Chapter 2 to add boxes, lines, or clip art as shown in the figure.

h. Add your name as an unbound control, indicating your status as the Loan Officer, then print the form shown in Figure 4.18. Submit the printed form to your instructor.

 Case Studies

Recreational Sports League

Design a database for a recreational sports league that will monitor players, coaches, and sponsors. There may be any number of teams in the league with each team having any number of players. A player is associated with only one team.

Each team has one or more coaches. The league also imposes the rule that a person may not coach more than one team. Each team has a sponsor such as a local business. One sponsor can be associated with multiple teams.

Your solution should make the system as realistic as possible. The player table, for example, requires not only the identifying information for each player (name, address, phone, and so on) but additional fields such as birth date (to implement age limits on various teams), ability ratings, and so on. Your system should be capable of producing reports that will display all information about a specific team such as its players, coach, and sponsor. The league administrators would also like master lists of all teams, players, coaches, and sponsors.

Show the required tables in the database, being sure to indicate the primary key and foreign keys in each table. Indicate additional fields in each table (you need not list them all).

The Personnel Director

You have been hired as a personnel director for a medium-sized company with offices in several cities. You require the usual personal data for each employee (birth date, hire date, home address, and so on). You also need to reach an employee at work, and must be able to retrieve the office address, office phone number, and office fax number for each employee. Each employee is assigned to only one branch office.

Your duties also include the administration of various health plans offered by the company. Each employee is given his or her choice of several health plans. Each plan has a monthly premium and deductible amount. Once the deductible is reached, each plan pays a designated percentage of all subsequent expenses.

Design a database that will include the necessary data to provide all of the information you need. Show the required tables in the database, being sure to indicate the primary key and foreign keys in each table. Indicate additional fields in each table (you need not list them all).

The Franchise

The management of a national restaurant chain is automating its procedure for monitoring its restaurants, restaurant owners (franchisees), and the contracts that govern the two. Each restaurant has one owner (franchisee). There is no limit on the number of restaurants an individual may own, and franchisees are encouraged to apply for multiple restaurants.

The payment from the franchisee to the company varies according to the contract in effect for the particular restaurant. The company offers a choice of contracts, which vary according to the length of the contract, the franchise fee, and the percentage of the restaurant's sales paid to the company for marketing and royalty fees. Each restaurant has one contract, but a given contract type may pertain to many restaurants.

The company needs a database capable of retrieving all data for a given restaurant such as its annual sales, location, phone number, owner, and type of contract in effect. It would also like to know all restaurants owned by one person as well as all restaurants governed by a specific contract type.

Widgets of America

Widgets of America gives its sales staff exclusive rights to specific customers. Each sales person has many customers, but a specific customer always deals with the same sales representative. The company needs to know all of the orders placed by a specific customer as well as the total business generated by each sales representative. The data for each order includes the date the order was placed and the amount of the order. Design a database capable of producing the information required by the company.

Show the required tables in the database, being sure to indicate the primary key and foreign keys in each table. Indicate additional fields in each table (you need not list them all).

5

Many-to-many Relationships: A More Complex System

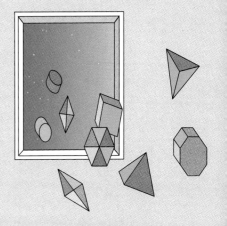

After reading this chapter you will be able to:

1. Define a many-to-many relationship and implement it in Access.
2. Use the Cascade Update and Cascade Delete options in the Relationships window to relax enforcement of referential integrity.
3. Create a main and subform based on a query; discuss the advantage of using queries rather than tables as the basis for a form or report.
4. Create a parameter query; explain how a parameter query can be made to accept multiple parameters.
5. Use aggregate functions in a select query.
6. Use the Import command to add external tables to an existing database.

OVERVIEW

This chapter introduces a new case study to give you additional practice in database design. The system extends the concept of a relational database that was introduced in Chapter 4 to include both a one-to-many and a many-to-many relationship. The case solution reviews earlier material on implementation in Access and the importance of referential integrity.

The chapter extends what you already know about subforms and queries and uses both to relate the tables to one another. The forms created in the chapter are based on multiple table queries rather than tables. The queries themselves are of a more advanced nature. We show you how to create a parameter query, in which you enter the criteria at the time you run the query. We also show you how to create queries that use the aggregate functions built into Access to perform calculations on groups of records.

The chapter contains four hands-on exercises to implement the case study. We think you will be pleased with what you have accomplished by the end of the chapter, working with a complex system that is typical of real-world applications.

CASE STUDY: THE COMPUTER SUPER STORE

The case study in this chapter is set within the context of a computer store that requires a database for its customers, products, and orders. The store maintains the usual customer data (name, address, phone, etc.). It also keeps data about the products it sells, storing for each product a product-id, description, quantity on hand, quantity on order, and cost. And finally, the store has to track its orders. It needs to know the date an order was received, the customer who placed it, the products that were ordered, and the quantity of each product.

Think, for a moment, about the tables that are necessary and the relationships between those tables, then compare your thoughts to our solution in Figure 5.1. You probably have no trouble recognizing the need for the Customers, Products, and Orders tables. Initially, you may be puzzled by the Order Details table, but you will soon appreciate why it is there and how powerful it is.

You can use the Customers, Products, and Orders tables individually to obtain information about a specific customer, product, or order, respectively. For example:

Query: What is Jeffrey Muddell's phone number?
Answer: Jeffrey Muddell's phone number is (305) 253-3909.

Query: What is the price of a Pentium 90 system? How many systems are in stock?
Answer: A Pentium 90 sells for $3895. Fifteen systems are in stock.

Query: When was Order O0003 placed?
Answer: Order O0003 was placed on March 15, 1994.

Other queries require you to relate the tables to one another. There is, for example, a *one-to-many relationship* between customers and orders. One customer can place many orders, but a specific order can be associated with only one customer. The tables are related through the CustomerID, which appears as the *primary key* in the Customers table and as a *foreign key* in the Orders table. Consider:

Query: What is the name of the customer who placed order number O0003?
Answer: Order O0003 was placed by Jeffrey Muddell.

Query: How many orders were placed by Jeffrey Muddell?
Answer: Jeffrey Muddell placed four orders: O0003, O0025, O0075, and O0110.

These queries are exactly like those in Chapter 4. To answer the first query, you would search the Orders table to find order O0003 and obtain the CustomerID (C0015 in this example). You would then search the Customers table for the customer with this Customer ID and retrieve the customer's name. To answer the second query, you would begin in the Customers table and search for Jeffrey Muddell to determine the CustomerID (C0015), then search the Orders table for all records with this CustomerID.

(a) Customers Table

Customer ID	First Name	Last Name	Address	City	State	Postal Code	Phone Number
C0002	Benjamin	Lee	1000 Call Street	Tallahassee	FL	33340	(904) 327-4124
C0003	Eleanor	Milgrom	7245 NW 8 Street	Margate	FL	33065	(305) 974-1234
C0004	Neil	Goodman	4215 South 81 Street	Margate	FL	33065	(305) 444-5555
C0009	Nicholas	Colon	9020 N.W. 75 Street	Coral Springs	FL	33065	(305) 753-9887
C0010	Michael	Ware	276 Brickell Avenue	Miami	FL	33131	(305) 444-3980
C0015	Jeffrey	Muddell	9522 S.W. 142 Street	Miami	FL	33176	(305) 253-3909
C0017	Ashley	Geoghegan	7500 Center Lane	Coral Springs	FL	33070	(305) 753-7830
C0019	Serena	Sherard	5000 Jefferson Lane	Gainesville	FL	32601	(904) 375-6442
C0020	Luis	Couto	455 Bargello Avenue	Coral Gables	FL	33146	(305) 666-4801
C0022	Derek	Anderson	6000 Tigertail Avenue	Coconut Grove	FL	33120	(305) 446-8900
C0031	Lauren	Center	12380 S.W. 137 Avenue	Miami	FL	33186	(305) 385-4432
C0033	Robert	Siane	4508 N.W. 7 Street	Miami	FL	33131	(305) 635-3454

(a) Customers Table

(b) Products Table

Product ID	Product Name	Units In Stock	Units On Order	Unit Price
P0001	Pentium/60 System	50	0	$2,899.00
P0002	486DX/33 System	25	5	$1,249.00
P0004	486DX2/66 System	125	15	$1,549.00
P0005	DX4/100 System	25	50	$2,795.00
P0007	Pentium/90 System	15	25	$3,895.00
P1002	17" SVGA Monitor	50	0	$1,199.00
P1050	14" SVGA Monitor	25	10	$299.00
P1075	15" MultiSync Monitor	50	20	$749.95
P2003	210 MB Hard Drive	15	20	$215.00
P2010	345 MB Hard Drive	25	15	$285.00
P2025	1 GB Hard Drive	10	0	$845.00
P2054	CD-ROM: 2X	40	0	$249.00
P2055	CD-ROM: 3X	50	15	$449.95
P5005	HD Floppy Disks	500	200	$9.99
P5010	HD Data Cartridges	100	50	$14.79
P5050	250 MB Tape Backup	15	3	$179.95
P5100	Serial Mouse	150	50	$69.95
P5105	Trackball	55	0	$59.95
P5110	Joystick	250	100	$39.95
P5301	Fax/Modem 14,400	35	10	$189.95
P5305	Fax/Modem 9,600	20	0	$65.95
P6005	Laser Printer	100	15	$1,395.00
P6006	24Pin Dot Matrix	50	50	$249.95
P6010	Color Printer	125	25	$569.95
P7001	Windows 3.1	400	200	$95.95
P7002	MS-DOS 6.2 Upgrade	150	50	$45.95
P7007	Norton Utilities 7.0	150	50	$115.95
P7015	Microsoft Scenes Screen Saver	75	25	$29.95
P7115	Microsoft Bookshelf	250	100	$129.95
P7120	Microsoft Cinemania	25	10	$59.95
P7122	Professional Photos on CD-ROM	15	0	$45.95

(b) Products Table

(c) Orders Table

Order ID	Customer ID	Order Date
O0001	C0002	03/31/94
O0002	C0019	03/10/94
O0003	C0015	03/15/94
O0010	C0033	04/03/94
O0018	C0003	04/08/94
O0021	C0009	04/15/94
O0025	C0015	04/15/94
O0029	C0017	04/16/94
O0030	C0031	04/18/94
O0033	C0004	04/18/94
O0049	C0022	04/25/94
O0050	C0020	05/01/94
O0051	C0017	05/06/94
O0055	C0002	05/10/94
O0058	C0003	05/10/94
O0070	C0002	05/11/94
O0075	C0015	05/12/94
O0090	C0031	05/20/94
O0100	C0019	05/25/94
O0110	C0015	06/10/94
O0177	C0017	06/13/94
O0200	C0009	06/15/94
O0275	C0003	06/21/94
O0300	C0033	06/30/94
O0305	C0022	07/01/94

(c) Orders Table

(d) Order Details Table

Order ID	Product ID	Quantity
O0001	P2055	1
O0001	P5005	4
O0001	P7007	1
O0002	P0001	1
O0002	P1002	1
O0002	P5301	1
O0002	P6005	1
O0003	P0007	1
O0003	P5301	1
O0003	P6005	1
O0010	P0004	1
O0010	P2010	1
O0010	P6005	2
O0018	P0004	2
O0018	P2054	2
O0018	P5050	2
O0021	P5005	10
O0021	P5010	2
O0025	P7015	1
O0025	P7120	3
O0029	P0001	1
O0029	P0005	3
O0029	P1075	4
O0029	P2025	2
O0029	P2054	1
O0030	P1002	1
O0033	P0002	2
O0033	P6005	1
O0033	P6006	1
O0049	P5050	2
O0049	P5301	2
O0050	P7115	10
O0050	P7120	10
O0050	P7122	10
O0051	P5050	4
O0051	P5100	10
O0051	P6010	2
O0055	P5110	2
O0055	P7015	1
O0058	P5105	1
O0058	P5301	1
O0070	P7115	2
O0075	P5110	2
O0090	P5100	1
O0090	P7001	2
O0090	P7002	2
O0100	P5005	25
O0110	P6010	1
O0177	P0005	1
O0200	P7007	1
O0275	P7015	1
O0275	P7115	1
O0275	P7122	1
O0300	P2055	1
O0300	P5005	5
O0300	P5010	3
O0300	P5050	1
O0305	P2054	2
O0305	P7115	2

(d) Order Details Table

FIGURE 5.1 Super Store Database

The system is more complicated than the examples in Chapter 4 in that there is a *many-to-many relationship* between orders and products. One order can include many products, and at the same time, a specific product can appear in many orders. The implementation of a many-to-many relationship requires an additional table, the Order Details table, containing (at a minimum) the primary keys of the individual tables.

The Order Details table will contain many records with the same OrderID, because there is a separate record for each product in a given order. It will also contain many records with the same ProductID, because there is a separate record for every order pertaining to that product. However, the *combination* of OrderID and ProductID is unique and this **combined key** becomes the primary key in the Order Details table. The Order Details table also contains an additional field (Quantity) whose value depends on the primary key (the combination of OrderID and ProductID). Thus:

Query: How many units of product P5005 were included in order O0001?
Answer: Order O0001 included four units of product P5005. (The order also included one unit of Product P2055 and one unit of P7007.)

The Order Details table has four records with a ProductID of P5005. It also has three records with an OrderID of O0001. There is, however, only one record with a ProductID P5005 *and* an OrderID O0001 because the combination of ProductID and OrderID is unique. Four units of product P5005 are in this order.

The Order Details table makes it possible to determine all products in one order or all orders for one product. Consider:

Query: Which products are included in Order O0003?
Answer: Order O0003 consists of products P0007, P5301, and P6005.

Query: Which orders include P0001?
Answer: Product P0001 appears in order O0002 and O0029.

To answer the first query, you would search the Order Details table for an OrderID of O0003, finding three records with ProductIDs P0007, P5301, and P6005, respectively. The second query is processed in similar fashion except that you would search the Order Details table for the records containing a ProductID of P0001.

We've emphasized that the power of a relational database comes from the inclusion of multiple tables and the relationships between those tables. As you already know, you can use data from several tables to compute the answer to more complex queries. For example:

Query: What is the total cost of order O0003?
Answer: Order O0003 costs $5479.95

To determine the cost of an order, you must first identify all of the products associated with that order, the quantity of each product, and the price of each product. The previous queries have shown how you would find the products in an order and the associated quantities. The price of a specific product is obtained from the Products table, which enables you to compute the invoice by multiplying the price of each product by the quantity. Thus, the total cost of order O0003 is $5479.95. (One unit of product P0007 at $3895, one unit of P5301 at $189.95, and one unit of product P6005 at $1395.)

THE ORDER DETAILS TABLE

Each entity in a database requires its own table. To determine whether the "obvious" tables are sufficient to implement the database, look at the individual fields to see where each field originates. The quantity of a particular product in a particular order is not determined by (just) the ProductID, and thus does not belong in the Products table. Nor is it dependent on (just) the OrderID and so should not be placed in the Orders table. It is determined by the *combination* of the OrderID and the ProductID; hence the need for the Order Details table whose primary key is the combination of primary keys of the individual tables.

Implementation in Access

The Relationships window in Figure 5.2 shows the Computer Store database as it will be implemented in Access. The database contains the Customers, Orders, Products, and Order Details tables as per the previous discussion. The field lists display the fields within each table with the primary key shown in bold. The OrderID and ProductID are both shown in bold in the Order Details table, to indicate that the primary key consists of the combination of these fields.

The many-to-many relationship between Orders and Products is implemented by a *pair* of one-to-many relationships. There is a one-to-many relationship between the Orders table and the Order Details table. There is a second one-to-many relationship between the Products table and the Order Details table. In other words, the Orders and Products tables are not related to each other directly, but indirectly through the pair of one-to-many relationships with the Order Details table.

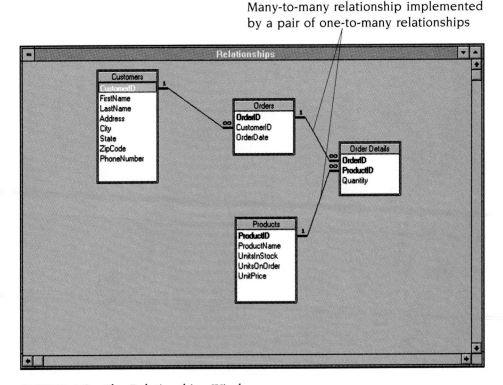

FIGURE 5.2 The Relationships Window

The join lines show the relationships between the tables. The number 1 appears next to the Orders table on the join line connecting the Orders table and the Order Details table. The infinity symbol appears at the end of the line next to the Order Details table. The one-to-many relationship between these tables means that each record in the Orders table can be associated with many records in the Order Details table. Each record in the Order Details table, however, is associated with only one record in the Orders table.

In similar fashion, there is a second one-to-many relationship between the Products table and the Order Details table. The number 1 appears on the join line next to the Products table. The infinity symbol appears at the end of the join line next to the Order Details table. Each record in the Products table can be associated with many records in the Order Details table, but each record in the Order Details table is associated with only one product.

PEDAGOGY VERSUS REALITY

Our database requires the CustomerID, OrderID, and ProductID to begin with the letters C, O, and P, respectively, to emphasize the tables in which these fields are found and to facilitate data entry in the hands-on exercises. A working system, on the other hand, might use a counter field for any (or all) of these fields to permit any number of records in the table. Alternatively, it might use an inherently unique number such as a social security number. It could also use an identification number based on an algorithm to create a unique number such as a magazine subscription number.

Referential Integrity

The concept of *referential integrity* was introduced in Chapter 4 to ensure that the records in related tables are consistent with one another. Enforcement of referential integrity prevents you from adding a record to the related table when there is no associated record in the primary table. It means, for example, that you cannot add a record to the Orders table unless there is a corresponding Customer record. Or stated another way, you must add a Customer record before assigning an order to that customer. Enforcement of referential integrity will also prevent you from deleting a record in the primary (Customers) table when there are corresponding records in the related (Orders) table.

Consider, for example, the application of referential integrity to the one-to-many relationship between the Orders table and the Order Details table. Referential integrity prevents the addition of a record to the related (Order Details) table unless there is a corresponding record in the Orders table. It also prevents the deletion of an order when there are corresponding records in the Order Details table.

There may be times, however, when you want to delete an order and simultaneously delete the corresponding records in the Order Details table. This is accomplished by enabling the *cascaded deletion* of related records, so that when you delete a record in the primary (Orders) table, Access will automatically delete the associated records in the related (Order Details) table. You will still be prevented, however, from adding a record to the Order Details table unless there is a corresponding order.

You might also want to enable the *cascaded updating* of related records under certain conditions—for example, to correct the value of an OrderID after the record has been entered into the Orders table. Enforcement of referential integrity would ordinarily prevent you from changing the value of the *join field* in the primary (Orders) table when there are corresponding records in the related (Order Details) table. You could, however, request the cascaded updating of related records so that if you were to change the OrderID in the Orders table, the corresponding records in the Order Details table would be changed as well.

HANDS-ON EXERCISE 1:

Relationships and Referential Integrity

Objective To create relationships between existing tables in order to demonstrate referential integrity; to edit an existing relationship to allow the cascaded deletion of related records. Use Figure 5.3 as a guide in the exercise.

Step 1: Add the tables

➤ Load Access. If you are using a floppy disk (instead of the hard drive), you must copy **SUPRSTOR.MDB** and **SUPRSTOR.LDB** from the data disk to a working disk. You must also copy the **SALESSTF.MDB** and **SALESSTF.LDB** files for use in a later hands-on exercise.

➤ Click the **Open Database icon** on the toolbar. Open the **SUPRSTOR.MDB** database in the ACCSDATA directory.

➤ Pull down the **Edit menu** and click **Relationships** to open the Relationships window, which is presently empty. Click the **Maximize button** to maximize the window as shown in Figure 5.3a.

➤ Pull down the **Relationships menu** and click **Add Table** (or click the Add Table icon).

➤ The **Customers table** is already selected. Click the **Add command button** (or double click the table name) to add the Customers table to the Relationships window.

➤ Add the **Order Details, Orders,** and **Products** tables in similar fashion. Click the **Close command button** to close the Add Table dialog box.

Step 2: Move and size the field lists

➤ Point to the bottom border of the Customers field list (the mouse pointer changes to a double arrow), then click and drag the border until all of the fields are visible. (The vertical scroll bar will disappear.)

➤ If necessary, click and drag the bottom border of the other tables until all of their fields are visible.

➤ Click and drag the title bars to move the field lists so that they are positioned as in Figure 5.3a.

Step 3: Create the relationships

➤ Click and drag the **CustomerID field** in the Customers field list to the **CustomerID field** in the Orders field list. You will see the Relationships dialog box in Figure 5.3a when you release the mouse.

➤ Click the **Enforce Referential Integrity** check box. The **One-to-many option button** is selected automatically.

➤ Click the **Create command button** to establish the relationship and close the Relationships dialog box. You should see a line indicating a one-to-many relationship between the Customers and Orders tables.

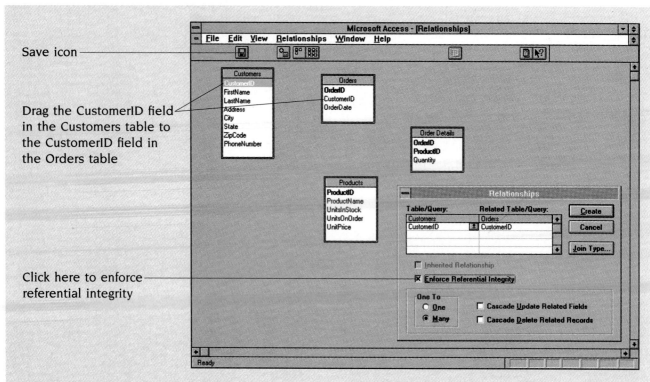

Save icon

Drag the CustomerID field in the Customers table to the CustomerID field in the Orders table

Click here to enforce referential integrity

(a) Create the Relationships (steps 1, 2, and 3)

FIGURE 5.3 Hands-on Exercise 1

> Click and drag the **OrderID field** in the Orders field list to the **OrderID field** in the Order Details field list. Click the **Enforce Referential Integrity** check box (the **One-to-many option button** is selected), then click the **Create command button.**

> Click and drag **ProductID** in the Products field list to the **ProductID field** in the Order Details field list. Click the **Enforce Referential Integrity** check box (the **One-to-many option button** is selected), then click the **Create command button.**

> Click the **Save icon** to save the relationships.

> Click the **Restore button** on the Relationships window, then click its **Minimize button** to minimize the window. You should see the minimized Relationships icon at the bottom of the desktop as shown in Figure 5.3b.

JOIN FIELDS

The join fields on both sides of a relationship must be the same data type—for example, both number fields or both text fields. (Number fields must also have the same field size setting.) You cannot, however, have two counter fields. Thus if a join field is a counter field in one table, the join field in the other table must have the Number data type with the Field Size property set to Long integer.

Step 4: Open the Orders and Order Details tables

➤ You should be in the Database window. Click the **Table button.** Open the **Orders table.**
➤ Return to the Database window:
   — Click in the **Database window** (if it is visible)
   — *or* pull down the **Window menu** and click **Database:SUPRSTOR.**
➤ Open the **Order Details table.** Your desktop should resemble Figure 5.3b although the precise arrangement of the open windows will be different.
➤ Click the **Minimize button** in the Database window to reduce the window to an icon and reduce the clutter on the desktop.

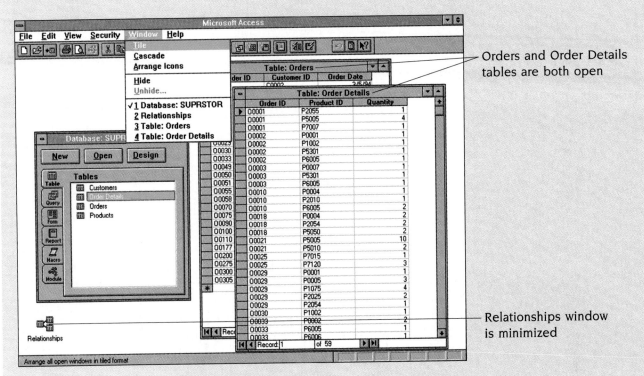

(b) Arranging the Desktop (step 4)

FIGURE 5.3 Hands-on Exercise 1 (continued)

Step 5: Delete an Order Details record

➤ Pull down the **Window menu.** Click **Tile** to display the Orders table and the Order Details table side by side as in Figure 5.3c. (It doesn't matter whether the Orders table appears on the left or right.)
➤ Click the **Order Details window.** Click the **row selector column** for the last Order Details record for order O0002. You should have selected the record for product P6005 in order O0002.
➤ Press the **Del key.** You will see a message indicating that you have just deleted one record. Click **OK** to delete the record. The Delete command works because you are deleting a "many" record in a one-to-many relationship.

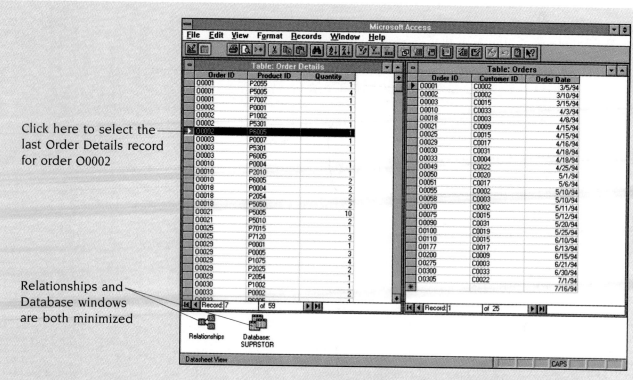

Click here to select the last Order Details record for order O0002

Relationships and Database windows are both minimized

(c) Delete an Order Detail Record (step 5)

FIGURE 5.3 Hands-on Exercise 1 (continued)

Step 6: Referential Integrity

➤ Click the **Orders window.** Click the **row selector column** for **Order O0002** as shown in Figure 5.3d. Press the **Del key** to (attempt to) delete the record.

➤ You will see the message in Figure 5.3d, indicating that you cannot delete the record. The Delete command does not work because you are attempting to delete the "one" record in a one-to-many relationship. Click **OK.**

Step 7: Edit a relationship

➤ You must close the tables in the relationship you wish to change.
 — Double click the **control-menu box** in the Orders table to close the table.
 — Double click the **control-menu box** in the Order Details table to close this table also.

➤ Double click the **minimized Relationships icon** to open the Relationships window.

➤ Click the line connecting the Orders and Order Details tables as shown in Figure 5.3e. The line turns bold, indicating the relationship has been selected.

➤ Pull down the **Relationships menu.** Click **Edit Relationship.** Check the box to **Cascade Delete Related Records.** Click **OK.**

➤ Click the **Save icon** to save the edited relationship. Minimize the Relationships window.

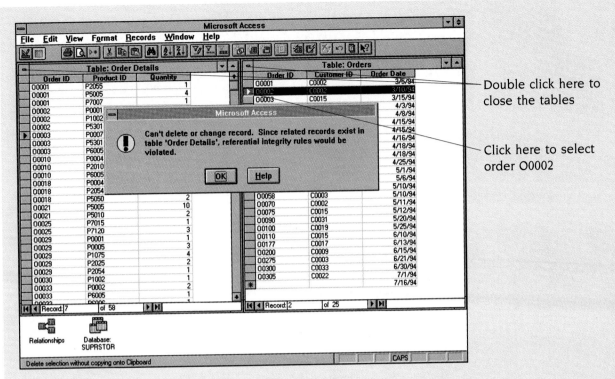

Double click here to close the tables

Click here to select order O0002

(d) Referential Integrity (step 6)

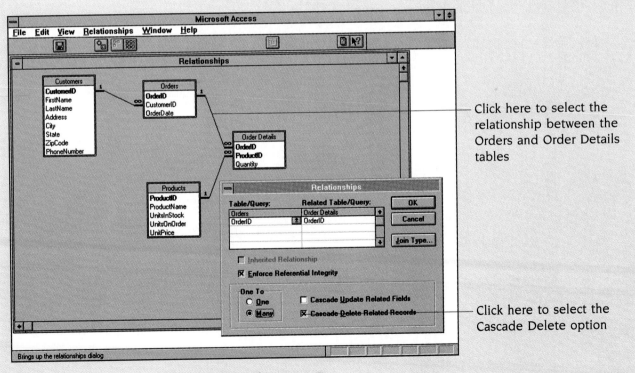

Click here to select the relationship between the Orders and Order Details tables

Click here to select the Cascade Delete option

(e) Edit a Relationship (step 7)

FIGURE 5.3 Hands-on Exercise 1 (continued)

Step 8: Delete the related records

➤ Double click the **minimized Database window icon** to return to the Database window. Open the **Orders table** and the **Order Details table**. Minimize the Database window, then tile the open windows.

➤ Click the **Orders window** and select the record for **Order O0002.** Press the **Del key** to delete the record.

➤ You will see a message indicating that you have just deleted one record in this table and additional records in related tables. Click **OK.** Order O0002 is gone from the Orders table.

➤ The related records in the Order Details table have also been deleted but are displayed with the #Deleted indicator as shown in Figure 5.3f. (The records will be gone the next time the Order Details table is opened.)

➤ The Delete command works this time (unlike the attempt in step 6) because the relationship was changed to permit the deletion of related records.

Step 9: The Print Definition command

➤ Double click the **minimized Relationships icon.**

Record O0002 has been deleted

Related records are marked with #Deleted indicator

Relationships and Database windows are both minimized

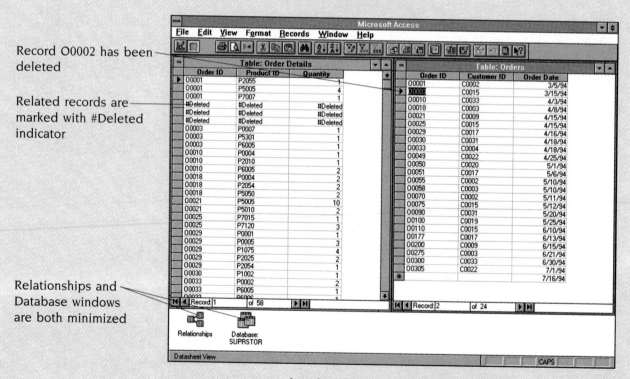

(f) Deleted Related Records (step 8)

FIGURE 5.3   Hands-on Exercise 1 (continued)

➤ Pull down the **File menu**. Click **Print Definition.** The status bar indicates that Access will print information about the selected object, then displays a message indicating that Access is examining relationships.

➤ You should see the Object Definition window in Figure 5.3g. Maximize the window. Scroll through the report to note the relationship between the Orders and Order Details tables (one to many, enforced, cascade deletes).

➤ Click the **Print icon.** Click **OK.** Click the **Close Window icon.**

➤ Exit Access. Click **Yes** if prompted to save the tables or relationships.

THE PRINT DEFINITION COMMAND

The Print Definition command can be used to print information about the design of a table, query, form, or report. Select the object in the Database window or open the object in the Design view. Pull down the File menu, click the Print Definition command, then select the desired options.

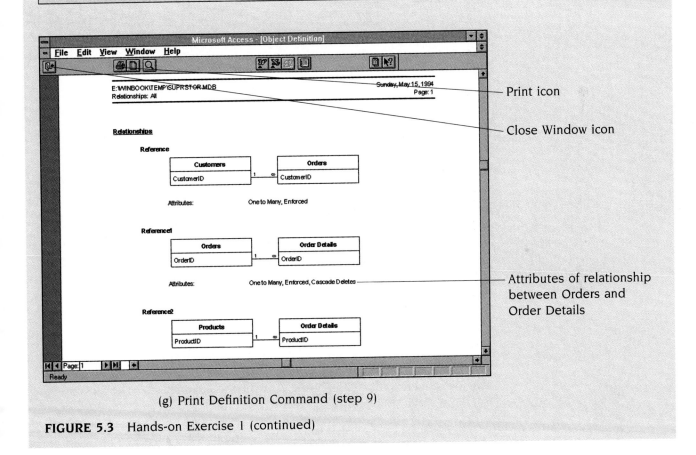

(g) Print Definition Command (step 9)

FIGURE 5.3 Hands-on Exercise 1 (continued)

SUBFORMS, QUERIES, AND AUTOLOOKUP

The main and subform combination in Figure 5.4 is used by the store to enter a new order for an existing customer. The forms are based on queries (rather than tables) for several reasons. A query enables you to display data from multiple tables, to display a calculated field, and to take advantage of Autolookup, a feature that is explained shortly.

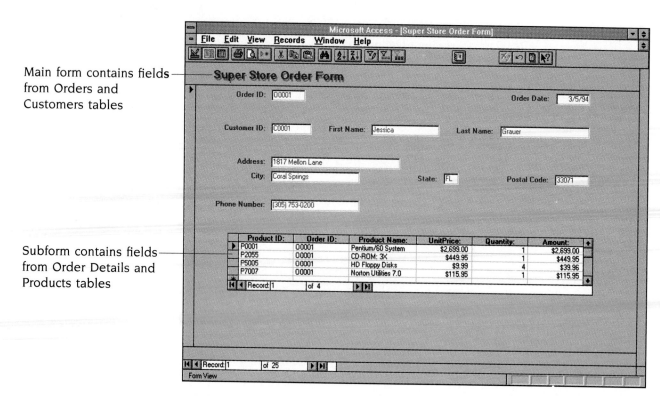

Main form contains fields from Orders and Customers tables

Subform contains fields from Order Details and Products tables

FIGURE 5.4 The Super Store Order Form

The ***main form*** contains fields from both the Orders table and the Customers table. The OrderID, OrderDate, and CustomerID (the join field) are taken from the Orders table. The other fields are taken from the Customers table. The query is designed so that you do not have to enter customer information when an existing customer places an order. Just enter the CustomerID, and Access will automatically look up (***Autolookup***) the corresponding customer data.

The ***subform*** is based on a second query containing fields from the Order Details table and the Products table. The OrderID, Quantity, and ProductID (the join field) are taken from the Order Details table. The ProductName and Unit-Price fields are from the Products table. Autolookup works here as well so that when you enter the ProductID, Access automatically displays the Product Name and Unit Price. You then enter the quantity, and the amount (a calculated field) is determined automatically.

The queries for the main form and subform are shown in Figures 5.5a and 5.5b, respectively. The upper half of the Query window displays the field list for each table and the relationship between the tables. The lower half of the Query window contains the QBE grid. Any query intended to take advantage of Autolookup must adhere to the following:

1. The tables in the query must have a one-to-many relationship such as Customers to Orders in Figure 5.5a or Products to Order Details in Figure 5.5b.
2. The join field on the "one" side of the relationship must have a unique value in the primary table. The CustomerID in Figure 5.5a and the ProductID in Figure 5.5b are primary keys in their respective tables and therefore unique.
3. The join field in the query must be taken from the "many" side of the relationship. Thus CustomerID is from the Orders table in Figure 5.5a rather than the Customers table. In similar fashion, ProductID is taken from the Order Details table in Figure 5.4b, not the Products table.

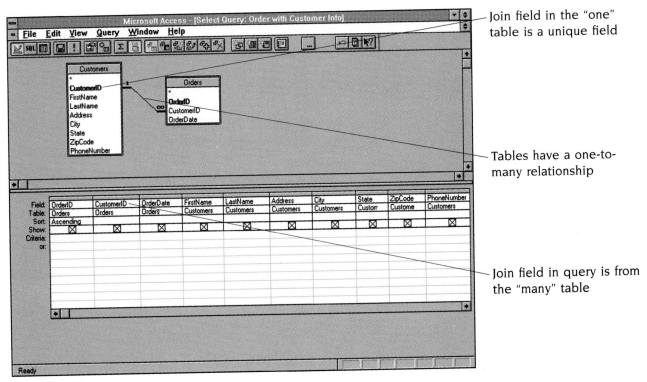

Join field in the "one" table is a unique field

Tables have a one-to-many relationship

Join field in query is from the "many" table

(a) Order with Customer Info Query (used for the main form)

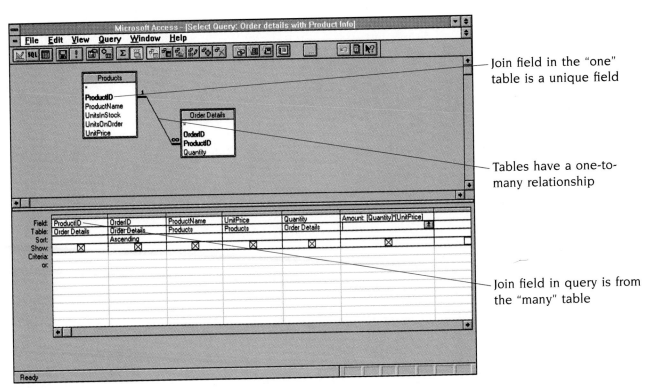

Join field in the "one" table is a unique field

Tables have a one-to-many relationship

Join field in query is from the "many" table

(b) Order Details with Product Info Query (used for the subform)

FIGURE 5.5 Multiple Table Queries

The next exercise has you create the main and subform in Figure 5.4. We supply the query in Figure 5.5a, but ask you to create the query in Figure 5.5b. The form will enable you to add a new order for an existing customer, but you cannot use it to add a new customer. Thus the exercise begins by having you enter the data for a new customer through a separate customer form. The form contains command buttons and clip art and is similar to those you developed in Chapter 2.

HANDS-ON EXERCISE 2:

Subforms and Multiple Table Queries

Objective To use multiple table queries as the basis for a main form and its associated subform; to create the link between a main form and subform manually. Use Figure 5.6 as a guide in the exercise.

Step 1: Add a new customer
➤ Open the **SUPRSTOR.MDB** database from the previous exercise.
➤ Click the **Form button** in the Database window. Double click the **Customers form** to open the form.
➤ Maximize the window. Click the **Add New Customer button** to move to an empty form and add a new customer. Click the **CustomerID** text box, then enter **C0001** as shown in Figure 5.6a. Complete the form, using your name, address, and phone.
➤ Click the **Close Customer Form button** when you have completed the form.

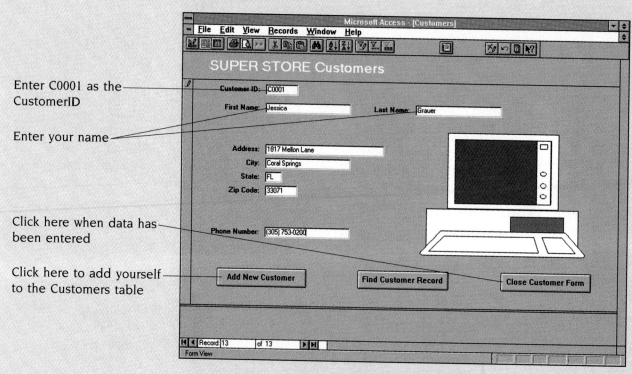

Enter C0001 as the CustomerID

Enter your name

Click here when data has been entered

Click here to add yourself to the Customers table

(a) Enter a Customer Record (step 1)

FIGURE 5.6 Hands-on Exercise 2

YOU'RE NUMBER ONE

It's hard to keep track of customer numbers, order numbers, and so on. To make things easier to remember, we have made you Customer Number One (C0001) and will (in the next step) place Order Number One (O0001) in your name. Later in the exercise we will add Product P0001 to your order. This way, whenever you go into the Super Store database, you will remember your CustomerID (C0001) and can expect to find a familiar address and phone number.

Step 2: Autolookup
➤ Click the **Query button** in the Database window and open the query, **Order with Customer Info.** You should see the dynaset in Figure 5.6b, which presently contains 24 orders.

➤ Press the **Tab (enter** or **right arrow) key** to move to the CustomerID field for Order O0001. Type **C0001** (your CustomerID) to associate yourself with this order.

➤ Press **enter.** Your name, address, and phone number have been placed into the dynaset since you are now the customer who has placed Order O0001.

➤ Double click the **control-menu box** to close the query and return to the Database window.

Enter C0001 as the CustomerID

Your data is automatically reflected as a result of Autolookup

(b) Autolookup (step 2)

FIGURE 5.6 Hands-on Exercise 2 (continued)

Step 3: Create the subform query

➤ If necessary, click the **Query button** in the Database window. Click the **New button** to produce the New Query dialog box. Click the **New Query button** since you are creating a select query and cannot use the Query Wizard.

➤ You will see the QBE grid in Figure 5.6c and the open list box containing the tables within the database. Double click the **Products table** to add this table to the query.

➤ Double click the **Order Details table** to add this table to the query. A join line showing the one-to-many relationship between the Products and Order Details tables appears automatically.

➤ Click the **Close command button** to close the Add Table dialog box. If necessary, click the **maximize button** to begin working in the query.

CUSTOMIZE THE QUERY WINDOW

The Query window displays the field list and QBE grid in its upper and lower halves, respectively. To increase (decrease) the size of either portion of the window, drag the line dividing the upper and lower sections. Drag the title bar to move a field list. You can also size a field list by dragging a border just as you can size any other window.

Click and drag here to increase/decrease the size of the upper and lower portions of the window

Double click here to add the Order Details table to the query

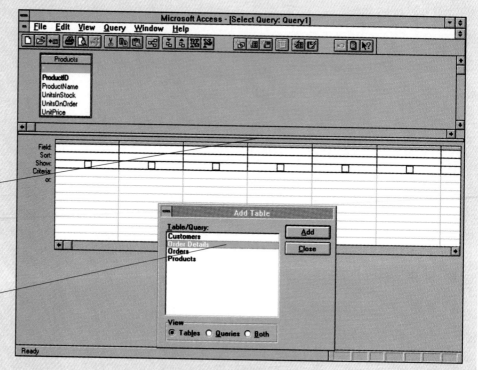

(c) Add the Tables (step 3)

FIGURE 5.6 Hands-on Exercise 2 (continued)

Step 4: Create the subform query (continued)

➤ Pull down the **View menu.** Click **Table names** to include the Table row in the QBE grid. Add the fields to the query as follows:
  — Double click the **ProductID** and **OrderID** fields in that order from the Order Details table.
  — Double click the **ProductName** and **UnitPrice** fields in that order from the Products table.
  — Double click the **Quantity** field from the Order Details table.

➤ Click the **Sort row** under the **OrderID** field. Specify an **ascending** sequence.

➤ Click the first available cell in the Field row. Type **=[Quantity]*[UnitPrice].** Do not be concerned if you cannot see the entire expression, but be sure you put square brackets around each field name.

➤ Press **enter.** Access has substituted Expr1: for the equal sign you typed. Drag the column selector boundary so that the entire expression is visible as in Figure 5.6d. (You will have to make the other columns narrower in order to see all of the fields in the QBE grid.)

➤ Click and drag to select **Expr1.** (Do not select the colon). Type **Amount** to substitute a more meaningful field name.

➤ Point to the expression and click the **right mouse button** to display a short-cut menu. Click **Properties** to display the Field Properties dialog box in Figure 5.6d.

➤ Click the box for the **Format property.** Click the **drop down arrow,** then scroll until you can choose **Currency.** Double click the **control-menu box** to close the Field Properties dialog box.

➤ Save the query as **Order Details with Product Info.**

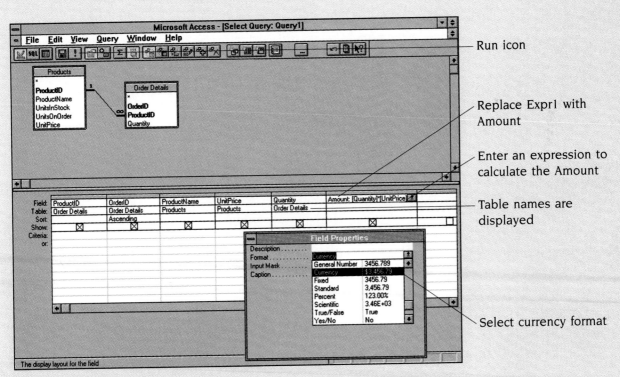

(d) Create the Subform Query (step 4)

FIGURE 5.6 Hands-on Exercise 2 (continued)

THE ZOOM BOX

Creating a long expression can be confusing in that you cannot see the entire expression as it is entered. Access anticipates the situation and provides a *Zoom box* to increase the space in which you can work. Press Shift+F2 as you enter the expression (or select Zoom from the shortcut menu) to display the Zoom box. Click OK to close the Zoom box and continue working in the QBE grid.

Step 5: Run the query

➤ Click the **Run icon** to run the query and change to the Datasheet view as shown in Figure 5.6e.

➤ Scroll to the end and click the **ProductID** field in the last row to add a new record. Type **P0001** (the record selector changes to a pencil), then press the **Tab key** to move to the OrderID field. The product information (Product Name and Unit Price) is entered automatically by Access because of the Autolookup feature.

➤ Type **O0001** as the order number for this product, which adds a Pentium system to Order O0001. (Order O0001 has several existing records for other products.)

➤ Tab to the **Quantity field** and type **1**; press **enter.** The cost of the item appears automatically in the last column.

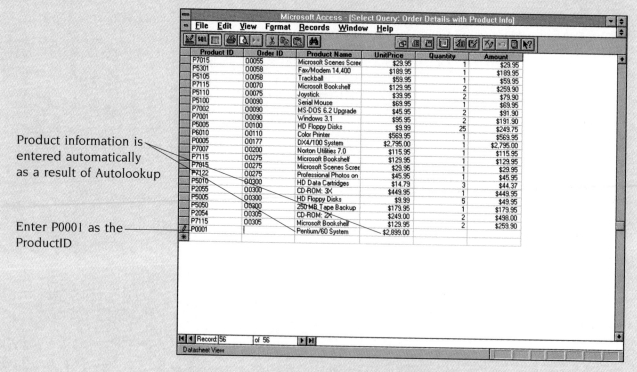

Product information is entered automatically as a result of Autolookup

Enter P0001 as the ProductID

(e) The Dynaset (step 5)

FIGURE 5.6 Hands-on Exercise 2 (continued)

Step 6: The Dynaset

➤ Click the **UnitPrice** field for your Pentium system. Click and drag to select the existing entry, then type **2699** and press **enter.**

➤ Pull down the **Records menu.** Click **Refresh** to rerun the query. The price change of the Pentium system is reflected throughout the dynaset.

➤ Double click the **control-menu box** to close the query. Click **Yes** if you are prompted to save changes to the query.

Step 7: The Main/Subform Wizard

➤ Click the **Form button** in the Database window. Click **New** to produce the New Form dialog box.

➤ Click the arrow next to the **Select A Table/Query** text box. Click **Order with Customer Info** to select the query for the main form.

➤ Click the **Form Wizards button** to open the Form Wizards. Choose **Main/Subform** as the type of form. Click **OK.**

➤ The next several screens ask questions about the Main/Subform you want to create.

— Click the **Queries option button** to display the existing queries as shown in Figure 5.6f. Choose **Order Details with Product Info** as shown in the figure. Click the **Next command button.**

— The Wizard indicates that data for the main form comes from the Order with Customer Info query. Click the **>> button** to select all available fields. Click the **Next command button.**

— The Wizard indicates that data for the subform comes from the Order Details with Product Info query. Click the **>> button** to select all available fields. Click the **Next command button.**

— The Wizard indicates that there is a matching field in the Orders table. Click the **Next command button.**

— Click **Embossed** for the style of the form. Click the **Next command button.**

— Type **Super Store Order Form** as the title of the form. Click the option button to **Modify the form's design.**

— Click the **Finish command button.**

➤ You will see a message indicating that you must save the subform before the Main/Subform Wizard can proceed. Click **OK.** Type **Order Details with Product Info** in the Save As dialog box. Click **OK.**

Step 8: Create the link

➤ You will see a message indicating that the Wizard could not establish a link between the main form and the subform. Click **OK.** You should be in the Design view as shown in Figure 5.6g. Click the **Maximize button.**

Select the Form object
button

Data for main form comes
from Order with Customer
Info query

Data for subform comes
from Order Details with
Product Info query

Queries option button is
selected

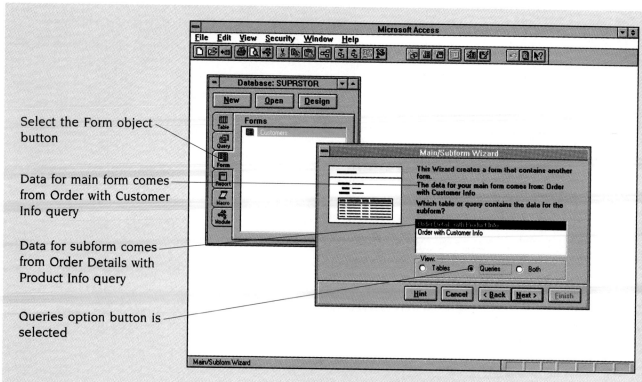

(f) The Main/Subform Wizard (step 7)

Form View icon

Double click here to
close the dialog box

Enter OrderID as the
linking field

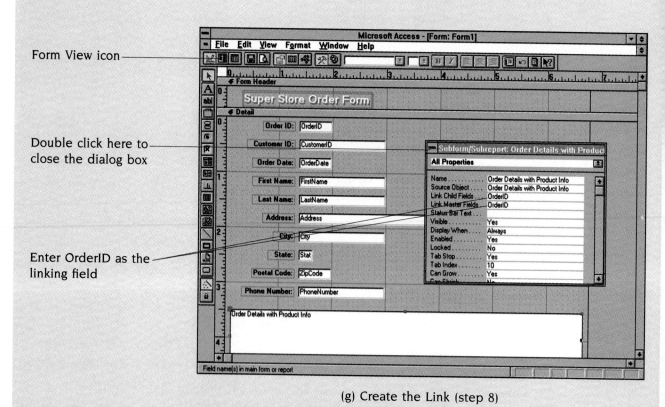

(g) Create the Link (step 8)

FIGURE 5.6 Hands-on Exercise 2 (continued)

- ► Scroll if necessary to see the subform. Point anywhere inside the subform (the large white rectangular box), then click the **right mouse button** to display a shortcut menu.
- ► Click **Properties** to display the Subform properties box shown in Figure 5.6g.
- ► Click the **Link Child Fields** property. Type **OrderID.** Click the **Link Master Fields** property. Type **OrderID** to link the main and subform by the value of the OrderID field.
- ► Double click the **control-menu box** to close the Subform properties box.
- ► Save the form as **Super Store Order Form.**

Step 9: The completed form
- ► Click the icon to switch to the Form view. Click the **Maximize button** so that the form takes the entire window as shown in Figure 5.6h. You should see your order displayed on the monitor.
- ► The status bar at the bottom of the window (corresponding to the main form) displays record 1 of 24 records (yours is the first order in the Orders table).

CUSTOMIZE THE MAIN FORM

Practice what you know about moving and aligning controls within a form, changing colors, adding lines and boxes, and so on. Add your name somewhere in the form (as the designer), then submit it to your instructor to prove you did the exercise.

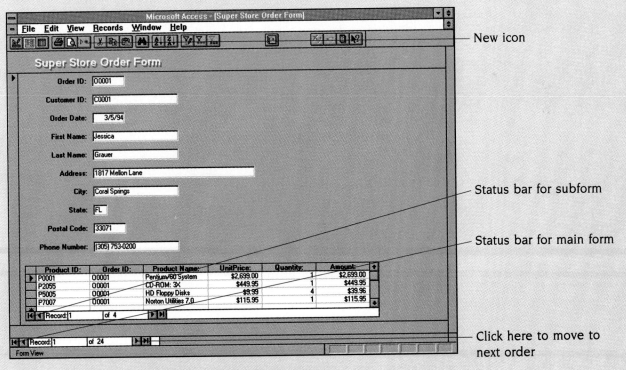

(h) The Completed Form (step 9)

FIGURE 5.6 Hands-on Exercise 2 (continued)

➤ The status bar for the subform displays record 1 of 4 records (you have four items in your order).

➤ Click the ▶ **button** on the status bar for the main form to move to the next order (Order O0003). The subform is updated automatically to display the items in this order.

Step 10: Enter a new order

➤ Click the **New icon** on the toolbar. Enter **O0400** as the new order number, then press the **Tab key** to move to the CustomerID field. (Today's date is entered automatically as the date of the order.)

➤ Type **C0001** (your CustomerID) and press **enter.** Your customer information is entered automatically.

➤ Click the subform to enter the products for your new order:
 — Enter **P7115** as the first ProductID in your order, then press the **Tab key** four times. The OrderID (O0400), ProductName (Microsoft Bookshelf), and UnitPrice ($129.95) are entered automatically. Enter **1** as the quantity and press **enter.** The cost of this item ($129.95) is computed automatically by multiplying the quantity by the unit price.
 — Complete your order by ordering one unit of product **P7015** and three units of Product **P5005.**

➤ Pull down the **File menu.** Click **Print Setup** to produce the Print Setup dialog box. Change the Left and Right margins to **.75 inch** so that the form fits on one page. Click **OK** to close the Print Setup dialog box.

➤ Click the **Print icon** to display the Print dialog box. Click the **Selection option button** to print only the current order. Click **OK.**

➤ Exit Access if you do not want to continue with the next exercise at this time.

ADDING A CUSTOMER

The main form enables you to add an order for an existing customer or modify data for an existing customer. It will *not* let you add a new customer because it does not contain the primary key from the Customers table. To use the main form to add a customer, you would have to modify both the form and its underlying query to include the CustomerID from *both* the Customers table and the Orders table.

ADVANCED QUERIES

A select query, powerful as it is, has its limitations. It requires you to enter the criteria directly into the query, which means you have to change the query every time you vary the criteria. What if you wanted to use a different set of criteria (e.g., a different customer's name) every time you ran the "same" query?

A second limitation of select queries is that they do not produce summary information about groups of records. How many orders have we received this month? What was the largest order? What was the smallest order?

This section introduces two additional types of queries to overcome both limitations.

Parameter Queries

A *parameter query* prompts you for the criteria each time you execute the query. It is created by using the QBE grid in similar fashion to a select query and is illustrated in Figure 5.7. The difference between a parameter query and an ordinary select query is the way in which the criteria are specified. In a select query you enter the actual criteria. In a parameter query you enter a *prompt* (message) requesting the criteria.

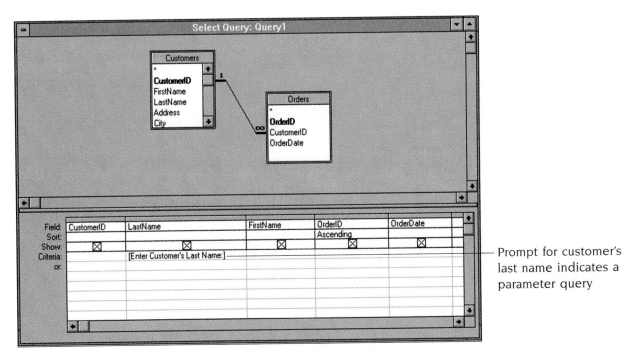

Prompt for customer's last name indicates a parameter query

(a) QBE Grid

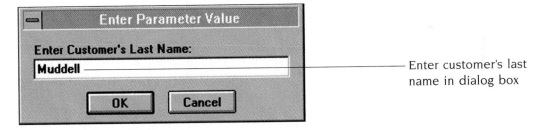

Enter customer's last name in dialog box

(b) Dialog Box

Customer ID	Last Name	First Name	Order ID	Order Date
C0015	Muddell	Jeffrey	O0003	3/15/94
C0015	Muddell	Jeffrey	O0025	4/15/94
C0015	Muddell	Jeffrey	O0075	5/12/94
C0015	Muddell	Jeffrey	O0110	6/10/94

Record: 1 of 4

(c) Dynaset

FIGURE 5.7 Parameter Query

The QBE grid in Figure 5.7a creates a parameter query that will display the orders for a particular customer. The query does not contain the customer's name, but a prompt for that name. The prompt is enclosed in square brackets and is displayed in a dialog box when the query is executed. The user enters the customer's name in the dialog box (Figure 5.7b), and the query displays the resulting dynaset (Figure 5.7c). This enables you to run the same query with different criteria; that is, you can enter a different customer name every time you execute the query.

A parameter query may prompt for any number of variables (parameters), which are entered in successive dialog boxes. The parameters are requested in order from left to right according to the way in which they appear in the QBE grid.

PARAMETER QUERIES, FORMS, AND REPORTS

A parameter query can be used as the basis for a form or report. Create the form or report in the normal way (with or without a wizard), but specify the parameter query when asked which table or query to use. Then, when you open the form or report, Access will display a dialog box with the prompt(s) contained within the parameter query. Supply the requested information, and the form or report is created, based on the criteria you entered.

Total Queries

A *total query* performs calculations on a *group of* records using one of several *aggregate functions* available within Access. These are the same functions available within a *Group/Total report* as described in Chapter 3:

Sum— The total of all values in a field
Avg— The average of values in a field
Min— The minimum value in a field
Max— The maximum value in a field
Count—The number of records with an entry in the field

Figure 5.8 illustrates the use of a total query to compute the amount of each order. Figure 5.8a displays a dynaset containing fields from both the Products and Order Details tables. There is one record for each product in each order. Each record contains the price of the product, the quantity ordered, and the amount for that product. There are, for example, four products in order O0001. The first and second products cost $2699 and $449.95, respectively. The third product costs $39.96 (four units at $9.99 each), and the fourth product is $115.95. The total for the order comes to $3304.86.

The QBE grid in Figure 5.8b creates a total query to perform the calculation for the total cost of the order. The *Group By entry* in the *Total Row* indicates that records are to be grouped (aggregated) according to the value in that field. The *Sum function* in the Total row specifies the arithmetic operation to be performed on the group of records.

The dynaset in Figure 5.8c shows the result of the total query and displays *aggregate* records as opposed to *individual* records. There are, for example, four individual records for order O0001 in Figure 5.8a, but only one aggregate record in Figure 5.8c. This is because each record in a total query contains the result of a calculation based on a group of individual records.

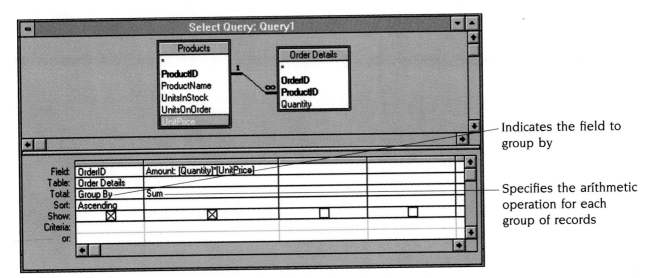

Order ID	Product ID	Product Name	Quantity	UnitPrice	Amount
00001	P0001	Pentium/60 System	1	$2,699.00	$2,699.00
00001	P2055	CD-ROM: 3X	1	$449.95	$449.95
00001	P5005	HD Floppy Disks	4	$9.99	$39.96
00001	P7007	Norton Utilities 7.0	1	$115.95	$115.95
00003	P0007	Pentium/90 System	1	$3,895.00	$3,895.00
00003	P5301	Fax/Modem 14,400	1	$189.95	$189.95
00003	P6005	Laser Printer	1	$1,395.00	$1,395.00
00010	P0004	486DX2/66 System	1	$1,549.00	$1,549.00
00010	P2010	345 MB Hard Drive	1	$285.00	$285.00
00010	P6005	Laser Printer	2	$1,395.00	$2,790.00
00018	P0004	486DX2/66 System	2	$1,549.00	$3,098.00
00018	P2054	CD-ROM: 2X	2	$249.00	$498.00
00018	P5050	250 MB Tape Backup	2	$179.95	$359.90

Record: 1 of 59

(a) Orders with Products Dynaset

(b) QBE Grid

Indicates the field to group by

Specifies the arithmetic operation for each group of records

Order ID	Amount
00001	$3,304.86
00003	$5,479.95
00010	$4,624.00
00018	$3,955.90

Record: 1 of 25

(c) Dynaset

FIGURE 5.8 Total Query

THE UNMATCHED QUERY WIZARD

The **Unmatched Query Wizard** identifies records in one table that do not have matching records in another table. It can, for example, tell you whether there are products in inventory that have never been ordered; that is, it will find the records in the Products table that do not appear in the Order Details table. Such information is extremely useful and can be used to reduce the cost of inventory. The Unmatched Query Wizard is explored in problem 4 at the end of the chapter.

The following exercise begins by having you create the Group/Total report in Figure 5.9. The report is a detailed analysis of all orders, listing every product in every order. The report is based on a query containing fields from the Orders, Products, and Order Details tables. Thus, the exercise provides a review of Group/Total reports and multiple table queries; it also provides practice in creating parameter queries and total queries.

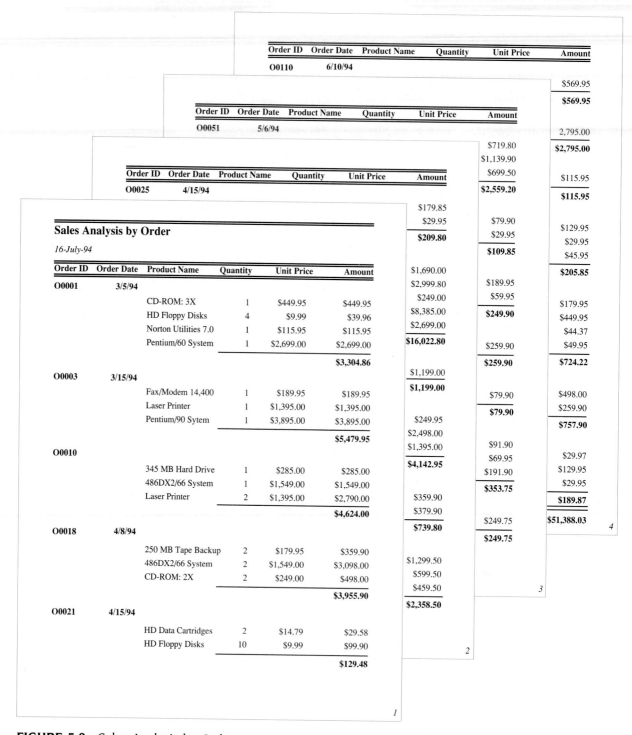

FIGURE 5.9 Sales Analysis by Order

HANDS-ON EXERCISE 3:

Advanced Queries

Objective To copy an existing query; to create a parameter query; to create a total query by using the aggregate Sum function. Use Figure 5.10 as a guide in the exercise.

Step 1: Create the query

➤ Open the **SUPRSTOR** database from the previous exercise.

➤ Click the **Query button** in the Database window. Click the **New button** to produce the New Query dialog box. Click the **New Query button** to produce the Add Table dialog box in Figure 5.10a. (The tables have not yet been added.)

➤ By now you have had sufficient practice creating a query, so we will just outline the steps:

— Add the **Orders, Products,** and **Order Details** tables as shown in Figure 5.10a. Move and size the field lists within the Query window to match Figure 5.10a. Maximize the window.

— Pull down the **View menu.** Click **Table Names** to include the Tables row in the QBE grid as shown in Figure 5.10a.

— Add the indicated fields to the QBE grid. Be sure to take each field from the appropriate table (field list), or else the Group/Total report will not work properly.

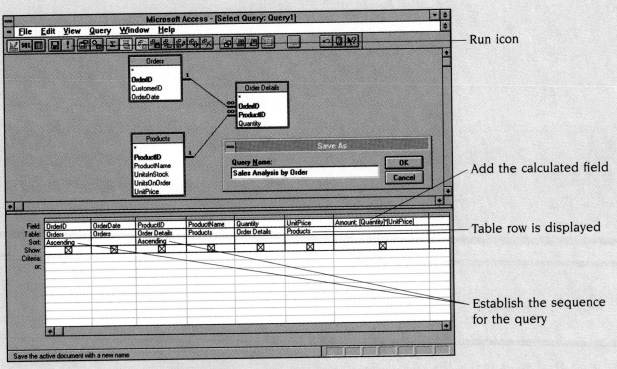

(a) Create the Query (step 1)

FIGURE 5.10 Hands-on Exercise 3

— Sort the query in **ascending order** by OrderID and by ProductID within OrderID. (The OrderID field must appear to the left of the ProductID field in the QBE grid.)
— Add the calculated field to compute the amount by multiplying the quantity by the unit price. Point to the expression, click the **right mouse button** to display a shortcut menu, then change the Format property to **Currency.**
— Check that your query matches Figure 5.10a. Save the query as **Sales Analysis by Order.**
➤ Click the **Run icon** (the exclamation point) to run the query. The dynaset contains one record for every item in every order.
➤ Double click the **control-menu box** to close the query.

Step 2: The Report Wizard
➤ Click the **Report button** in the Database window. Click the **New command button.** Click the **down arrow** and scroll until you can select **Sales Analysis by Order** (the query you just created). Click the **Report Wizards button.** Click **Group/Totals.** Click **OK.**
➤ By now you have had sufficient practice using the Report Wizard, so we will just outline the steps:
— Add the **OrderID, OrderDate, ProductName, Quantity, UnitPrice,** and **Amount** fields from the Available fields list box to the report.
— Group the report by **OrderID,** then accept Normal grouping as suggested by the Wizard.
— Sort by **ProductName.**
— Click the option buttons for the **Executive style** and **Portrait orientation.**
— Check the box to **See all the fields on one page.** Remove the check from the box to calculate percentages.
— Click the option button to **Modify the report's design.** Click the **Finish command button.** You should see the Report Design view as shown in Figure 5.10b. **Maximize** the Report window.
➤ Save the report as **Sales Analysis by Order.**

Step 3: Complete and print the report
➤ Press and hold the **Shift key** to select the group and report totals for Quantity and Unit Price as shown in Figure 5.10b. Press the **Del key** to delete the selected controls.
➤ Click the **Print Preview icon** to view the completed report as shown in Figure 5.10c. Click the **Zoom icon** to see the entire page. Click the **Zoom icon** a second time to return to the higher magnification, which lets you read the report. (You may want to return to the Design view to move and/or size the ProductName and other controls in the report.)
➤ Click the **Printer icon** to display the Print dialog box. The All option button is already selected under Print Range. Click **OK** to print the report.
➤ Double click the **control-menu box** to close the report and return to the Database window. Click **Yes** if asked whether to save the report.

Step 4: Copy a query
➤ Click the **Query button** in the Database window. Click the **Sales Analysis by Order** query to select the query as shown in Figure 5.10d.
➤ Pull down the **Edit menu.** Click **Copy.** (The query has been copied to the clipboard.)

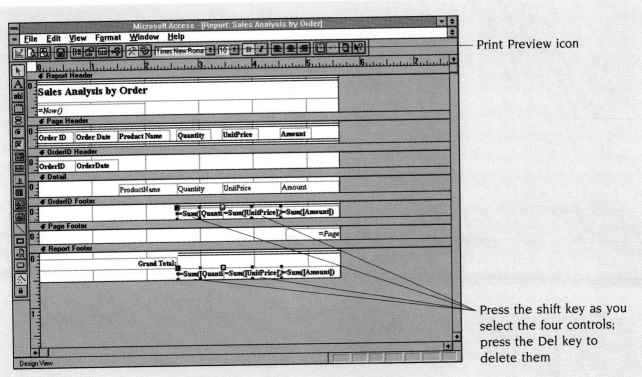

Print Preview icon

Press the shift key as you select the four controls; press the Del key to delete them

(b) Modify the Report (steps 2 and 3)

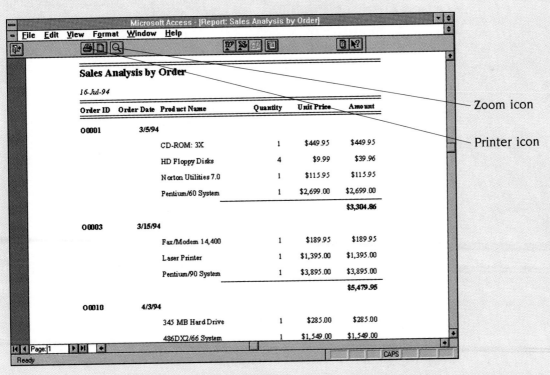

Zoom icon

Printer icon

(c) The Completed Report (step 3)

FIGURE 5.10 Hands-on Exercise 3 (continued)

Select the Query button ─

Select the Sales Analysis ─
by Order query

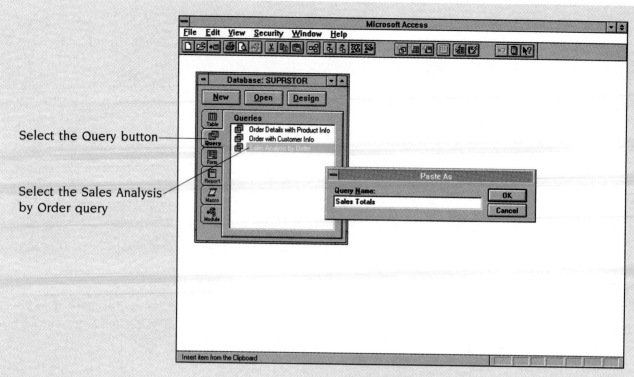

(d) Copy an Existing Query (step 4)

FIGURE 5.10   Hands-on Exercise 3 (continued)

➤ Pull down the **Edit menu.** Click **Paste** to produce the Paste As dialog box in
Figure 5.10d. Type **Sales Totals.** Click **OK.** The Database window contains
both the original query (Sales Analysis by Order) as well as the copied version (Sales Totals) you just created.

COPY, DELETE, OR RENAME AN OBJECT

The Database window enables you to copy, delete, or rename any object
(a table, form, query, or report) in an Access database. To copy an object,
select the object, pull down the Edit menu, and click Copy. Pull down the
Edit menu a second time, click Paste, then enter the name of the copied
object. To delete or rename an object, point to the object, then click the
right mouse button to display a shortcut menu and select the desired
operation.

Step 5: Create a total query
➤ Click the newly created **Sales Totals query.** Click the **Design command button** to open the Query Design window in Figure 5.10e. (The Customers table
has not yet been added to the query.)
➤ Pull down the **Query menu.** Click **Add Table** to produce the Add Table dialog box. Double click the Customers table to add it to the query. Click the
Close command button to close the dialog box.

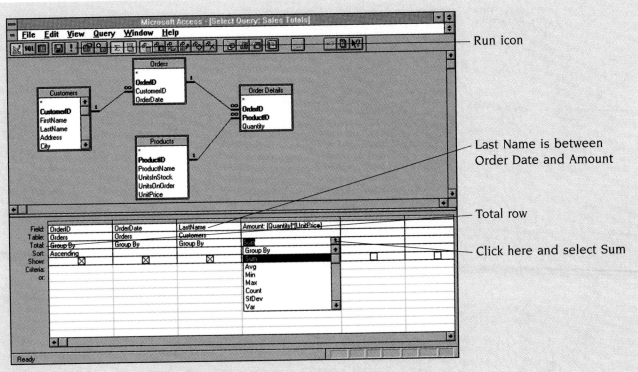

Run icon

Last Name is between
Order Date and Amount

Total row

Click here and select Sum

(e) Create a Total Query (step 5)

FIGURE 5.10 Hands-on Exercise 3 (continued)

➤ Click and drag the **title bars** of the various field lists to position them within the Query window and match the arrangement in Figure 5.10e.

➤ Click the **column selector** for the **ProductID** field to select the column. Press the **Del key** to delete the field from the query. Delete the **ProductName, Quantity,** and **UnitPrice** fields in similar fashion.

➤ Double click **LastName** in the Customers field list to add this field to the query. Click the **column selector** for the **LastName** field to select the column, then drag the column so that the LastName appears between the OrderDate and Amount fields. Check that the fields in your QBE grid match those in Figure 5.10e.

➤ Pull down the **View menu.** Click **Totals.** Click the **Total row** under Amount, then click the arrow to open the drop-down list box. Click **Sum** as shown in the figure.

➤ Save the query.

Step 6: Run the query

➤ Pull down the **Query menu** and click **Run** (or click the **Run icon**) to run the query. You should see the datasheet in Figure 5.10f, which contains one record for each order with the total amount of that order.

➤ Click any field and attempt to change its value. You will be unable to do so as indicated by the beep and the message in the status bar indicating that the record set is not updatable.

➤ Click the **Design View icon** to return to the Query Design view.

Design View icon—

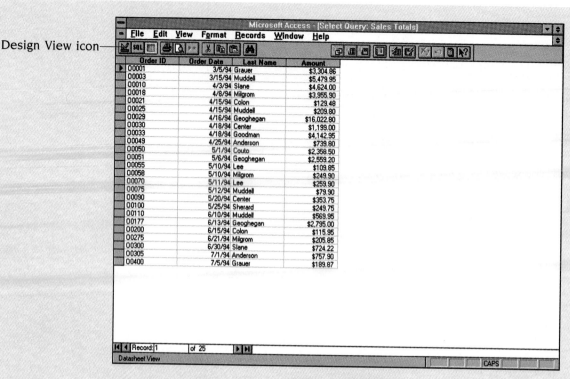

(f) The Dynaset (step 6)

FIGURE 5.10 Hands-on Exercise 3 (continued)

THE TOPVALUES PROPERTY

The *TopValues property* returns a designated number of records rather than the entire dynaset. Open the query in Design view, then click the right mouse button *outside* the QBE grid to display a shortcut menu. Click Properties, click the box for TopValues, and enter the desired value. You can enter either a number or a percent; for example, type 5 to list the top five records, or type 5% to list the records that make up the top five percent.

Step 7: Create a parameter query

➤ Click the **Criteria row** under **LastName.** Type **[Enter Customer's Last Name]** as shown in Figure 5.10g. Be sure to enclose the entry in square brackets, which are required to create a parameter query.

➤ Pull down the **File menu.** Click **Save As.** Save the query as **Customer Parameter Query.**

➤ Run the query. Access will display the dialog box in Figure 5.10g, asking for the Customer's last name. Type **your name** and press **enter.** Access displays your last name, OrderID(s), and the date and amount of your order(s).

➤ Double click the **control-menu box** to close the query.

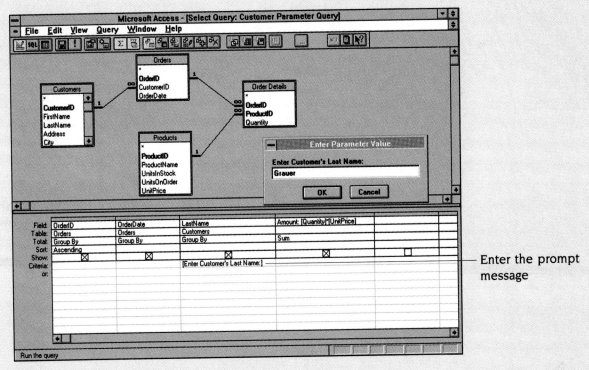

— Enter the prompt message

(g) Create a Parameter Query (step 7)

FIGURE 5.10   Hands-on Exercise 3 (continued)

UPDATING THE QUERY

The changes made in a query are automatically made in the underlying table(s). Not every field in a query is updatable, however, and the easiest way to determine if you can change a value is to run the query, view the dynaset, and attempt to edit the field. Access will prevent you from updating a calculated field, a field based on an aggregate function (such as Sum or Count), or the join field on the "one" side of a one-to-many relationship. If you attempt to update a field you cannot change, the status bar will display a message indicating why the change is not allowed.

Step 8: Exit Access
➤ Double click the **control-menu box** in the Database window to close the SUPRSTOR.MDB database.
➤ Double click the **control-menu box** in the Access window to exit Access and return to Windows. (Do not be concerned by the message indicating that closing Access will empty the clipboard.)

EXPANDING THE DATABASE

One of the advantages of an Access database is that it can be easily expanded to include additional data without disturbing the existing tables. The database used throughout the chapter consisted of four tables: a Customers table, a Products table, an Orders table, and an Order Details table. Figure 5.11 extends the database to include a Sales Staff table with data about each member of the sales staff.

The sales person helps the customer as he or she comes into the store, then receives a commission based on the order. There is a one-to-many relationship between the sales staff and orders. One sales person can generate many orders, but an order can have only one sales person. The Sales Staff and Orders tables are joined by the SalesPersonID field, which is common to both tables.

Figure 5.11 is similar to Figure 5.1 at the beginning of the chapter except that the Sales Staff table has been added and the Orders table has been expanded to include a SalesPersonID. This enables management to monitor the performance of the sales staff. Consider:

Query: How many orders has Linda Black taken?
Answer: Linda has taken six orders.

The query is straightforward and easily answered. You would search the Sales Staff table for Linda Black to determine her SalesPersonID (S01). You would then search the Orders table and count the records containing S01 in the SalesPersonID field.

Query: Which salesperson has the fewest orders?
Answer: Karen Ruenheck has only four orders.

The easiest way to answer this query would be to sort the Orders table by SalesPersonID, then count the number of orders for each salesperson. You could also create a total query using the aggregate count function.

The Sales Staff table is also used to generate a report listing the commissions due to each sales person. The store pays a 2.5% commission on every sale. Consider:

Query: What is the commission on Order O0018? Which salesperson gets the commission?
Answer: The commission for order O0018 is $98.90. Linda Black gets the commission.

To calculate the commission for order O0018, you must first determine the total amount of that order. You would begin in the Order Details table, find each product in order O0018, and multiply the quantity of that product by its unit price. The total cost of order O0018 comes to $3995.90 (two units of product P0004 at $1549, two units of product P2054 at $249, and two units of Product 5050 at $179.95). The commission is therefore $98.90 (.025 × $3995.90).

To determine the sales person, you would search the Orders table for Order O0018 to obtain the SalesPersonID (S01). You would then search the Sales Staff table for this value and find the corresponding name (Linda Black).

Figure 5.12a displays the commission report for the entire sales staff. The report was created by using the Group/Total Report Wizard and is based on the totals query in Figure 5.12b. The query references fields from all five tables in the database to produce the dynaset in Figure 5.12c, which is the basis of the report. The Sales Staff table is included on the data disk and is referenced in the next hands-on exercise as well as in several problems at the end of the chapter.

(a) Customers Table

Customer ID	First Name	Last Name	Address	City	State	Postal Code	Phone Number
C0001	Jessica	Grauer	1817 Mellon Lane	Coral Springs	FL	33071	(305) 753-0200
C0002	Benjamin	Lee	1000 Call Street	Tallahassee	FL	33340	(904) 327-4124
C0003	Eleanor	Milgrom	7245 NW 8 Street	Margate	FL	33065	(305) 974-1234
C0004	Neil	Goodman	4215 South 81 Street	Margate	FL	33065	(305) 444-5555
C0009	Nicholas	Colon	9020 N.W. 75 Street	Coral Springs	FL	33065	(305) 753-9887
C0010	Michael	Ware	276 Brickell Avenue	Miami	FL	33131	(305) 444-3980
C0015	Jeffrey	Muddell	9522 S.W. 142 Street	Miami	FL	33176	(305) 253-3909
C0017	Ashley	Geoghegan	7500 Center Lane	Coral Springs	FL	33070	(305) 753-7830
C0019	Serena	Sherard	5000 Jefferson Lane	Gainesville	FL	32601	(305) 375-6442
C0020	Luis	Couto	455 Bargello Avenue	Coral Gables	FL	33146	(305) 666-4801
C0022	Derek	Anderson	6000 Tigertail Avenue	Coconut Grove	FL	33120	(305) 446-8900
C0031	Lauren	Center	12380 S.W. 137 Avenue	Miami	FL	33186	(305) 385-4432
C0033	Robert	Siane	4508 N.W. 7 Street	Miami	FL	33131	(305) 635-3454

(a) Customers Table

(b) Products Table

Product ID	Product Name	Units In Stock	Units On Order	Unit Price
P0001	Pentium/60 System	50	0	$2,899.00
P0002	486DX/33 System	25	5	$1,249.00
P0004	486DX2/66 System	125	15	$1,549.00
P0005	DX4/100 System	25	50	$2,795.00
P0007	Pentium/90 System	15	25	$3,895.00
P1002	17" SVGA Monitor	50	0	$1,199.00
P1050	14" SVGA Monitor	25	10	$299.00
P1075	15" MultiSync Monitor	50	20	$749.95
P2003	210 MB Hard Drive	15	20	$215.00
P2010	345 MB Hard Drive	25	15	$285.00
P2025	1 GB Hard Drive	10	0	$845.00
P2054	CD-ROM: 2X	40	0	$249.00
P2055	CD-ROM: 3X	50	15	$449.95
P5005	HD Floppy Disks	500	200	$9.99
P5010	HD Data Cartridges	100	50	$14.79
P5050	250 MB Tape Backup	15	3	$179.95
P5100	Serial Mouse	150	50	$69.95
P5105	Trackball	55	0	$59.95
P5110	Joystick	250	100	$39.95
P5301	Fax/Modem 14,400	35	10	$189.95
P5305	Fax/Modem 9,600	20	0	$65.95
P6005	Laser Printer	100	15	$1,395.00
P6006	24Pin Dot Matrix	50	50	$249.95
P6010	Color Printer	125	25	$569.95
P7001	Windows 3.1	400	200	$95.95
P7002	MS-DOS 6.2 Upgrade	150	50	$45.95
P7007	Norton Utilities 7.0	150	50	$115.95
P7015	Microsoft Scenes Screen Saver	75	25	$29.95
P7115	Microsoft Bookshelf	250	100	$129.95
P7120	Microsoft Cinemania	25	10	$59.95
P7122	Professional Photos on CD-ROM	15	0	$45.95

(b) Products Table

(c) Orders Table

Order ID	Customer ID	Order Date	Sales Person ID
O0001	C0001	03/05/94	S01
O0003	C0015	03/15/94	S05
O0010	C0033	04/03/94	S03
O0018	C0003	04/08/94	S01
O0021	C0009	04/15/94	S04
O0025	C0015	04/15/94	S01
O0029	C0017	04/16/94	S03
O0030	C0031	04/18/94	S02
O0033	C0004	04/18/94	S02
O0049	C0022	04/25/94	S05
O0050	C0020	05/01/94	S01
O0051	C0017	05/06/94	S04
O0055	C0002	05/10/94	S03
O0058	C0003	05/10/94	S04
O0070	C0002	05/11/94	S03
O0075	C0015	05/12/94	S01
O0090	C0031	05/20/94	S02
O0100	C0019	05/25/94	S02
O0110	C0015	06/10/94	S05
O0177	C0017	06/13/94	S03
O0200	C0009	06/15/94	S05
O0275	C0003	06/21/94	S01
O0300	C0033	06/30/94	S05
O0305	C0022	07/01/94	S04
O0400	C0001	07/05/94	S02

(c) Orders Table

(d) Order Details Table

Order ID	Product ID	Quantity
O0001	P0001	1
O0001	P2055	1
O0001	P5005	4
O0001	P7007	1
O0003	P0007	1
O0003	P5301	1
O0003	P6005	1
O0010	P0004	1
O0010	P2010	1
O0010	P6005	2
O0018	P0004	2
O0018	P2054	2
O0018	P5050	2
O0021	P5005	10
O0021	P5010	2
O0025	P7015	1
O0025	P7120	3
O0029	P0001	1
O0029	P0005	3
O0029	P1075	4
O0029	P2025	2
O0029	P2054	1
O0030	P1002	1
O0033	P0002	2
O0033	P6005	1
O0033	P6006	1
O0049	P5050	2
O0049	P5301	2
O0050	P7115	10
O0050	P7120	10
O0050	P7122	10
O0051	P5050	4
O0051	P5100	10
O0051	P6010	2
O0055	P5110	2
O0055	P7015	1
O0058	P5105	1
O0058	P5301	1
O0070	P7115	2
O0075	P5110	2
O0090	P5100	1
O0090	P7001	2
O0090	P7002	2
O0100	P5005	25
O0110	P6010	1
O0177	P0005	1
O0200	P7007	1
O0275	P7015	1
O0275	P7115	1
O0275	P7122	1
O0300	P2055	1
O0300	P5005	5
O0300	P5010	3
O0300	P5050	1
O0305	P2054	2
O0305	P7115	2
O0400	P5005	3
O0400	P7015	1
O0400	P7115	1

(d) Order Details Table

(e) Sales Staff Table

Sales Person ID	FirstName	LastName	WorkPhone	HireDate
S01	Linda	Black	(305) 284-6105	02/03/93
S02	Michael	Vaughn	(305) 284-3993	02/10/93
S03	Cori	Rice	(305) 284-2557	03/15/93
S04	Karen	Ruenheck	(305) 284-4641	01/31/94
S05	Richard	Linger	(305) 284-4662	01/31/94

(e) Sales Staff Table

FIGURE 5.11   Super Store Database

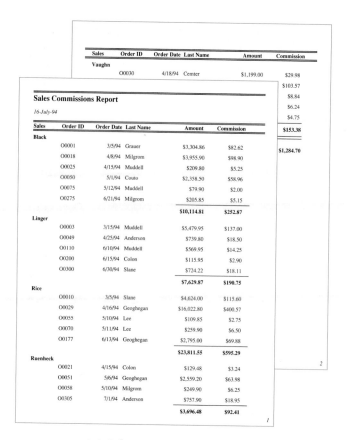

(a) Sales Commission Report

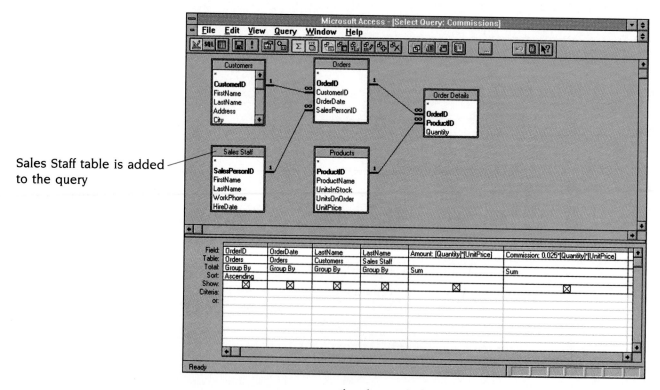

Sales Staff table is added to the query

(b) The Underlying Query

FIGURE 5.12 Sales Commissions

Order ID	Order Date	Last Name	Sales Staff.LastName	Amount	Commission
00001	3/5/94	Grauer	Black	$3,304.86	$82.62
00003	3/15/94	Muddell	Linger	$5,479.95	$137.00
00010	4/3/94	Slane	Rice	$4,624.00	$115.60
00018	4/8/94	Milgrom	Black	$3,955.90	$98.90
00021	4/15/94	Colon	Ruenheck	$129.48	$3.24
00025	4/15/94	Muddell	Black	$209.80	$5.25
00029	4/16/94	Geoghegan	Rice	$16,022.80	$400.57
00030	4/18/94	Center	Vaughn	$1,199.00	$29.98
00033	4/18/94	Goodman	Vaughn	$4,142.95	$103.57
00049	4/25/94	Anderson	Linger	$739.80	$18.50
00050	5/1/94	Couto	Black	$2,358.50	$58.96
00051	5/6/94	Geoghegan	Ruenheck	$2,559.20	$63.98
00055	5/10/94	Lee	Rice	$109.85	$2.75
00058	5/10/94	Milgrom	Ruenheck	$249.90	$6.25
00070	5/11/94	Lee	Rice	$259.90	$6.50
00075	5/12/94	Muddell	Black	$79.90	$2.00
00090	5/20/94	Center	Vaughn	$353.75	$8.84
00100	5/25/94	Sherard	Vaughn	$249.75	$6.24
00110	6/10/94	Muddell	Linger	$569.95	$14.25
00177	6/13/94	Geoghegan	Rice	$2,795.00	$69.88
00200	6/15/94	Colon	Linger	$115.95	$2.90
00275	6/21/94	Milgrom	Black	$205.85	$5.15
00300	6/30/94	Slane	Linger	$724.22	$18.11
00305	7/1/94	Anderson	Ruenheck	$757.90	$18.95
00400	7/5/94	Grauer	Vaughn	$189.87	$4.75

Record: 1   of 25

(c) The Dynaset

FIGURE 5.12 Sales Commissions (continued)

Importing Objects

Access allows only one database to be open at a time, but it allows you to import objects (tables, queries, forms, and reports) from other databases. This makes it possible to combine smaller databases into larger databases and/or divide the work in developing larger systems among many individuals.

The last exercise has you import the Sales Staff table from another Access database. It then directs you to modify the Orders table to include a SalesPersonID, which references the records in the Sales Staff table.

HANDS-ON EXERCISE 4:

Expanding the Database

Objective To import a table from another database; to modify the design of an existing table; to create a combined parameter/totals query. Use Figure 5.13 as a guide in the exercise.

Step 1: Import the Sales Staff Table
➤ Open the **SUPRSTOR.MDB** database. Click the **Table button.**
➤ Pull down the **File menu.** Click **Import.** Click **Microsoft Access** as the Data Source. Click **OK.**
➤ Select the **SALESSTF.MDB** database from the File Name list box. Click **OK.** You will see the Import Objects dialog box in Figure 5.13a.
➤ Tables is selected as the Object. Click **Sales Staff** (the only entry in the list box). The option button for **Structure and Data** is already selected. Click the **Import command button.**
➤ You should see a message indicating that the Sales Staff table has been successfully imported. Click **OK.** Click the **Close command button** in the Import Objects dialog box.

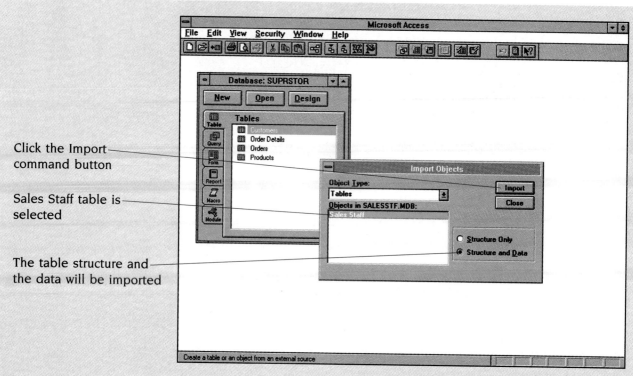

Click the Import command button

Sales Staff table is selected

The table structure and the data will be imported

(a) Import the Sales Staff Table (step 1)

FIGURE 5.13 Hands-on Exercise 4

Step 2: Modify the Orders table

➤ Select the **Orders table** from the Database window as shown in Figure 5.13b. Click the **Design command button.**

➤ Click the first available row in the **Field Name** column. Type **SalesPersonID** as shown in Figure 5.13b. Choose **text** as the data type for this field.

➤ Click the **Field Size** property. Replace 50 with **3.**

➤ Click the **Format** property. Enter a **greater than sign** (>).

➤ Click the **Validation Rule** property and enter **Like S##.** Click the **Validation Text** property and enter the message, **The SalesPersonID must begin with the letter S followed by two digits.**

➤ Click the **Save icon** to save the modified design of the Orders table. You will see a message indicating the data integrity rules have been changed and data may be lost.

➤ Click **No** since the newly entered validation rule does not affect existing data and you do not have to revalidate the data.

Step 3: Modify the Data in the Orders table

➤ Click the **Datasheet view icon** to change to the Datasheet view as shown in Figure 5.13c. Maximize the window.

➤ Enter the **SalesPersonID** for each existing order as shown in Figure 5.13c. Double click the **control-menu box** to close the Orders table.

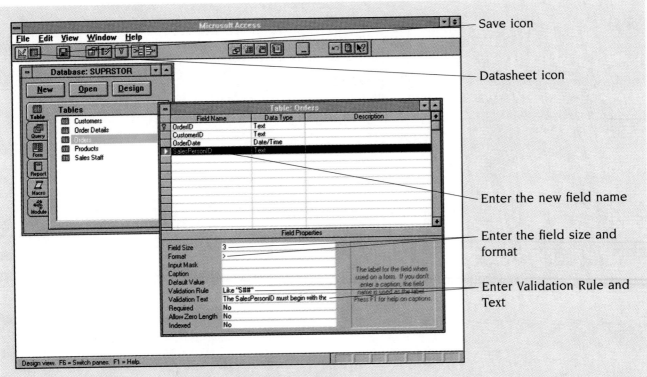

Save icon

Datasheet icon

Enter the new field name

Enter the field size and format

Enter Validation Rule and Text

(b) Modify the Orders Table (step 2)

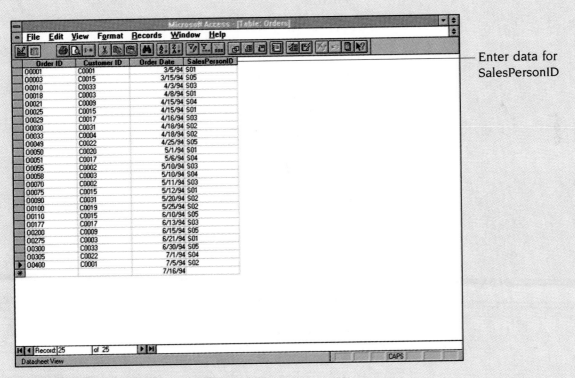

Enter data for SalesPersonID

(c) Add the Sales Person Data (step 3)

FIGURE 5.13 Hands-on Exercise 4 (continued)

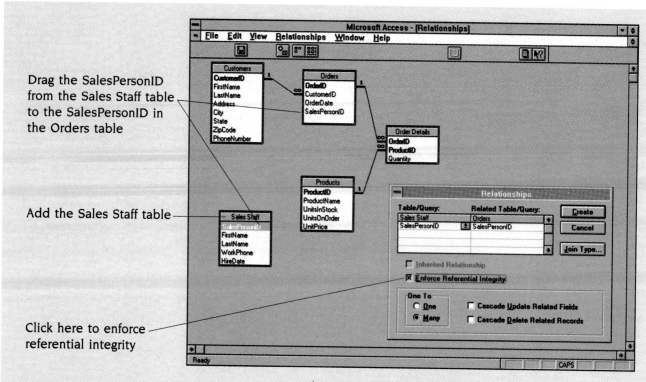

Drag the SalesPersonID from the Sales Staff table to the SalesPersonID in the Orders table

Add the Sales Staff table

Click here to enforce referential integrity

(d) Create the Relationships (step 4)

FIGURE 5.13   Hands-on Exercise 4 (continued)

Step 4: Add a relationship
➤ Pull down the **Edit menu.** Click **Relationships** to open the Relationships window as shown in Figure 5.13d. (The Sales Staff table is not yet visible.) Click the **Maximize button.**
➤ If necessary, drag the bottom border of the Orders table until you see the SalesPersonID (the field you added in step 2).
➤ Pull down the **Relationships menu.** Click **Add table.** Select the **Sales Staff table** from the Table/Query list. Click the **Add command button.** Click the **Close command button** to close the Add table dialog box.
➤ Drag the title bar of the Sales Staff table to position the table as shown in Figure 5.13d.
➤ Drag the **SalesPersonID** field from the Sales Staff table to the SalesPersonID in the Orders table. You will see the Relationships dialog box.
➤ Check the box to **Enforce referential integrity.** Click the **Create command button** to create the relationship.
➤ Click the **Save icon** to save the Relationships window. Double click the **control-menu box** to close the Relationships window.

Step 5: Create a Parameter/Totals Query
➤ Click the **Query button** in the Database window. Click the **Sales Totals query.** Pull down the **Edit menu.** Click **Copy.** Pull down the **Edit menu** a second time. Click **Paste.** Save the query as **Commission Parameter Query.**
➤ Click the newly created **Commission Parameter Query.** Click the **Design command button** to open the Query Design window in Figure 5.13e. Add the **Sales Staff table** to the query, then click and drag its title bar to match the layout in Figure 5.13e.

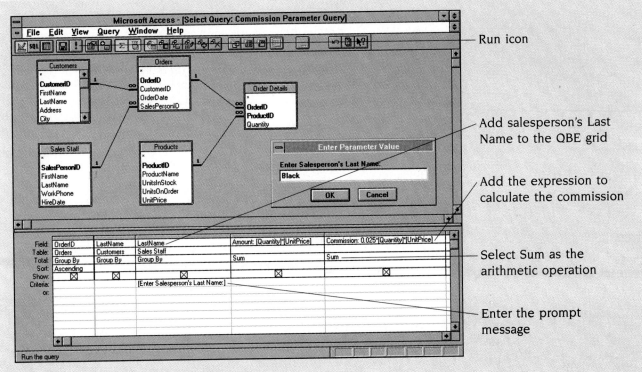

Run icon

Add salesperson's Last Name to the QBE grid

Add the expression to calculate the commission

Select Sum as the arithmetic operation

Enter the prompt message

(e) Create a Parameter/Total Query (step 5)

FIGURE 5.13 Hands-on Exercise 4 (continued)

➤ Double click **LastName** in the **Sales Staff field list** to add this field to the query. Click the column selector for this field to select the column, then drag the column so that it appears to the left of the Amount field.

➤ Click the first empty cell in the Field row to enter the commission. Type **=0.025*[Quantity]*[UnitPrice]** and press **enter,** then replace Expr1 with **Commission.** Click the **Total row** and select **Sum.** Click the right mouse button to change the **Format property** to **Currency.**

➤ Run the query. You should see a datasheet containing the total amount of each sale and the associated commission. Click the **Design View icon.**

➤ Click the **Criteria row** under **LastName** from the **Sales Staff table.** Enter **[Enter Salesperson's Last Name].** Save the query.

➤ Run the query to produce the dialog box in Figure 5.13e. Type **Black** as the name of the sales person and press **enter.** You will see all sales for the selected sales person (Black), the amount of each sale, and the commission in each sale.

➤ Close the SUPRSTOR database. Exit Access and return to Windows.

SUMMARY

The implementation of a many-to-many relationship requires an additional table whose primary key consists of (at least) the primary keys of the individual tables. The many-to-many table may contain additional fields whose values are dependent on the combined key.

A database can have any number of one-to-many relationships and any number of many-to-many relationships. All relationships are created in the Relationships window by dragging the join field from the primary table to the related table.

A many-to-many relationship is implemented through a pair of one-to-many relationships.

Enforcement of referential integrity prevents the deletion and/or updating of records on the "one" side of a one-to-many relationship when there are matching records in the related table. The deletion (updating) can take place, however, if the relationship is modified to allow the cascaded deletion (updating) of related records.

There are several reasons to base a form (or subform) on a query rather than a table. A query can contain a calculated field; a table cannot. A query can contain fields from more than one table and take advantage of Autolookup. A query can also contain selected records from a table and/or display those records in a different sequence from that of the table on which it is based.

A parameter query prompts you for the criteria each time you execute the query. The prompt is enclosed in square brackets and is entered in the Criteria row of the QBE grid. Multiple parameters may be specified within the same query.

Aggregate functions (Avg, Count, Min, Max, and Sum) perform arithmetic on groups of records. Execution of the query displays an aggregate record, and individual records do not appear. Updating of individual records is not possible in this type of query.

Tables may be added to an Access database without disturbing the data in existing tables. The Import command enables you to copy an object(s) from another database.

Key Words and Concepts

Aggregate functions
Autolookup
Cascaded Deletion
Cascaded Updating
Combined key
Foreign key
Group By entry
Group/Total report
Import command
Join field

Main form
Many-to-many relationship
One-to-many relationship
Parameter query
Primary key
Prompt
Referential integrity
Rename command

Subform
Sum function
Top Values property
Total query
Total row
Unmatched Query Wizard
Zoom box

Multiple Choice

1. The Relationships window in an Access database that contains a relationship between orders and products would most likely have:
   (a) A one-to-one join line between the Products table and the Orders table
   (b) A many-to-many join line between the Products table and the Orders table
   (c) Either (a) or (b)
   (d) Neither (a) nor (b)

2. Which of the following is necessary to add a record to the "one" side in a one-to-many relationship in which referential integrity is enforced?
   (a) A unique primary key for the new record
   (b) One or more matching records in the "many" table
   (c) Both (a) and (b)
   (d) Neither (a) nor (b)

3. Which of the following is necessary to add a record to the "many" side in a one-to-many relationship in which referential integrity is enforced?
   (a) A unique primary key for the new record
   (b) A matching record in the primary table
   (c) Both (a) and (b)
   (d) Neither (a) nor (b)

4. Under which circumstances can you delete a "many" record in a one-to-many relationship?
   (a) Under all circumstances
   (b) Under no circumstances
   (c) By enforcing referential integrity
   (d) By changing the relationship to permit the cascaded deletion of related records

5. Under which circumstances can you delete the "one" record in a one-to-many relationship?
   (a) Under all circumstances
   (b) Under no circumstances
   (c) By enforcing referential integrity
   (d) By changing the relationship to permit the cascaded deletion of related records

6. A database may contain:
   (a) One or more one-to-many relationships
   (b) One or more many-to-many relationships
   (c) Both (a) and (b)
   (d) Neither (a) nor (b)

7. Which type of relationship best describes the relationships between students and the courses they take?
   (a) One-to-one between students and courses
   (b) One-to-many between students and courses
   (c) One-to-many between courses and students
   (d) Many-to-many between courses and students

8. The implementation of the database in question 7 requires:
   (a) A Students table and a Courses table
   (b) A Students-Courses table
   (c) Both (a) and (b)
   (d) Neither (a) nor (b)

9. Which of the following would be suitable as the primary key in a Patients-Doctors table, where there is a many-to-many relationship between patients and doctors, and where the same patient can see the same doctor on different visits?
   (a) The combination of PatientID and DoctorID
   (b) The combination of PatientID, DoctorID, and the date of the visit
   (c) Either (a) or (b) is suitable
   (d) Neither (a) nor (b) is suitable

10. Which of the following is true about a main form and an associated subform?
   (a) The main form can be based on a query
   (b) The subform can be based on a query
   (c) Both (a) and (b)
   (d) Neither (a) nor (b)

11. A parameter query:
  (a) Is created through the Query Wizard
  (b) May contain more than one parameter
  (c) Both (a) and (b)
  (d) Neither (a) nor (b)

12. Which of the following is available as an aggregate function within a select query?
  (a) Sum, Avg, and Count
  (b) Min and Max
  (c) Both (a) and (b)
  (d) Neither (a) nor (b)

13. A query designed to take advantage of Autolookup requires:
  (a) A unique value for the join field in the "one" side of a one-to-many relationship
  (b) The join field to be taken from the "many" side of a one-to-many relationship
  (c) Both (a) and (b)
  (d) Neither (a) nor (b)

14. Which of the following can be imported from another Access database?
  (a) Tables and forms
  (b) Queries and reports
  (c) Both (a) and (b)
  (d) Neither (a) nor (b)

15. Which of the following is true of the TopValues query property?
  (a) It can be used to display only the top 10 records in a dynaset
  (b) It can be used to display only the top 10 percent of the records in a dynaset
  (c) Both (a) and (b)
  (d) Neither (a) nor (b)

ANSWERS

1. d	**6.** c	**11.** b
2. a	**7.** d	**12.** c
3. c	**8.** c	**13.** c
4. a	**9.** b	**14.** c
5. d	**10.** c	**15.** c

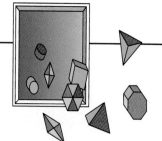

EXPLORING ACCESS

1. Use Figure 5.14 to match each action with its result. A given action may be used more than once or not at all.

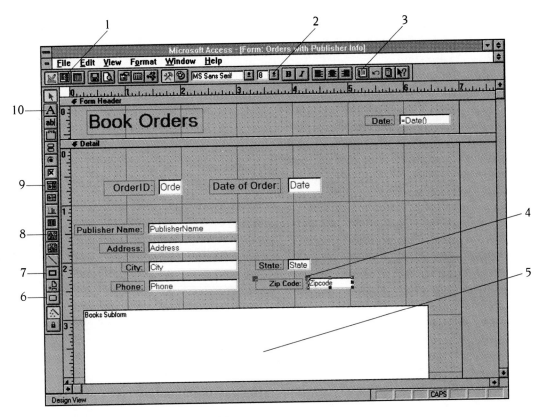

FIGURE 5.14 Screen for Problem 1

Action	Result
a. Click at 1	___ Add a command button to the form
b. Click at 2	___ Change to the Form view
c. Click at 3	___ Draw an object frame on the form for a graphic
d. Click and drag at 4	___ Change the font size for the selected control
e. Click the right mouse button at 5	___ Establish the linking fields for the main form and the subform
f. Click at 6	___ Move the selected control
g. Click at 7	___ Switch to the Database window
h. Click at 8	___ Add the name of the book store to the form
i. Click at 9	___ Draw a box around the OrderID and Date of Order controls
j. Click at 10	___ Create a combo box for the Publisher's Name

2. Relationships and referential integrity: Answer the following with respect to the Relationships window in Figure 5.15 :

    a. What relationships are shown in Figure 5.15?

    b. What is the primary key in the Students table? in the Courses table? How is this indicated in the diagram?

    c. What is the primary key in the Student Course table? Does this key permit a student to repeat a course?

    d. What foreign keys (if any) are present in the Students table? in the Courses table? in the Student Course table?

    e. Can you add a student to the Students table who hasn't taken any courses?

    f. Can you add a course to the Courses table prior to students enrolling in that course?

    g. Under what circumstances can you delete a student from the Students table and simultaneously delete the courses taken by that student from the Student Course table?

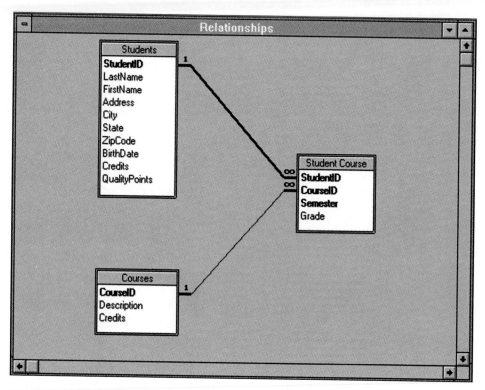

FIGURE 5.15 Screen for Problem 2

3. The database in Figure 5.16 is intended to monitor information about doctors and patients in an HMO.

    a. What is the primary key in the Patients table? in the Doctors table? in the Visits table?

    b. Which table(s) has a foreign key?

    c. Assume that referential integrity is enforced without cascading of any kind. Can you delete a record in the Patients table? in the Doctors table? in the Visits table?

    d. Use the data in the figure to answer the following questions.

        i. List all visits for Heather Warren, showing the doctor's name, complaint, and amount charged for each visit

(a) Patients Table

Patient ID	First Name	Last Name	Address	City	State	Zip Code	Phone Number	Birth Date	Sex
P001	Karen	Kinzer	5600 West 29 Court	Ft. Lauderdale	FL	33305	(305) 561-5347	07/02/65	F
P002	Brett	Gibson	9200 S.W. 142 Street	Miami	FL	33176	(305) 235-0506	05/01/90	M
P003	Matthew	Karlaftis	425 Segovia Avenue	Coral Gables	FL	33124	(305) 443-8976	02/03/47	M
P004	Daniel	Passacantilli	1200 Brickell Boulevard	Miami	FL	33021	(305) 595-0090	06/15/88	M
P005	Heather	Warren	7890 N.E. 71 Street	Miami	FL	33075	(305) 271-8008	09/30/55	F
P006	Rocio	Diaz	875 West 7 Street	Hialeah	FL	33390	(305) 874-6676	10/05/93	F
P007	Sandra	Anon	6220 Miracle Mile	Coral Gables	FL	33124	(305 284-6629	12/22/68	F
P008	William	Blaney	4777 S.W. 88 Street	Miami	FL	33152	(305)385-6656	04/18/25	M
P009	Rozelle	Marder	922 Queen Avenue	Hialeah	FL	33395	(305) 874-3309	05/31/87	F
P010	Florence	Hecht	1120 Main Highway	Coconut Grove	FL	33130	(305) 854-6789	08/22/41	F
P011	Frank	Costa	1210 Brickell Boulevard	Miami	FL	33021	(305) 595-2202	03/15/94	M
P012	Pat	Conroy	5090 South Island Road	Miami	FL	33021	(305) 595-7878	11/11/52	M
P013	Michelle	Lopez	8888 Kendall Drive	Miami	FL	33156	(305) 274-5665	12/02/72	F

(a) Patients Table

(b) Doctors Table

Doctor ID	First Name	Last Name	Address	City	State	Zip Code	Phone Number	Fax	Specialty
D001	Kenneth	Ficker	8700 S.W. 144 Street	Miami	FL	33156	(305) 235-5585	(305) 235-5590	Pediatrics
D002	Grace	Wolfe	2445 N.W. 12 Avenue	Miami	FL	33120	(305) 444-8990	(305) 444-9000	Cardiology
D003	Daniel	McLeod	9225 S.W. 88 Street	Miami	FL	33165	(305) 274-5500	(305) 274-5600	Obstetrics
D004	Phillip	Paul	8700 S.W. 144 Street	Miami	FL	33156	(305) 235-5585	(305) 235-5590	Pediatrics
D005	Victor	Dembrow	1415 N.W. 12 Avenue	Miami	FL	33120	(305) 446-6200	(305) 446-6205	General Practice

(b) Doctors Table

(c) Visits Table

Patient ID	Doctor ID	Visit Date	Complaint	Diagnosis	Lab Work	Amount	Paid
P002	D001	01/12/94	Annual Checkup	Annual Checkup	2	$145.00	No
P013	D003	01/12/94	Sore Throat	Pregnancy	3	$195.00	Yes
P012	D005	02/01/94	Fever/Aches	Flu	1	$95.00	No
P004	D004	02/03/94	Annual Checkup	Annual Checkup	2	$145.00	Yes
P008	D005	02/12/94	Sore Throat	Strep Throat	1	$95.00	Yes
P008	D005	02/19/94	Sore Throat	Strep Throat	0	$45.00	No
P010	D002	03/01/94	Chest Pains	Irregular Heart	1	$95.00	Yes
P001	D003	03/05/94	Pregnancy	Pregnancy	1	$95.00	Yes
P013	D003	03/12/94	Pregnancy	Pregnancy	3	$195.00	Yes
P002	D004	03/15/94	Fever	Flu	1	$95.00	Yes
P012	D005	03/15/94	Twisted Ankle	Broken Ankle	0	$45.00	Yes
P002	D004	03/21/94	Fever Follow-up	No follow up needed	0	$0.00	No
P005	D002	04/01/94	Chest Pains	Anxiety	3	$195.00	No
P001	D005	04/05/94	Sore Throat	Mild Flu Symptoms	1	$95.00	Yes
P007	D003	04/18/94	Nausea	Flu	1	$95.00	Yes
P003	D002	05/01/94	Palpitations	Cardiac Disease	3	$195.00	No
P005	D005	05/01/94	Fever	Flu	0	$45.00	Yes
P009	D004	05/01/94	Annual Checkup	Annual Checkup	2	$145.00	No
P001	D003	05/05/94	Pregnancy	Pregnancy	1	$95.00	Yes
P013	D003	05/12/94	Pregnancy	Pregnancy	3	$195.00	Yes
P003	D002	05/15/94	Palpitations	Cardiac Disease	0	$45.00	Yes
P011	D001	05/31/94	Well Baby Checkup	Well Baby Checkup	0	$45.00	No
P001	D003	06/05/94	Pregnancy	Pregnancy	1	$95.00	Yes
P010	D005	06/12/94	Annual Checkup	Annual Checkup	3	$195.00	Yes

(c) Visits Table

FIGURE 5.16 Tables for Problem 3

ii. When was Heather Warren's last visit?

iii. How much has Heather Warren paid to the HMO in 1994?

e. Use the HMO.MDB database on the data disk to create select queries for each question in part d. Print the dynaset for each query.

f. Create a report that lists the name, address, and telephone number for every patient in the database. List the patients in alphabetical order.

4. Use the Unmatched Query Wizard to tell management which products (if any) have not appeared in a single order.

a. Open the SUPRSTOR database. Click the Query button in the Database window. Click the New command button, then click Query Wizards. Choose Find Unmatched Query as the wizard you want and click OK.

b. Choose Products as the table whose records you want to see and click the Next command button.

c. Choose Order Details as the related table. Click the Next button.

d. ProductID is automatically selected as the related field. Click the Next command button.

e. Select every field from the Available Fields list. Click the Next command button.

f. Click the Finish command button to see the results of the query. What advice will you give to management regarding unnecessary inventory?

5. Expanding the database: Figure 5.17 contains a modified version of the Super Store Order Form created in the second hands-on exercise. The form has been modified to include the SalesPersonID, which is made necessary by inclusion of the Sales Staff table at the end of the chapter.

a. Modify the underlying query (Order with Customer Info) by including the SalesPersonID from the Orders table.

b. Run the modified query to make sure that the SalesPersonID is displayed in the dynaset.

c. Open the existing Super Store Order Form in the Design view.

d. Pull down the View menu. Click Field List to display the field list of the modified query, which now contains the SalesPersonID.

e. Drag the SalesPersonID field from the field list to the form.

f. Move and size the controls and add color as shown in Figure 5.17. Change the tab order as necessary. Save the form.

g. Import the Sales Staff form from the SALESSTF.MDB into the SUPRSTOR.MDB. Use that form to add Adam Moldof (305 755-6666) as a new sales associate with SalesPersonID S06. Use today's date as the date of hire.

h. Use the modified Order form to enter a new order (O0401) for customer C0004 for one unit each of products P0007, P1002, and P2055. Give Adam Moldof credit for this order by entering a SalesPersonID of S06.

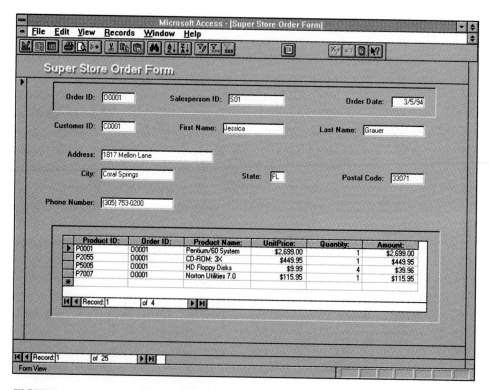

FIGURE 5.17 Screen for Problem 5

i. Rerun the Sales Commission Report of Figure 5.12 (which will now include Adam Moldof). Print the report and submit it to your instructor.

6. Combo boxes: Expand upon the form in problem 5 to include a combo box to choose the SalesPersonID from the drop-down list of names as shown in Figure 5.18. The combo box is different from the ones created earlier because it consists of two columns. Follow the steps below to create the combo box shown in the figure.

   a. Delete the control for the SalesPersonID and its associated label.

   b. Click the Combo box tool on the Toolbox. Click and drag in the form where you want the combo box to go. Release the mouse.

   c. You will see the first screen in the Combo Box Wizard. Check the option that indicates you want to look up values in a table or query. Click the Next command button.

   d. Choose the Sales Staff table in the next screen. Click the Next command button.

   e. Select the SalesPersonID and LastName from the Available fields list box for inclusion in the Combo box columns list. Click the Next command button.

   f. Adjust the column widths. Click the Next command button.

   g. Choose SalesPersonID as the column containing the value you want to store in the database.

   h. Click the option button to store the value in the field. Select the Sales-PersonID field. Click the Next command button.

   i. Type Salesperson: as the label for the combo box. Click the Finish command button.

   j. Point to the combo box, click the right mouse button to display a short-cut menu, and click Properties. Change the name of the box to Sales Person.

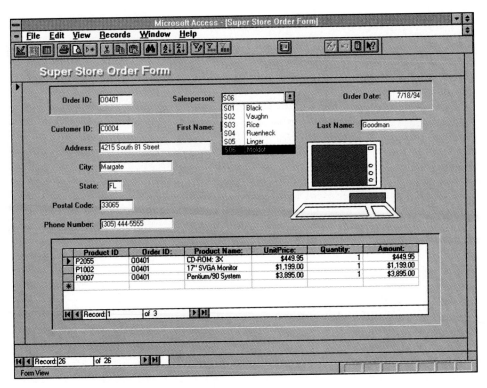

FIGURE 5.18   Screen for Problem 6

k. Pull down the Edit menu and click Tab Order to change the tab order so that the box is accessed in sequence.

l. Change the color of the controls as shown in the figure. Add a graphic to complete the form.

7. Repeat the steps in problem 6 to create a two-column combo box to display the ProductID and associated Product Name in the subform of Figure 5.18. When you complete problems 5, 6, and 7, you will have a truly powerful form that relates data from five tables to one another.

8. Back to the bookstore: The form in Figure 5.19 is based on the college bookstore described at the end of Chapter 1.

a. Which tables are in the database? What is the primary key in each table?

b. What are the relationships between the tables?

c. Is the main form based on a query or a table?

d. Is the subform based on a query or a table?

e. Open the BOOKPROB.MDB database on the data disk and create the form in Figure 5.19.

f. Add your name to the form as the Bookstore Manager. Print the order form in Figure 5.19 and submit it to your instructor.

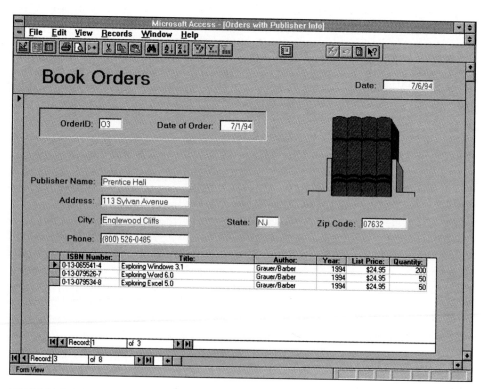

FIGURE 5.19   Screen for Problem 8

Case Studies

Medical Research

Design a database for a medical research project that will track specific volunteers and/or specific studies. A study will require several subjects, but a specific person may participate in only one study. The system should also be able to track physicians. Many physicians can work on the same study. A given physician may also work on multiple studies.

The system should be able to display all facts about a particular volunteer (subject) such as the name, birth date, sex, height, weight, blood pressure, cholesterol level, and so on. It should be able to display all characteristics associated with a particular study—for example, the title, beginning date, ending date, as well as the names of all physicians who work on that study. It should also show whether the physician is a primary or secondary investigator in each study.

Show the required tables in the database, being sure to indicate the primary key and foreign keys in each table. Indicate additional fields in each table as appropriate (you need not list them all).

The Stockbroker

You have been hired as a consultant to a securities firm that wants to track its clients and the stocks they own. The firm prides itself on its research and maintains a detailed file for the stocks it follows. Among the data for each stock are its symbol (ideal for the primary key), the industry it is in, its earnings, dividend, and so on.

The firm requires the usual client data (name, address, phone number, social security number, etc.). One client can hold many different stocks, and the same stock can be held by different clients. The firm needs to know the date the client purchased the stock, the number of shares that were purchased, and the purchase price.

Show the required tables in the database, being sure to indicate the primary key and foreign keys in each table. Indicate additional fields in each table (you need not list them all).

The Video Store

You have been hired as a database consultant to the local video store, which rents and/or sells tapes to customers. The store maintains the usual information about every customer (name, address, phone number, and so on). It also has detailed information about every movie such as its duration, rating, rental price, and purchase price. One customer can rent several tapes, and the same tape will (over time) be rented to many customers.

The owner of the store needs a detailed record of every rental that identifies the movie, the customer, the date the rental was made, and the number of days the customer may keep the movie without penalty.

Class Scheduling

Class scheduling represents a major undertaking at any university. It entails the coordination of course offerings as published in a registration schedule together with faculty assignments. All courses have a formal title but are more commonly known by a six-position course-id. Microcomputer Applications, for example, is better known as CIS120. The first three characters in the course-id denote the department (e.g., CIS stands for Computer Information Systems). The last three indicate the particular course.

The university may offer multiple sections of any given course at different times. CIS120, for example, is offered at four different times: at 9:00, 10:00, 11:00, and 12:00, with all sections meeting three days a week (Mondays, Wednesdays, and Fridays). The information about when a class meets is summarized in the one-letter section designation; for example, section A meets from 9:00 to 9:50 on Mondays, Wednesdays, and Fridays.

The published schedule should list every section of every course together with the days, times, and room assignments. It should also display the complete course title, number of credits, and the name of the faculty member assigned to that section. It should be able to list all classes taught by a particular faculty member or all sections of a particular course. Design a relational database to satisfy these requirements.

Appendix A:
Database Design: Getting the Most from Microsoft Access

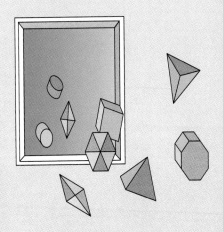

OVERVIEW

An Access database consists of multiple tables. Each table in the database stores data about a specific subject. To use Access effectively, you must relate the tables to one another. To do so requires a knowledge of database design and an understanding of the principles of a relational database under which Access operates.

Our approach to teaching database design is to present two *case studies*, each of which covers a common application. (Additional case studies are presented in Chapters 4 and 5.) The first case centers on franchises for fast-food restaurants and incorporates the concept of a one-to-many relationship. One person can own many restaurants, but a given restaurant is owned by only one person. The second case is based on a system for student transcripts and incorporates a many-to-many relationship. One student takes many courses, and one course is taken by many students.

Each case study is introduced by a case preview to familiarize you with the essential elements of the case. The intent in both cases is to design a database capable of producing the desired information.

CASE PREVIEW: FAST-FOOD FRANCHISES

The case you are about to read is set within the context of a national corporation offering franchises for fast-food restaurants. The concept of a franchise operation is a familiar one and exists within many industries. The parent organization develops a model operation, then franchises that concept to qualified individuals (franchisees) seeking to operate their own businesses. The national company teaches the franchisee to run the business, aids the person in site selection and staffing, coordinates national advertising, and so on. The franchisee pays an initial fee to open the business, followed by subsequent royalties and marketing fees to the parent corporation.

The essence of the case is how to relate the data for the various entities or subjects—that is, the *restaurants*, *franchisees*, and *contracts*—to one another. One approach is to develop a single restaurant table, with each restaurant record containing data about the owner and contract arrangement. As we shall see, that design leads to problems of **redundancy** whenever the same person owns more than one restaurant or when several restaurants are governed by the same contract type. A better approach is to develop separate tables, one for each of the objects (restaurants, franchisees, and contracts).

The objects in the case have a definite relationship to one another, which must be reflected in the database design. The corporation encourages individuals to own multiple restaurants, creating a **one-to-many relationship** between franchisees and restaurants. In similar fashion, each restaurant is governed by one of three contract types, producing a second one-to-many relationship between contracts and restaurants.

CASE STUDY

Fast-Food Franchises

The management of a national chain is seeking to automate its restaurant, franchisee, and contract data. The company wants a database that can retrieve all data for a given restaurant such as the annual sales, type of contract in effect (contract types are described below), and/or detailed information about the restaurant owner. The company also needs reports that reflect the location of each restaurant, all restaurants in a given state, and all restaurants managed by a particular contract type. The various contract arrangements are described below:

> **Contract 1:** 99-year term, requiring a one-time fee of $250,000 payable at the time the franchise is awarded. In addition, the franchisee must pay a royalty of 2 percent of the restaurant's gross sales to the parent corporation, and contribute an additional 2 percent of sales to the parent corporation for advertising.

> **Contract 2:** 5-year term (renewable at franchisee's option), requiring an initial payment of $50,000. In addition, the franchisee must pay a royalty of 4 percent of the restaurant's gross sales to the parent corporation, and contribute an additional 3 percent of sales to the parent corporation for advertising.

> **Contract 3:** 10-year term (renewable at franchisee's option), requiring an initial payment of $75,000. In addition, the franchisee must pay a royalty of 3 percent of the restaurant's gross sales to the parent corporation, and contribute an additional 3 percent of sales to the parent corporation for advertising.

Other contract types may be offered in the future. The company currently has 500 restaurants, of which 200 are company owned. Expansion plans call for opening an additional 200 restaurants each year for the next three years, all of which are to be franchised. There is no limit on the number of restaurants an individual may own, and franchisees are encouraged to apply for multiple restaurants.

Design a database to accommodate all of the above, and in addition enable the company to do all of the following:

Single Table Solution

The initial concern in this, or any other, system is how best to structure the data so that the solution satisfies the information requirements of the client. We present two solutions. The first is based on a single restaurant table and will be shown to have several limitations. The second introduces the concept of a relational database and consists of three tables (for the restaurants, franchisees, and contracts).

The single table solution is shown in Figure A.1a. Each record within the table contains data about a particular restaurant, its franchisee (owner), and contract type. There are five restaurants in our example, each with a *unique* restaurant number. At first glance, Figure A.1a appears to satisfy the case requirements, yet there are three specific types of problems associated with this solution:

1. Difficulties in the changing of data for an existing franchisee or contract type.
2. Difficulties in the addition of a new franchisee or contract type, in that these entities must first be associated with a particular restaurant.
3. Difficulties in the deletion of a restaurant, in that data for a particular franchisee or contract type may be deleted as well.

The first problem, modification of data about an existing franchisee or contract type, stems from redundancy, which in turn requires that any change to duplicated data be made in several places. In other words, any modification to a duplicated entry, such as a change in data for a franchisee with multiple restaurants (e.g., Grauer, who owns restaurants in Miami and Fort Lauderdale), requires a search through the entire table to find *all* instances of that data so that the *identical modification* can be made to each of the records. A similar procedure would have to be followed should data change about a duplicated contract (e.g., a change in the royalty percentage for contract type 1, which applies to restaurants R1, R2, and R4). This is, to say the least, a time-consuming and error-prone procedure.

Restaurant Number	Restaurant Data (Address, annual sales . . .)	Franchisee Data (Name, telephone, address . . .)	Contract Data (Type, term, initial fee . . .)
R1	Restaurant data for Miami . . .	Franchisee data (Grauer . . .)	Contract data (Type 1 . . .)
R2	Restaurant data for Coral Gables . . .	Franchisee data (Moldof . . .)	Contract data (Type 1 . . .)
R3	Restaurant data for Fort Lauderdale . . .	Franchisee data (Grauer . . .)	Contract data (Type 2 . . .)
R4	Restaurant data for New York . . .	Franchisee data (Glassman . . .)	Contract data (Type 1 . . .)
R5	Restaurant data for Coral Springs . . .	Franchisee data (Coulter . . .)	Contract data (Type 3 . . .)

(a) Single Table Solution

FIGURE A.1 Single versus Multiple Table Solution

The addition of a new franchisee or contract type poses a different type of problem. It is quite logical, for example, that potential franchisees must qualify for ownership *prior* to having a restaurant assigned to them. It is also likely that the corporation would develop a new contract type *prior* to offering that contract to an existing restaurant. Neither of these events is easily accommodated in the table structure of Figure A.1a, which would require the creation of a "dummy" restaurant record to accommodate the new franchisee or contract type.

The deletion of a restaurant creates yet another type of difficulty. What happens, for example, if the company decides to close restaurant R5 because of insufficient sales? The record for this restaurant would disappear as expected, but so too would the data for the franchisee (Coulter) and the contract type (C3). The corporation might want to award Coulter another restaurant in the future and/or offer this contract type to other restaurants. Neither situation is possible as the relevant data has been lost with the deletion of the restaurant record.

Multiple Table Solution

A much better solution appears in Figure A.1b, which uses a different table for each of the entities (restaurants, franchisees, and contracts). Every record in the restaurant table is assigned a unique restaurant number (e.g., R1 or R2), just as every record in the franchisee table is given a unique franchisee number (e.g., F1 or F2) and every contract record a unique contract number (e.g., C1 or C2).

The tables are linked to one another through the franchisee and/or contract numbers, which also appear in the restaurant table. Every record in the restaurant table is associated with its appropriate record in the franchisee table through the franchisee number common to both tables. In similar fashion, every restaurant is tied to its appropriate contract through the contract number, which appears in the

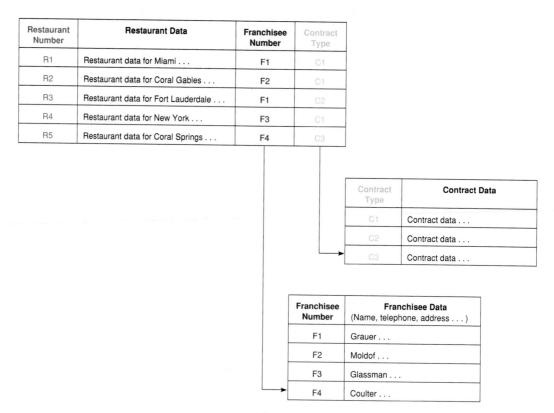

Restaurant Number	Restaurant Data	Franchisee Number	Contract Type
R1	Restaurant data for Miami . . .	F1	C1
R2	Restaurant data for Coral Gables . . .	F2	C1
R3	Restaurant data for Fort Lauderdale . . .	F1	C2
R4	Restaurant data for New York . . .	F3	C1
R5	Restaurant data for Coral Springs . . .	F4	C3

Contract Type	Contract Data
C1	Contract data . . .
C2	Contract data . . .
C3	Contract data . . .

Franchisee Number	Franchisee Data (Name, telephone, address . . .)
F1	Grauer . . .
F2	Moldof . . .
F3	Glassman . . .
F4	Coulter . . .

(b) Multiple Table Solution

FIGURE A.1   Single versus Multiple Table Solution (continued)

restaurant record. This solution may seem complicated, but it is really quite simple and elegant.

Assume, for example, that we want the name of the franchisee for restaurant R5, and further, that we need the details of the contract type for this restaurant. We retrieve the appropriate restaurant record, which contains franchisee and contract numbers of F4 and C3, respectively. We then search through the franchisee table for franchisee F4 (obtaining all necessary information about Coulter) and search again through the contract table for contract C3 (obtaining the data for this contract type). The process is depicted graphically in Figure A.1b.

The multiple table solution may require slightly more effort to retrieve information, but this is more than offset by advantages of table maintenance. Consider, for example, a change in data for contract type 1, which currently governs restaurants R1, R2, and R4. All that is necessary is to go into the contract table, find record C1, and make the changes. The records in the restaurant table are *not* affected because the restaurant records do not contain contract data per se, only the number of the corresponding contract record. In other words, the change in data for contract type 1 is made in one place (the contract table), yet that change would be reflected for all affected restaurants. This is in contrast to the single table solution of Figure A.1a, which would require the identical modification in three places.

The addition of new records for franchisees or contracts is done immediately in the appropriate tables of Figure A.1b. The corporation simply adds a franchisee or contract record as these events occur, without the necessity of a corresponding restaurant record. This is much easier than the approach of Figure A.1a, which required an existing restaurant in order to add one of the other entities.

The deletion of a restaurant is also easier than with the single table organization. You could, for example, delete restaurant R5 without losing the associated franchisee and contract data as these records exist in different tables.

Queries to the Database

By now you should be convinced of the need for multiple tables within a database and that this type of design facilitates all types of table maintenance. However, the ultimate objective of any system is to produce information, and it is in this area that the design excels. Consider now Figure A.2, which expands upon the multiple table solution to include additional data for the respective tables.

To be absolutely sure you understand the multiple table solution of Figure A.2, use it to answer the following questions. Check your answers with those provided.

QUESTIONS
1. Who owns restaurant R2? What contract type is in effect for this restaurant?
2. What is the address of restaurant R4?
3. Which restaurants are owned by Mr. Grauer?
4. List all restaurants with a contract type of C1.
5. Which restaurants in Florida have gross sales over $300,000?
6. List all contract types.
7. Which contract type has the lowest initial fee? How much is the initial fee? Which restaurant is governed by this contract?
8. How many franchisees are there? What are their names?
9. What are the royalty and advertising percentages for restaurant R3?

1. Restaurant R2 is owned by Moldof and governed by contract C1.
2. Restaurant R4 is located at 1700 Broadway, New York, NY 10293.
3. Mr. Grauer owns restaurants R1 and R3.
4. R1, R2, and R4 are governed by contract type C1.
5. The restaurants in Florida with gross sales over $300,000 are R1 ($600,000) and R2 ($450,000).
6. The existing contract types are C1, C2, and C3.
7. Contract type C2 has the lowest initial fee ($50,000); restaurant R3 is governed by this contract type.
8. There are four franchisees: Grauer, Moldof, Glassman, and Coulter.
9. Restaurant R3 is governed by contract C2, with royalty and advertising expenses of 4 and 3 percent, respectively.

Restaurant Number	Street Address	City	State	Zip Code	Annual Sales	Franchisee Number	Contract Type
R1	1001 Ponce de Leon Blvd	Miami	FL	33361	$600,000	F1	C1
R2	31 West Rivo Alto Road	Coral Gables	FL	33139	$450,000	F2	C1
R3	333 Las Olas Blvd	Fort Lauderdale	FL	33033	$250,000	F1	C2
R4	1700 Broadway	New York	NY	10293	$1,750,000	F3	C1
R5	1300 Sample Road	Coral Springs	FL	33071	$50,000	F4	C3

(a) Restaurant Table

Franchisee Number	Franchisee Name	Telephone	Street Address	City	State	Zip Code
F1	Grauer	(305) 755-1000	2133 NW 102 Terrace	Coral Springs	FL	33071
F2	Moldof	(305) 753-4614	1400 Le Jeune Blvd	Miami	FL	33365
F3	Glassman	(212) 458-5054	555 Fifth Avenue	New York	NY	10024
F4	Coulter	(305) 755-0910	1000 Federal Highway	Fort Lauderdale	FL	33033

(b) Franchisee Table

Contract Type	Term (years)	Initial Fee	Royalty Pct	Advertising Pct
C1	99	$250,000	2%	2%
C2	5	$50,000	4%	3%
C1	10	$75,000	3%	3%

(c) Contract Table

FIGURE A.2 Fast-Food Franchises

THE RELATIONAL MODEL

A *relational database* requires a separate *table* for every entity in a physical system (restaurants, franchisees, and contracts). Each occurrence of an *entity* (a specific restaurant, franchisee, or contract type) appears as a *row* within a table. The properties of an entity (a restaurant's address, owner, or sales) appear as *columns* within a table.

Every row in every table of a relational database must be distinct. This is accomplished by including a column (or combination of columns) to uniquely identify the row. The unique identifier is known as the *primary key.* The restaurant number, for example, is different for every restaurant in the restaurant table. The franchisee number is unique in the franchisee table. The contract type is unique in the contract table.

The same column can, however, appear in multiple tables. The franchisee number, for example, appears in both the franchisee table, where its values are unique, and in the restaurant table, where they are not. The franchisee number is the primary key in the franchisee table, but it is a *foreign key* in the restaurant table. (A foreign key is simply the primary key of a related table.)

The inclusion of a foreign key in the restaurant table enables us to implement the one-to-many relationship between franchisees and restaurants. We enter the franchisee number (the primary key in the franchisee table) as a column in the restaurant table, where it (the franchisee number) is a foreign key. In similar fashion, contract type (the primary key in the contract table) appears as a foreign key in the restaurant table to implement the one-to-many relationship between contracts and restaurants.

It is helpful, perhaps, to restate these observations about a relational database in general terms:

1. Every entity in a physical system requires its own table in a database.
2. Each row in a table is different because of a unique column (or combination of columns) known as a primary key.
3. The primary key of one table can appear as a foreign key in another table.
4. The order of rows in a table is immaterial.
5. The order of columns in a table is immaterial, although the primary key is generally listed first.
6. The number of columns is the same in every row of the table.

Referential Integrity

The concept of *referential integrity* requires that the tables in a database be consistent with one another. Consider once again the first row in the restaurant table of Figure A.2a, which indicates that the restaurant is owned by franchisee F1 and governed by contract type C1. Recall also how these values are used to obtain additional information about the franchisee or contract type from the appropriate tables in Figures A.2b and A.2c, respectively.

What if, however, the restaurant table referred to franchisee number F1000 or contract type C9, neither of which exists in the database of Figure A.2? We would have a problem because the tables are inconsistent with one another; that is, the restaurant table refers to rows in the franchisee and contract tables that do not exist. Suffice it to say, therefore, that data validation is critical when establishing or maintaining a database, and that no system, relational or otherwise, can compensate for inaccurate or incomplete data.

CASE PREVIEW: STUDENT TRANSCRIPTS

Our second case is set within the context of student transcripts and expands the concept of a relational database to implement a ***many-to-many relationship.*** The system is intended to track students and their courses. The many-to-many relationship occurs because one student takes many courses, while at the same time, one course is taken by many students. The objective of this case is to relate the student and course tables to one another to produce desired information. The database must be able to answer queries about a particular student or course, as well as list all courses taken by one student or all students in one course.

CASE STUDY

Student Transcripts

The registrar of a major university is seeking to convert its enrollment and course data to a relational database in order to facilitate on-line registration. The student table will contain the student's name, address, major, date of entry into the school, cumulative credits, and cumulative quality points. The course table is to contain the unique six-character course identifier, the course title, and the number of credits.

The system should be able to display information about a particular student as well as information about a particular course. It should also display information about a student-course combination such as when a student took the course and the grade he or she received.

Design a database to accommodate all of the above, being sure to indicate which columns are unique. Your solution should enable a user to, at a minimum, do all of the following:

1. List all courses currently offered in alphabetical order by course identifier
2. List all courses taken by a particular student
3. List all students in alphabetical order
4. List all students who took a specific course in a specific semester
5. List all students who received an A in a specific course regardless of when the course was taken
6. Display the course description of a particular course
7. List all four-credit courses

Solution

The initial solution of Figure A.3 consists of two tables, one for courses and one for students, corresponding to the two entities in the physical system. There are no problems of redundancy. The data for a particular course (its title and number of credits) appears only once in the course table, just as the data for a particular student appears only once in the student table. New courses will be added directly to the course table, just as new students will be added to the student table.

The design of the student table makes it easy to list all courses for one student. It is more difficult, however, to list all students in one course. Even if this were not the case, the solution is complicated by the irregular shape of the student table. The rows in the table are of variable length, according to the number of courses taken by each student. Not only is this design awkward, but how do we know in advance how much space to allocate for each student?

Course Number	Course Title	Credits
ACC101	Introduction to Accounting	3
CHM100	Survey of Chemistry	3
CHM101	Chemistry Lab	1
CIS120	Microcomputer Applications	3
ENG100	Freshman English	3
MTH100	Calculus with Analytic Geometry	4
MUS110	Music Appreciation	2
SPN100	Spanish I	3

(a) Course Table

Student Number	Student Data	Courses taken, with grade and semester														
S1	Student data (Adams . . .)	ACC101	SP94	A	CIS120	FA93	A	MU100	SP93	B						
S2	Student data (Fox . . .)	ENG100	SP94	B	MTH100	SP94	B	SPN100	SP94	B	CIS120	FA93	A			
S3	Student data (Baker . . .)	ACC101	SP94	C	ENG100	SP94	B	MTH100	FA93	C	CIS120	FA93	B			
S4	Student data (Jones . . .)	ENG100	SP94	A	MTH100	SP94	A									
S5	Student data (Smith . . .)	CIS120	SP94	C	ENG100	SP94	B	CIS120	FA93	F						

(b) Student Table

FIGURE A.3   Registration System (repeating groups)

The problems inherent in Figure A.3 stem from the many-to-many relationship that exists between students and courses. The solution is to eliminate the *repeating groups* (course number, semester, and grade), which occur in each row of the student table in Figure A.3, in favor of the additional table shown in Figure A.4. Each row in the new table is unique because the *combination* of student number, course number, and semester is unique. Semester must be included since students are allowed to repeat a course. Smith (student number S5), for example, took CIS120 a second time after failing it initially.

The implementation of a many-to-many relationship requires an additional table, with a **combined key** consisting of (at least) the keys of the individual entities. The many-to-many table may also contain additional columns that exist as a result of the combination of the individual keys. The combination of student S5, course CIS120, and semester SP94 is unique and results in a grade of C.

Note, too, how the design in Figure A.4 facilitates table maintenance as discussed in the previous case. A change in student data is made in only one place (the student table) regardless of how many courses the student has taken. A new student may be added to the student table prior to taking any courses. In similar fashion, a new course can be added to the course table before any students have taken the course.

To be absolutely sure that you understand the solution, and to illustrate once again the power of the relational model, use Figure A.4 to answer the following questions about the student database.

QUESTIONS
1. How many courses are currently offered?
2. List all three-credit courses.
3. Which courses has Smith taken during his stay at the university?
4. Which students have taken MTH100?
5. Which courses did Adams take during the Fall 1993 semester?

Course Number	Course Title	Credits
ACC101	Introduction to Accounting	3
CHM100	Survey of Chemistry	3
CHM101	Chemistry Lab	1
CIS120	Microcomputer Applications	3
ENG100	Freshman English	3
MTH100	Calculus with Analytic Geometry	4
MUS110	Music Appreciation	2
SPN100	Spanish I	3

(a) Course Table

Student Number	Student Data
S1	Student data (Adams . . .)
S2	Student data (Fox . . .)
S3	Student data (Baker . . .)
S4	Student data (Jones . . .)
S5	Student data (Smith . . .)

(b) Student Table

Student Number	Course Number	Semester	Grade
S1	ACC101	SP94	A
S1	CIS120	FA93	A
S1	MU100	SP93	B
S2	ENG100	SP94	B
S2	MTH100	SP94	B
S2	SPN100	SP94	B
S2	CIS120	FA93	A
S3	ACC101	SP94	C
S3	ENG100	SP94	B
S3	MTH100	FA93	C
S3	CIS120	FA93	B
S4	ENG100	SP94	A
S4	MTH100	SP94	A
S5	CIS120	SP94	C
S5	ENG100	SP94	B
S5	CIS120	FA93	F

(c) Student-Course Table

FIGURE A.4   Registration System (improved design)

6. Which students took Microcomputer Applications in the Fall 1993 semester?
7. Which students received an A in Freshman English during the Spring 1994 semester?

ANSWERS

1. Eight courses are offered.
2. The three-credit courses are: ACC101, CHM100, CIS120, ENG100, and SPN100.
3. Smith has taken CIS120 (twice) and ENG100.
4. Fox, Baker, and Jones have taken MTH100.
5. Adams took CIS120 during the Fall 1993 semester.
6. Adams, Fox, Baker, and Smith took Microcomputer Applications in the Fall 1993 semester.
7. Jones was the only student to receive an A in Freshman English during the Spring 1994 semester.

SUMMARY

A relational database consists of multiple two-dimensional tables. Each entity in a physical system requires its own table in the database. Every row in a table is unique due to the existence of a primary key. The order of the rows and columns in a table is immaterial. Every row in a table contains the same columns in the same order.

A one-to-many relationship is implemented by including the primary key of one table as a foreign key in the other table. Implementation of a many-to-many relationship requires an additional table whose primary key combines (at a minimum) the primary keys of the individual tables. Referential integrity ensures that the information in a database is internally consistent.

THE KEY, THE WHOLE KEY, AND NOTHING BUT THE KEY

The theory of a relational database was developed by *Dr. Edgar Codd*, giving rise to the phrase, *"The key, the whole key, and nothing but the key . . . so help me Codd."* The sentence effectively summarizes the concepts behind a relational database and helps to ensure the validity of a design. Simply stated, the value of every column other than the primary key depends on the key in that row, on the entire key, and on nothing but that key.

Key Words and Concepts

Column	One-to-many relationship	Repeating group
Combined key	Primary key	Row
Entity	Redundancy	Table
Foreign key	Referential integrity	
Many-to-many relationship	Relational database	

Case Studies

One-to-many Relationships

Chapter 4 focuses on one-to-many relationships and develops a case study for consumer loans. The database is designed at the beginning of the chapter, then implemented in Access through four hands-on exercises. Four additional case studies appear at the end of the chapter (pages 172–174) and provide additional practice in database design.

Many-to-many Relationships

Chapter 5 focuses on many-to-many relationships and develops a case study for a computer store. The database is designed at the beginning of the chapter, then implemented in Access through four hands-on exercises. Four additional case studies appear at the end of the chapter (pages 226–228) and provide additional practice in database design.

Appendix B: Toolbars

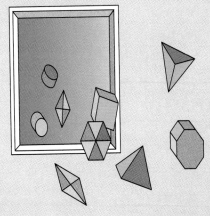

Microsoft Access 2.0 offers eighteen predefined toolbars to provide access to commonly used commands. Thirteen of the toolbars are tied to a specific view, and are displayed automatically when you work in that view. Eleven of the thirteen are displayed in Figure B.1 and are listed here for convenience:

Database   Form Design
Relationships   Form View
Table Design   Report Design
Table Datasheet   Print Preview
Query Design   Filter/Sort
Query Datasheet

The Macro and Module toolbars are not displayed as they are beyond the scope of this text. The remaining five toolbars are not tied to a specific view and can be displayed when needed. They are:

Toolbox
Palette
Utility 1
Utility 2
Microsoft

These are displayed in Figure B.2. The Toolbox and Palette are typically used in the design of forms and reports. The Utility 1 and Utility 2 toolbars are used to create custom toolbars that can be displayed with any database. The Microsoft toolbar is used to quickly access other Microsoft applications.

The icons on the toolbars are intended to be indicative of their function. For example, clicking on the printer executes the Print command. If you are unsure of the purpose of any icon, point to it, and a Tool Tip will appear that displays its name.

You can display multiple toolbars at one time, move them to new locations on the screen, customize their appearance, or suppress their display. The name of a toolbar is displayed in the far left corner of the status bar when you point to the toolbar.

➤ To display or hide a toolbar, pull down the View menu and click Toolbars. Select the toolbar to be displayed (hidden) and click the Show (Hide) command button to display (hide) the toolbar. You can continue to display (hide) additional toolbars until you click the Close command button. The selected toolbar(s) will be displayed in the same position as when last displayed. Note that when you explicitly show a predefined toolbar, it is displayed in every view. In similar fashion, when you explicitly hide a predefined toolbar from within its default view, it will remain hidden in every view.

Alternatively, you may point to any toolbar and click with the right mouse button to bring up a shortcut menu. You may then select the Toolbars command or toggle on/off the listed toolbars, which include the toolbar appropriate to the current view, the Microsoft toolbar, and any custom toolbars.

➤ To change the size of the tools, display them in monochrome rather than color, or suppress the display of the Tool Tips, pull down the View menu, click Toolbars, and then select/deselect the appropriate check box at the bottom of the dialog box.

➤ Toolbars may either be docked (along the edge of the window) or left floating (in their own window). A toolbar moved to the edge of the window will dock along that edge. A toolbar moved anywhere else in the window will float in its own window. (You can double click the gray background area of a toolbar to toggle it between docked and floating.) Docked toolbars are one tool wide (high), whereas floating toolbars can be resized by clicking and dragging a border/corner as you would any window.
 — To move a docked toolbar, click anywhere in the gray background area and drag the toolbar to its new location.
 — To move a floating toolbar, drag its title bar to its new location.

➤ To customize (modify) one or more toolbars, display the toolbars on the screen, pull down the View menu, click Toolbars, and click the Customize command button. Alternatively, you can click on any toolbar with the right mouse button and select Customize from the shortcut menu.
 — To move a tool, drag the tool to its new location on that toolbar or any other displayed toolbar.
 — To delete a tool, drag the tool off of the toolbar and release the mouse button.
 — To add a tool, select the category from the Categories list box and drag the tool to the desired location on the toolbar. (To see a description of a tool's function prior to adding it to a toolbar, point to the tool in the Customize dialog box and read the displayed description.)
 — To restore a predefined toolbar to its default appearance, pull down the View menu, click Toolbars, select the desired toolbar, and click the Reset command button.

➤ To create a new toolbar that can be displayed for any database, pull down the View menu and click Toolbars, then select either the Utility 1 or Utility 2 toolbar, which is initially one tool wide and empty. (Alternatively, you can click any toolbar with the right mouse button and select Toolbars from the shortcut menu.) Add, move, and delete tools following the same procedures as outlined above. The toolbar will automatically size itself as new tools are added and deleted.

➤ To create a new toolbar that can be displayed only in the database in which it is created, pull down the View menu and click Toolbars, then click the New command button. (Alternatively, you can click any toolbar with the right mouse button and select Toolbars from the shortcut menu.)
 — Enter a name for the toolbar in the dialog box that follows. The name can be up to 64 characters in length and can contain spaces. The new toolbar will appear at the upper left of the screen and initially it will be big enough to hold only one tool. Click the Customize command button.

— Add, move, and delete tools following the same procedures as outlined above. The toolbar will automatically size itself as new tools are added and deleted.

— To delete a custom toolbar, pull down the View menu, click Toolbars, select the toolbar to be deleted, and click the Delete command button. Click Yes to confirm the deletion.

— You may also quickly create a new toolbar by dragging a button from the Customize window to any location on the screen other than a toolbar. The new toolbar will initially be one tool wide and it will be empty. It will be named Custom Toolbar x, where x is the next sequential number available, starting with Custom Toolbar 1.

MICROSOFT ACCESS 2.0 TOOLBARS

Database Toolbar

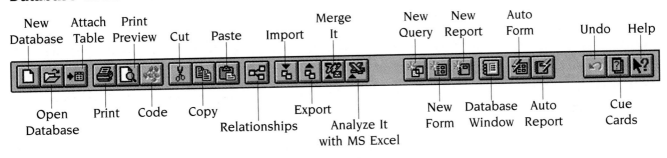

Relationships Toolbar

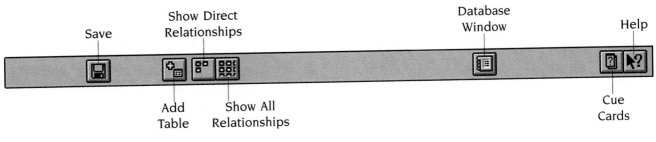

Table Design Toolbar

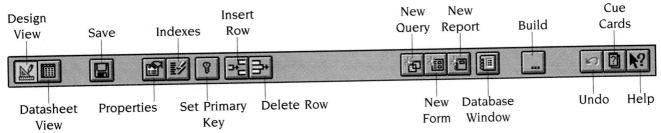

FIGURE B.1 Access 2.0 Toolbars Tied to a Specific View

Table Datasheet Toolbar

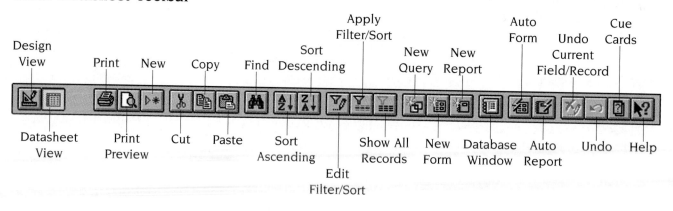

Query Design Toolbar

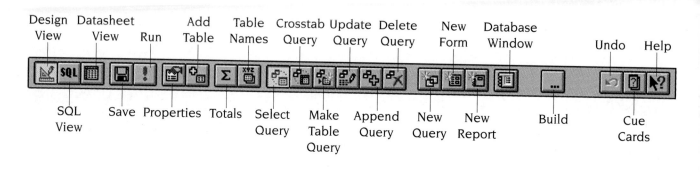

Query Datasheet Toolbar

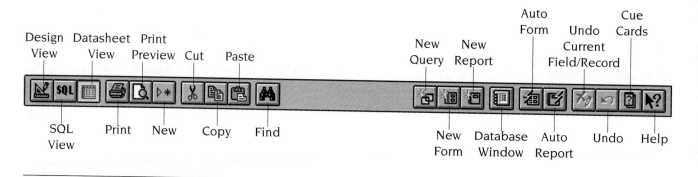

Form Design Toolbar

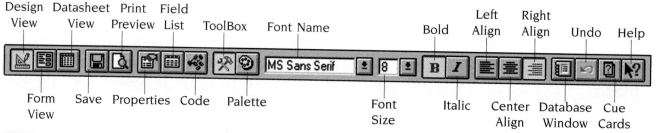

FIGURE B.1 Access 2.0 Toolbars Tied to a Specific View (continued)

Form View Toolbar

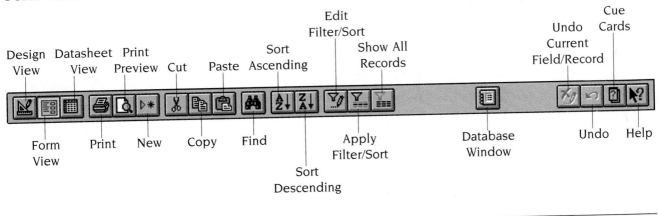

Design View · Form View · Datasheet View · Print Preview · Print · Cut · New · Paste · Copy · Sort Ascending · Find · Sort Descending · Edit Filter/Sort · Apply Filter/Sort · Show All Records · Database Window · Undo Current Field/Record · Undo · Cue Cards · Help

Report Design Toolbar

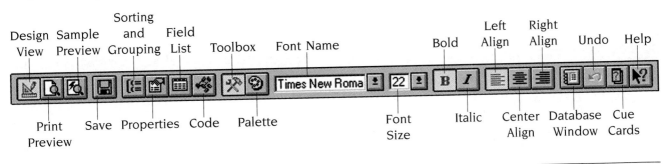

Design View · Sample Preview · Print Preview · Save · Sorting and Grouping · Properties · Field List · Code · Toolbox · Palette · Font Name · Font Size · Bold · Italic · Left Align · Center Align · Right Align · Database Window · Undo · Cue Cards · Help

Print Preview Toolbar

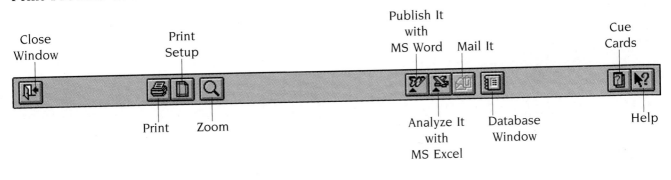

Close Window · Print Setup · Print · Zoom · Publish It with MS Word · Analyze It with MS Excel · Mail It · Database Window · Cue Cards · Help

Filter/Sort Toolbar

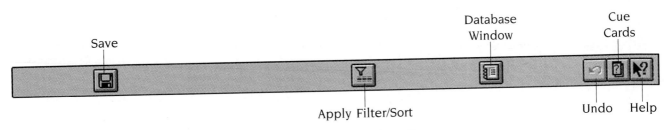

Save · Apply Filter/Sort · Database Window · Undo · Cue Cards · Help

FIGURE B.1   Access 2.0 Toolbars Tied to a Specific View (continued)

MICROSOFT ACCESS 2.0 TOOLBARS

Toolbox Toolbar

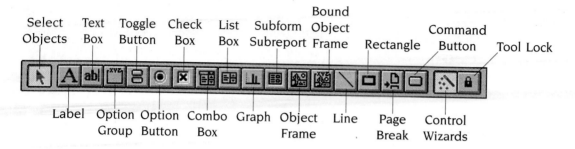

Palette Toolbar

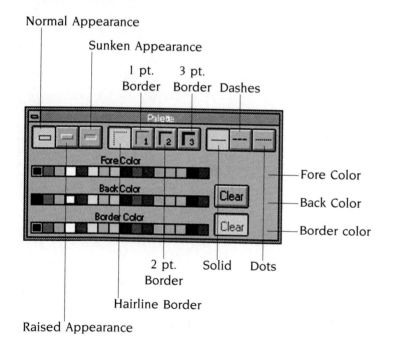

Microsoft Toolbar

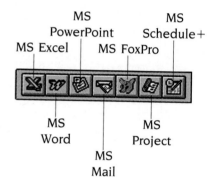

Utility 1 and Utility 2 Toolbars

FIGURE B.2   Access 2.0 Toolbars Not Tied to a Specific View